# Reimagining Change

How do organisations change, and how do we, as individuals, make sense of it? This textbook addresses that vital question by offering a comprehensive framework of perspectives on organisational transformation. Built on the idea that all change theories rest on important underlying beliefs and assumptions, it invites students and practitioners to explore seven distinct ways of understanding change. Rather than advocating for a single model, the book encourages readers to navigate between perspectives, deepening their ability to interpret, communicate, and act in times of transformation. Drawing on decades of research and practice, it blends conceptual rigour with illustrative examples, accessible language, and real-world case studies, making it an ideal resource for management students, change practitioners, and educators alike. Supplementary materials include lecture slides, tutorial slides, and teaching schedules for instructors, and reading lists, video resources, and extra cases for students.

**Bart De Keyser** is a lecturer in strategy, innovation, and entrepreneurship at the University of Sydney. He holds a PhD from the University of Antwerp, has conducted research at HEC Montréal and Columbia University, and is a recipient of multiple teaching awards. His work – spanning industries from banking to diamond trading – explores how organisations navigate transformation, disruption, and strategy.

# Reimagining Change

## Gaining Perspective on Transforming Organisations

**Bart De Keyser**
University of Sydney

CAMBRIDGE
UNIVERSITY PRESS

CAMBRIDGE
UNIVERSITY PRESS

Shaftesbury Road, Cambridge CB2 8EA, United Kingdom

One Liberty Plaza, 20th Floor, New York, NY 10006, USA

477 Williamstown Road, Port Melbourne, VIC 3207, Australia

314–321, 3rd Floor, Plot 3, Splendor Forum, Jasola District Centre,
New Delhi – 110025, India

Cambridge University Press is part of Cambridge University Press & Assessment,
a department of the University of Cambridge.

We share the University's mission to contribute to society through the pursuit of
education, learning and research at the highest international levels of excellence.

www.cambridge.org
Information on this title: www.cambridge.org/highereducation/isbn/9781009686846

DOI: 10.1017/9781009686860



When citing this work, please include a reference to the DOI 10.1017/9781009686860

First published 2026

Cover image: Credit: Air Creative / Moment / Getty Images

*A catalogue record for this publication is available from the British Library*

*A Cataloging-in-Publication data record for this book is available from the Library of Congress*

ISBN 978-1-009-68684-6 Hardback
ISBN 978-1-009-68682-2 Paperback

Additional resources for this publication at www.cambridge.org/DeKeyser

# Contents

# Figures

# Tables

# Preface

Few organisational topics have been as intensely scrutinised as change. For decades, managers and scholars alike have grappled with the concept of organisations in motion, often declaring their own era to be the most susceptible to change. Whether in the eloquent writings of the early theorists in the 1940s, the introductions to change management models of the 1980s, or the textbooks that have shaped generations of today's managers – the narrative has consistently emphasised the uniquely dynamic nature of the times. Contemporary discussions on change continue this trend, if not amplifying it. With rapid developments in geopolitics, customer interactions, and technology, we are now said to be living in the 'age of change' – an era of unprecedented adaptation, where both the speed and the magnitude of developments threaten to upend any market participant at a moment's notice.

But perhaps the 'age of change' is not unique to our time, nor has it ever been. Perhaps we are simply perpetually surprised by new developments while becoming accustomed to those already in place. This cyclical pattern may lead us to believe, somewhat ironically, that our era is the most dynamic of all. Maybe we have lost sight of the fact that change is not a novel phenomenon but an ever-present force. In our self-centred view of history, we may overlook one of the most enduring insights: that the only constant is, in fact, change itself.

So, what's the issue here? Is it truly problematic to assume that one's own era is the most turbulent of all? Is there harm in believing that the clock of change is ticking louder now than ever before? I believe that the answer might be yes – not simply because such a belief is somewhat arrogant or brash, but because it risks undervaluing the countless insights and experiences that have emerged from previous generations. Change has captivated managers and theorists for decades, and there is a wealth of knowledge available for anyone interested in the topic. This book is not an urgent call to action because change has suddenly stormed the organisational stage, guns blazing and costumes shining – rather, it exists because change has always been a part of the organisational landscape, inspiring countless valuable ideas.

The aim of this book is to highlight those ideas, exploring seven different approaches to understanding, discussing, and managing organisational change. In this book, we'll reimagine change by continually shifting our approach to it; in this book, we'll reimagine change by exploring the different ways in which we can make sense of and work with it.

## On the Reasons behind This Book

Going out into 'the field', I've always been struck by how perceptive people can be about change, yet equally amazed at how we all seem to diverge on its core meaning. It's not uncommon to witness people becoming defensive, tuning out, or showing frustration when someone else presents a different view on change. Heated debates are frequent, and on rare occasions I've witnessed even fists being raised (yes, really). When it comes to change, people often end up talking past each other – not out of malice but because they base their understanding on fundamentally different interpretations of what change means.

This same fragmentation is evident in the literature. Numerous books address the topic, yet many are confined to a narrow interpretation, presenting change as either one thing or another, with little room for alternative views. I suspect that this is not due to ill intent; rather, authors tend to stick with the understanding that resonates most with their experiences. A consultant might focus on leader-driven change, while someone with a background in labour relations might emphasise change being born out of conflict. Similarly, a writer who has experienced grassroots movements first-hand might view change as emerging from the bottom up. As a result, our understanding of organisational change and transformation is often split into isolated camps, where adherents of one approach dismiss others.

I believe that the field needs a book that interconnects and harmonises the different 'gospels' on change we currently have available. To reimagine organisational change, we must accept and internalise the different angles from which the phenomenon can be approached. To reimagine change, we must come to terms with the various possible ways of understanding it.

Beyond this core purpose, let me also clarify what this book certainly does *not* intend to do. First, this book has *not* been written as an all-inclusive summary of interesting thoughts on change in an organisational context: given the fantastic plethora of texts disseminated on the topic, I believe that any ambition to do something similar should be considered ludicrous at best. Instead, this book is intended to provide an essential overview of those perspectives on change deemed most common or useful, thus helping you to dig deeper into your sub-stream(s) of interest.

Next, this book does *not* seek to discredit or undermine certain views on change. While I will take the opportunity to highlight standing challenges and pitfalls for every perspective on organisational change, it is up to you to decide what to do with them eventually. In this regard, the value of this book lies not in offering prescriptive advice but in presenting different viewpoints to challenge and expand your thinking.

Finally, this book does *not* intend to offer easy fixes for success. Too often have I encountered texts that claim to provide their readers with an easy pathway to stellar business results or instant gratification. While having the advantage of being attractive, I believe that such short-cuts on change hold very little merit whatsoever – representing an idealised picture of change that is devoid of the nuance that makes the real world out there so much more challenging. This book does not claim to lay bare the proverbial pot of gold at the end of the rainbow, nor is it a foolproof success formula. It merely intends to offer an essential overview of different ways of thinking about organisational change – leaving it up to you to balance different insights in the specific situations you encounter.

## Who Should Pick Up This Text

This book is for anyone interested in organisational change, whether from a theoretical or a practical standpoint. While I welcome readers from all backgrounds, I believe that the ideas presented here will be most valuable to the following groups:

- Business/management students – this book systematically explores various perspectives on change, offering a framework for understanding it within organisational contexts. Whether your focus is on management, finance, accounting, marketing, or logistics, having a solid grasp of change will be a significant asset.
- Managers – despite the critical role of leaders in guiding organisational change, it's often surprising how little many executives know about transformation. This book aims to enhance executives' understanding by distilling key concepts and ideas into a concise format – providing a structured overview for selective reading while offering enough depth to provoke meaningful reflection.
- Employees – traditionally, change has been viewed mostly from the position of corporate executives. However, this book is designed not only for those in leadership positions but also for non-executive employees. After all, change often has a profound impact on non-executives, who are frequently the ones tasked with implementing new policies and adapting to shifts in the workplace. Catering to the needs of 'regular' employees is essential for fostering a more inclusive, collaborative approach to organisational transformation.
- Researchers – the field of change research is vast but often fragmented, with scholars working in isolated silos. While this book does not claim to be an exhaustive academic resource, it does offer a clear delineation of major change concepts from multiple perspectives. This structure may help researchers by clarifying existing ideas and inspiring new avenues of inquiry.

In sum, this book bridges theory and practice to offer a comprehensive yet accessible exploration of organisational change. Whether you are a student, a manager, an employee, or a researcher, it provides insights to help you navigate, implement, and understand change more effectively.

## How to Use This Book

This book is designed with a modular structure, allowing flexibility in how readers engage with its content. Each chapter is crafted to stand on its own, offering insights into specific aspects of organisational change. However, when read together, the chapters weave a cohesive narrative, providing a comprehensive understanding of the field. As a result, there are two primary ways to approach this book, depending on your goals and interests:

- The 'full-menu' approach – in this approach, you explore the book in its entirety, from start to finish. This method is ideal for those who want to gain a deep, holistic perspective on organisational change. By reading all the chapters in sequence, you will see how the various

perspectives connect, interact, and build upon one another, creating a rich tapestry of ideas. This approach is particularly valuable for students, educators, or professionals seeking a thorough grounding in the subject matter or those teaching or designing curricula based on the book's framework.
- The 'plug-and-play' approach – for those with more specific interests or immediate needs, the book's modular design allows for a more targeted reading experience. You can jump directly to the chapters or themes that resonate most with your current challenges or questions. Whether you're navigating a crisis, exploring strategies for sustaining innovation, or delving into the nuances of stakeholder politics, this approach lets you pick and choose the content that's most relevant to you. This flexibility ensures that the book serves as both a quick reference tool and a practical guide.

Regardless of the approach you choose, the book is crafted to offer value in a way that aligns with your goals. Whether you seek full immersion or targeted insights, this modular design ensures accessibility, practicality, and depth.

## How to Navigate This Book's Sections

Each chapter follows a consistent structure, starting with four foundational elements highlighted in a 'Perspective in Brief' callout box:

- Concepts related to the perspective – understanding the concepts tied to each perspective is crucial for any meaningful exploration. This section identifies the concepts most closely associated with the perspective under discussion.
- Keep reading to learn more about – for most of us interested in change, practice matters. In this section, I'll uncover the practical themes nested most directly under the perspectives, allowing you to easily identify the perspective that suits your immediate needs.
- Prime contributors – delving deeper into any school of thought requires knowing who shaped it. This section highlights the key figures, that is, those whose ideas have been most influential, whether they are celebrated or contested.
- Guiding metaphor – finally, to allow for a first notion of how streams of thought relate to change, this section includes an analogical depiction: how can one connect to the perspective in terms of imagery?

Beyond these introductory highlights, each chapter delves into the perspective by advancing the following structure:

- 'The Genesis of Thought' – what are the roots of this perspective on change? Perspectives on change often arise from challenges to conventional ideas. This section explores the origins of each perspective, examining the questions that led to its development.
- 'Unpacking the Heart' – what is the essence of the perspective? Despite perspectives' evolutions, core ideas often remain consistent. This section distils the perspective's essence, discussing fundamental assumptions about (i) the capacity of change, (ii) the development of change, (iii) the drivers of change, and (iv) the goals of change.

- 'Extending Your Toolkit' – how can you get hands-on with the perspective? Each perspective has generated frameworks and models that translate ideas into practice. This section introduces each perspective's key tools, equipping you with practical methods to apply its principles.
- 'Impact on the Ground' – how can you benefit from drawing on the perspective? Ideas are powerful when they shape real-world outcomes. This section examines how each perspective can help influence reality, illustrating its practical implications.
- 'Drawbacks and Pitfalls' – what challenges should you be aware of with the perspective? Every perspective has its challenges. This section outlines the major criticisms, providing an overview of what to be cautious about when handling the perspective in question.
- 'Case' – how does the perspective work in practice? To ground each perspective on change in lived experience, every chapter concludes with a case study that brings the ideas to life. These real-world scenarios help you see how abstract concepts unfold in practice. Each case is followed by a set of reflective questions that prompt you to interrogate the perspective's assumptions and connect the case to your own context or experiences.

Finally, each chapter includes several integrated features embedded throughout the text, designed to prompt reflection and support critical engagement with the material:

- 'The Point?' – these callout paragraphs distil the core message or takeaway of a section, helping you pause and ask: 'Why does this matter?'. They serve as checkpoints for understanding and relevance.
- 'Practical Advice' – these callouts suggest how to translate theory into action, offering concrete tips or strategies that you can apply in real-world settings or in your own professional practice.
- 'Be Aware!' – these notes highlight common blind spots or controversial aspects of the topic at hand, encouraging you to think critically and avoid simplistic interpretations of change dynamics.

Taken as a whole, this structure ensures that each chapter equips you with the means to critically engage with its origins, assumptions, tools, and practical relevance in the world of change.

## Leveraging This Book's Online Resources

To deepen engagement, each chapter will be supported by a suite of online resources. These materials are designed to reinforce key concepts, illustrate applications, and offer extended discussions beyond what is covered in the text. The online resources (www.cambridge.org/De Keyser) accompanying this book include:

- Reading lists – for those looking to explore perspectives on change in greater depth, each chapter will be accompanied by a curated list of readings. These include seminal works, contemporary research, and practitioner-oriented insights, helping readers navigate the broader landscape of thought related to each perspective.

- Video references – to bring perspectives on change to life, the book's online resources include curated third-party video content. These references feature interviews with thought leaders, case study documentaries, and conceptual explainers that reinforce the book's key themes. Whether used for individual exploration or in classroom discussions, these videos help translate abstract ideas into concrete, real-world examples.
- Extra cases – while each chapter includes a case study to illustrate its perspective in practice, the online platform offers additional case studies. These extra cases provide further opportunities to analyse how different perspectives on change unfold across various contexts, such as reorganisations, cultural changes, mergers and acquisitions, downsizings, digital transformations, and so on – allowing readers to compare, contrast, and apply insights to real-world scenarios.
- Lecture slides – designed for instructors, these slides summarise key points from each chapter, providing a structured overview that facilitates discussion and retention. They highlight foundational concepts, guiding metaphors, and core frameworks, making them useful for classroom instruction.
- Tutorial slides – to encourage active engagement with the material, tutorial slides contain discussion prompts, case-based exercises, and thought-provoking questions. They are meant for instructors and are particularly valuable for facilitating group discussions, problem-solving activities, and reflective learning exercises. Often, they build directly on the end-of-chapter cases, as for Chapters 2–8.
- Teaching schedules – finally, teaching schedules are available to support instructors in planning and delivering the material across different formats. Whether you are teaching in a trimester-based system, a semester-based course, or using intensive or half-semester formats, you will find sample schedules that outline how the material can be structured and paced.

Together, these online resources serve as an interactive extension of the book, ensuring that learning remains dynamic, practical, and engaging.

## Moving Forward

With this framework in place, I hope that you will find this book both informative and inspiring. Take from it the insights that resonate with you and use them to fuel your own ideas and curiosity. Whether you are a student, a leader, a researcher, or a practitioner, my hope is that these perspectives will help you approach change not as a problem to be solved but as a phenomenon to be understood, engaged with, and even embraced. Ultimately, this book is an invitation to see change through different eyes – to learn, to lead, and to make a meaningful difference in the organisations and systems you are, or will be, a part of.

# Acknowledgements

This book would not have been possible without the support, encouragement, and generosity of many people. I'm deeply grateful to my colleagues, whose thoughtful feedback and energising conversations helped shape the ideas throughout these pages – and whose willingness to entertain half-formed thoughts over coffee (or corridor chats) often sparked the best insights. To the many students I've had the privilege to teach – thank you for your curiosity and challenging questions, which have consistently pushed me to think more clearly and critically (and occasionally forced me to rethink everything mid-lecture).

A special thanks to Valerie Appleby at Cambridge University Press for championing this project from its earliest proposal through to production – your belief in the book and your steady encouragement along the way meant more than I can say. I'm also deeply thankful to Rowan Groat for her calm guidance, sharp editorial eye, and steady hand through every twist and turn of the publishing process.

Yet this book stands on the shoulders of many others. I'm indebted to the scholars and practitioners whose ideas and frameworks are woven throughout these pages. Some I've had the privilege to meet and learn from directly; many more I've encountered through their writing. Their insights, debates, and provocations have shaped not just the text but the way I think – and I hope I've done justice to their work here.

I also want to acknowledge the anonymous reviewers who took the time to read early drafts with care and generosity. Their thoughtful critiques helped surface what was unclear, sharpen what was murky, and make the text stronger, page by page. I believe that thoughtful feedback is a rather rare gift, and I'm genuinely grateful for the clarity and rigour they brought to the process.

And finally, to my family and friends, thank you for your patience, humour, and unflagging support – and, from some, for the kind of unwavering belief that echoes long after they're gone. Whether you offered encouragement, distractions, unsolicited pep talks, or just pretended to listen while I over-explained some obscure point – you played a bigger role than you probably intended. This book has a lot of me in it, but more of you than you realise – and I wouldn't have it any other way.

## Ethics and Transparency

In accordance with publishing transparency and ethical standards, the author acknowledges the use of AI-assisted tools to support grammar correction and stylistic refinement. All substantive content, interpretations, and editorial decisions were developed independently by the author and remain entirely his responsibility.

# Part I

# Getting Started

**IN THIS PART, YOU WILL LEARN TO . . .**

- ► recognise the historical and ongoing significance of change;
- ► identify the key reasons why organisations devote attention to change;
- ► clarify what change actually means in an organisational context.

Before diving into any theory or framework, it's important to halt momentarily and ask ourselves a basic question: what exactly are we dealing with when we talk about change? It's easy to assume that we know. After all, we hear about it constantly – whether it's about adapting to new technologies, responding to new regulations, or navigating leadership transitions. But, in reality, people often mean very different things when they talk about change.

The first part of this book is designed to clear some of that initial fog. Rather than rushing into techniques or models, we'll begin by laying down the conceptual basics. We'll explore why change matters, why it persists as a topic of concern, and what makes it such a complex phenomenon. From the roots of organisational change to the layered ways in which it can be understood, this part sets out to sharpen our language and deepen our understanding. Think of it as learning to read the terrain before setting off on a demanding hike: not a detour but a necessary orientation.

If we can better grasp what change is, why we care about it, and how we can talk about it more clearly, then we're much more likely to navigate it well. So, consider this part your compass: a way to ground yourself before we begin examining the many different lenses through which change can be interpreted and worked with. From there, you'll be better prepared not just to tackle change but to think critically about it, to challenge easy answers, and to engage with it on your own terms.

# 1 What Is Change and Why Should We Care?

## Introduction

Change is often described as the only constant in life – a phrase so familiar that it has become cliché. And yet, in the world of organisations, few statements ring truer. Whether it arrives like a tidal wave or creeps in gradually like erosion, change is unavoidable. It shapes how we work, how we lead, and how we imagine the future. For some, it sparks opportunity and reinvention; for others, it brings uncertainty, resistance, or even decline. Regardless of how it is perceived, change is seldom absent; it is a constant presence and it falls to us to make sense of it and respond.

In this opening chapter, I aim to lay the groundwork for the journey ahead. First, I will illustrate how change is not a recent development or a passing phase; it is a force that has always shaped the evolution of organisations, from the earliest institutions to today's digital and global enterprises. Next, I will explore why change remains at the heart of organisational debates, tracing its growing importance in a world defined by volatility, complexity, and interdependence. Third, I will confront the deceptively simple question: what do we mean by change? Here, I will consider the conceptual terrain that scholars and practitioners alike have used to make basic sense of it. Finally, I will touch upon how to approach perspectives yet to come.

By the end of this chapter, my hope is that you will have a strong foundation on which to build the insights ahead. Change, as we will see, is not merely something to be managed; it is something to be understood, questioned, and reimagined. And the way we choose to approach it will shape not only our organisations but ourselves.

## 1.1 The Only Constant Is Change

In today's world, change seems to be everywhere. Whether you're talking to employees or managers across different industries, you're likely to hear phrases like 'things are changing faster than ever' or 'it was never like this before'. But is that really the case?

Consider, for instance, the way we transport ourselves. For one, it's certainly true that there's a lot happening right now, with advancements in electric and autonomous vehicles making headlines. But if we look back, we see that even more seismic shifts have occurred. Take the introduction of the combustion engine, for example. For carriage makers, this must have been a shocking development. Few of them likely imagined that such a technology was possible and, as a result, many were wiped out.

Similarly, think about everyday products like washing machines. Before they were invented, families did laundry in tubs, and tools like wringers were indispensable. Yet, as washing machines became commonplace, wringer manufacturers quickly went out of business. At the time, it might have seemed absurd to imagine a world without wringers, but, as time progressed, so did the tools we relied on.

Or consider the once-ubiquitous snuff boxes of the eighteenth century. In many parts of the world, no distinguished person would leave home without their snuff tobacco. Yet today these items are nearly non-existent. For the companies that made them, being at the height of fashion in the eighteenth century clearly didn't guarantee survival into the present day.

More recently, the way organisations structure themselves has also undergone major transformation. Traditional hierarchical models, where authority and decision-making flow from the top down, are increasingly giving way to flatter, more agile arrangements. Many organisations now prioritise cross-functional collaboration, rapid iteration, and decentralised decision-making. This shift reflects a growing recognition that, in fast-moving environments, responsiveness and adaptability often matter more than rigid control.

Or simply consider the nature of work itself: the rise of remote and hybrid work arrangements has altered not just where people work but how they relate to their teams, their leaders, and their organisations. Some departments that once thrived on co-location have had to rethink workflows, adopt new technologies, and reconsider what effective collaboration looks like. Alongside this, many roles have become more fluid, with employees expected to take on a mix of responsibilities rather than staying confined to a narrowly defined job description.

Moreover, entire industries have recently witnessed shifts in how value is created and captured. Organisations that once relied on owning physical assets – such as factories, stores, or vehicles – are now adapting to models that prioritise platforms, data, or networks. And, ironically, industries that once relied on asset-light business models – such as tech – are now increasingly investing in physical assets like energy and data infrastructure. These changes often demand not only new strategies but new internal capabilities and cultural norms.

Layered onto this are broader forces – technological and geopolitical – that have recently accelerated the pace and scope of organisational change. Breakthroughs in artificial intelligence, automation, and biotechnology are not only enabling new products and services but also redefining the very nature of competition. At the same time, global instability, shifting trade alliances, and supply chain disruptions are pushing organisations to rethink where and how they operate. These external shifts are not simply 'context' for change; they are often its very engine.

### Box 1.1 The Point?

No matter how successful an organisation might be at any given moment, it must remember that few things are as constant as change. Keep an open mind about what's happening and evolving today, and don't cling too tightly to what was – for it is very possible that it will not matter as much tomorrow as it did the day before.

## 1.2 Why Do Organisations Fuss Over Change?

So, why do organisations fuss over change? What do managers and scholars find so enticing about the phenomenon to be willing to churn it over and over again, instead of just 'letting it rip'? While an all-inclusive answer to questions of purpose can of course never be claimed, I would like to highlight what I consider to be five major motives underlying much of our past, present, and future dealings with change.

### 1.2.1 Because Change Results from Being Tied to Context

No organisation ever exists in a vacuum: for every group of people that collaborate, there are ties and relationships with an outside world that matter. Such ties can be fairly directly related to the organisation's reason for existence – think customers or suppliers – but they can also relate to a more general context, such as the political or social background. As such context develops, so will it press the organisations connected to it to develop as well. In this way, the motive to change may not necessarily lie with organisations themselves – it may merely be the inevitable consequence of organisations dealing with an ever-evolving context.

Think about the impact of environmental regulations on the automotive industry. As governments worldwide imposed stricter emissions standards, automakers had to develop more fuel-efficient and environmentally friendly vehicles. This external pressure has driven significant changes in product design, manufacturing processes, and even business models, as companies shifted towards electric vehicles and hybrid technology to meet these new requirements. Change, in this sense, was underscored not by personal appetite but by organisations' connections to an ever-evolving context.

### 1.2.2 Because Change Is Necessary for Survival

Closely related to the inevitability of change is the idea that it is necessary for survival. Organisations must adapt to their environments not just to thrive but to avoid being left behind. As such, the survival rationale stresses that change is not merely an option; it is a necessity for organisations to stay standing in a competitive marketplace.

Consider, for one, the case of video stores, which once were an integral part of the larger film industry. Despite early signs of a shift towards digital streaming, many of these stores failed to adapt their business model, leading to their eventual decline and bankruptcy. Others, in contrast, recognised the same shift and transformed their businesses from DVD rental services to streaming platforms. The difference in outcomes between these two types of player highlights the survival rationale: organisations must adapt to changing circumstances to continue operating, and failure to do so can lead to extinction.

### 1.2.3 Because Change Supports the Idea of Being in Control

Furthermore, the act of initiating change often serves as a validation of management itself. By discussing, analysing, and implementing changes, we create the perception that organisations can be shaped and directed. For those involved in managing organisations at any level, the idea of control is a crucial consideration; it is often what motivates managers to devote their time, energy, and resources to the organisation they are part of. Embracing change reinforces the belief that we can influence and shape the trajectory of organisational development. This sense of control is vital for most people working within organisations – for without it, the effort invested in managing would seem purposeless.

Think about a retail company facing declining sales due to shifting consumer preferences and the rise of e-commerce. Management decides to initiate a comprehensive change programme, including revamping the product line, investing in online sales channels, and retraining staff to enhance customer experience. These actions create a sense of control, signalling to stakeholders that the company is actively responding to external challenges and reshaping its future. By driving these changes, management validates its role, demonstrating that it can steer the organisation through turbulent times and ultimately reinforcing the belief in its ability to influence outcomes.

### 1.2.4 Because Change Implies Improvement

Moreover, change is often seen as a source of aspiration. From this angle, talking about change is elementary to our conception of the organisation as an entity of success: we consider change to be necessary not merely to safeguard the firm's survival but to ensure that it reaches its maximum potential. Change helps us believe that things can always improve, and that we have the power to actively facilitate such improvements. In this sense, dealing with change becomes a catalyst for performance: for if results today are not what we hoped for, who says we can't do better tomorrow?

For example, for many companies, conveying a sense of potential change is critical to maintaining shareholder trust. If anything, investors and stakeholders are more likely to remain confident in a company that demonstrates adaptability and a forward-looking mindset. When firms emphasise their ability to evolve – whether through innovation, restructuring, or strategic shifts – they signal resilience and a commitment to continuous improvement. This is particularly important in industries where disruption is frequent, such as technology and finance, where the expectation of progress drives market valuation. In this way, change is not just a means of survival but a fundamental driver of long-term performance and competitive advantage.

### 1.2.5 Because Change Legitimises People and Their Actions

Finally, change is often tapped into as a vehicle for legitimisation: by emphasising the importance as well as the complexity of the topic, many self-proclaimed experts validate the advice they can offer to the disoriented aspirant. Over time, such change experts have come to take many forms, and may vary from management consultants to scholars, to corporate executives or those writing books on the issue – not unlike myself, to be fair.

Question yourself for a moment: would change be as big a topic if industries such as management consultancy had not been able to seize and capitalise on it? Probably not. In this capacity, the conversation on change is utilised as a constant call-to-arms, ringing consistently and loudly to justify enquiries, actions being taken, and money being spent.

**Box 1.2 The Point?**

While I have little doubt that some motives for talking about organisational change might come across as more respectable than others, I want to stress that such evaluations may be beyond the point: for all these motives – whatever their moral qualities – have stimulated us to talk and write about change to the extent that interesting stuff has emerged. And that, in my belief, is something to be genuinely grateful for.

## 1.3 What Is Change?

Yet gratitude alone does not resolve a deeper issue: even though change has turned into a very common topic of conversation nowadays, it is surprising how often people spend their time talking about very different things. Consequentially, before delving into an extensive text on the matter, it's useful to set some clear boundaries on its basic 'what'. Here, I'll discuss three major angles: dimensions, classifications, and levels of change.

### 1.3.1 Dimensions of Change

A first way in which we can try to define change is by considering its **dimensions**, or the different parts by which change is ultimately composed. In general, four major dimensions crop up:[1, 3, 5, 6]

- Content – when referring to change in terms of content, we typically relate to which elements in the organisation are effectively altered: is it, for example, the organisation's structure, its culture, its strategic orientation, or is it something else?[1, 3, 5, 6]
- Context – next, talking about change in terms of context means relating to factors in the organisation's internal/external environment that can impact how a change is being dealt with. A wide variety of determinants can be thought of, such as governmental regulations and technological advances (external), or degree of specialisation and prior change experience (internal).[1, 3, 5, 6]
- Process – furthermore, when considering change along the process dimension, we usually refer to how a change trajectory is being addressed. This dimension relates to change from an implementation angle – that is, getting it done – and how people will respond to it along the way.[1, 3, 5, 6]

- Outcome – finally, we can talk about change in terms of envisioned results: what goals do we intend to reach when pushing for change? Note that such consequences can be attributable to the organisation itself (e.g. profits, turnover) as well as to the people making up that organisation (e.g. behaviours, attitudes).[1, 3, 5, 6]

To make better sense of the differences between dimensions, consider a technology firm that decides to shift from a traditional hierarchical structure to a more agile, team-based approach. In this scenario, the content of the change revolves around the structural transformation within the organisation, where rigid departmental silos are dismantled in favour of cross-functional teams that are empowered to make decisions independently. The context for this change is shaped by the rapid pace of technological advancements in the industry, which necessitates quicker decision-making and greater innovation to stay competitive. As the company embarks on the process of change, careful planning, and execution are critical. This involves training managers and employees in agile methodologies, reconfiguring reporting lines, and introducing new collaboration tools that facilitate the new team-based approach. Ultimately, the outcome of change involves the organisation anticipating an increase in innovation, faster time-to-market for new products, and improved employee satisfaction due to the enhanced autonomy and collaboration inherent in the new structure.

**Box 1.3 The Point?**

To avoid talking past each other, discussions on change should never be limited to a single dimension. When addressing change, it's crucial to remember that it involves more than just the content of the change itself; the context, the process, and the intended outcomes are equally important. Focusing on only one dimension can lead to misunderstandings: effective communications about change must consider how these elements interact and influence each other.

### 1.3.2 Classifications of Change

While dimensions highlight the different aspects that make up any change effort, another helpful step is to consider how change can be **classified**. Scholars often distinguish change along recurring categories such as scope, speed, and magnitude, each offering further nuance for how we think about and manage change:[2, 7, 8]

- Scope of change, that is, operational to strategic – where lies the focus of the change enacted by the organisation; does it aim to render current processes more efficient or does it intend to overhaul the firm's long-term way of doing business?[2, 7, 8] For instance, a retail chain might decide to focus on operational changes by implementing new inventory management software to improve efficiency in tracking stock levels. On the other hand, a strategic change could involve the company shifting from a bricks-and-mortar focus to a predominantly online business model, fundamentally altering how it operates in the long term.

- Speed of change, that is, incremental to radical – how fast does the organisation go about change; does it tackle developments in bits and pieces or does it opt for a big-bang approach?[2, 7, 8] A manufacturing company might choose an incremental approach by gradually introducing automation into its production line, allowing employees to adapt to each new piece of technology over time. Conversely, a radical approach would be if the company decided to fully automate its entire production process in one sweeping move, requiring immediate and comprehensive adjustments from all employees.
- Magnitude of change, that is, evolutionary to revolutionary – to what extent does the change adapt the current way of working; does it intend to alter only minor features or does it aim to re-examine the business's entire way of working?[2, 7, 8] An evolutionary change could involve a software company making continuous updates to its existing product, enhancing features based on customer feedback. In contrast, a revolutionary change might be the company deciding to pivot entirely, moving away from its traditional software offerings to develop a completely new and disruptive product, thereby redefining its market position.

**Box 1.4 Be Aware!**

When pondering the different classifications, remember that none of these represents a hard choice – either A or B. Rather, they represent a continuum of options according to which real-life changes can be categorised. Strategic changes, for example, very often also include operational developments; and most operational developments will – to some extent – either reinforce or redirect the organisation's strategic trajectory. In this sense, you should never consider classifications as representing strict opposites, between which you are to make harsh decisions. They rather represent a continuum of decisions, of which no one side is either better or worse.

### 1.3.3 Levels of Change

Beyond dimensions and classifications, another crucial lens is the **level of analysis**. In an organisational context, four levels are generally distinguished:[2, 4]

- Micro-level, that is, the individual – change in an organisation can strongly relate to the individual: how do singular people alter (or refuse to alter) their behaviour? With topics at this level of analysis often relating to notions of behaviour, cognition, and neurology, it shouldn't surprise that this level is strongly affiliated with psychology and medicine.[2, 4] Consider a large multinational corporation facing pressure to become more sustainable due to increasing regulatory demands and shifting consumer preferences. At the micro-level, this change begins with individuals within the company: employees must adopt new behaviours, such as reducing waste in their daily tasks or embracing more sustainable practices in product development. The challenge here lies in how each person processes and responds to these changes, with some employees quickly adapting while others may resist due to ingrained habits or cognitive dissonance.

- Meso-level, that is, the group/team – next, change can relate to the level represented by the group or the team. At this level, group dynamics, communication, networks, and leadership claim key roles, with references to fields such as sociology.[2, 4] In our sustainability example, the meso-level focus would cover how teams and groups within the organisation manage this change. For instance, a product development team may need to redefine its collaboration processes to incorporate sustainability into every phase of its work. A meso-level focus would emphasise that group dynamics, communication patterns, and leadership within the team play crucial roles in ensuring that the new sustainability goals are met. We may want to consider how team leaders foster an environment that encourages open dialogue about the change and address any conflicts that arise from differing opinions or resistance within the group.
- Macro-level, that is, the organisation – at a macro-level, change generally relates to the adaptation of an overarching system. Topics covered include structure, culture, performance, and politics, with fields such as political sciences and anthropology typically being tapped into.[2, 4] At the macro-level of our sustainability example, we would focus on how the corporation as a whole undergoes a more profound transformation. The organisation may need to restructure its operations, redefine its corporate culture to emphasise sustainability, and realign its performance metrics to reflect these new priorities. This level of change might involve looking into significant shifts in organisational politics, as various departments vie for resources and influence in the new sustainability-driven strategy.
- Meta-level, that is, the context – finally, the meta-level of considering change relates to the interlinkage between an organisation and the context in which it operates. Topics can vary from industry analyses to regulatory reactions and assessments of the national culture's impact.[2, 4] At the meta-level, the sustainability example includes looking at how the corporation navigates its broader context, including how it analyses the industry's overall direction, complies with evolving regulations, and understands the cultural expectations of sustainability in different markets. The organisation might engage in industry-wide collaborations to set new standards or lobby for favourable regulatory conditions. Additionally, it may assess how national cultures influence the perception and implementation of sustainability practices, ensuring that its approach is both globally consistent and locally relevant.

### Box 1.5 Be Aware!

While it is essential to understand which level of analysis you chiefly envision when talking about change in an organisational setting, always try to remain appreciative of the interconnections running between levels. It's rare that change remains strictly confined to one level of analysis: spillovers almost naturally occur and are (to a large extent) responsible for the phenomenon's complexity. This is not to say that all discussions on change must necessarily be multi-levelled – sometimes, focus may be necessary to bring a point home. Yet, such a need for focus notwithstanding, don't be tempted to consider these levels as starkly partitioned: in many cases, they represent divisions of the mind, rather than reality.

## 1.4 How to Make Sense of Perspectives to Come

Section 1.3 examined the question 'What is change?' by breaking it down into its dimensions, classifications, and levels. Yet knowing what change is only gets us part of the way. To fully understand organisational change, we also need to recognise that it can be approached from multiple perspectives, each highlighting different facets of the phenomenon.

This book explores seven such perspectives: the managerial perspective, the organic perspective, the tension perspective, the reactive perspective, the capability perspective, the paradox perspective, and the persistence perspective. Each of these perspectives offers a unique lens through which to view the complexities of change, presenting a diverse array of insights that together form a rich tapestry of understanding.

At their core, perspectives reflect fundamentally different assumptions about what organisational change is, how it unfolds, and what purposes it serves. They guide us in asking critical questions: What drives change? Who controls it? How is success defined? While all perspectives address the phenomenon of organisational change, their interpretations often diverge sharply, offering contrasting narratives and emphases.

These perspectives are not merely academic exercises; they are powerful tools for interpreting and navigating the reality of organisational change. As you engage with this book, you will see how each perspective provides a framework for identifying problems, articulating solutions, and shaping actions. They function like specialised goggles, enabling us to see organisational change through different filters, each revealing truths that might otherwise remain hidden.

I believe that this way of continuously 'reimagining' organisational change is not just important; it is essential for today's complex and dynamic environments. Too often have I seen people approach organisational change as a simple phenomenon that can easily be realised if only we have the right checklists at hand. It rarely, if ever, works – and, often, such limited understandings leave a significant amount of damage in their wake.

By adopting a perspective-based approach, this book equips readers with a more versatile and adaptive mindset. It acknowledges that no single framework can address all of the challenges of change, and instead emphasises the value of considering diverse viewpoints. I believe that this plurality is critical in a world where organisations face rapid technological advancements, shifting market dynamics, and increasing stakeholder diversity. Understanding change from multiple angles allows leaders and practitioners to craft strategies that are not only more robust but also more inclusive and contextually relevant.

By the end of this book, you will have not only a deeper understanding of each perspective but also an appreciation of how they collectively enrich our understanding of change. As you move forward, consider these perspectives as tools in your professional toolkit, each suited to specific situations and challenges. Equipped with these insights, you will be prepared to address the nuanced realities of change with greater clarity, confidence, and creativity.

## SUMMARY

Chapter 1 set the stage for understanding change, its significance, and why organisations devote so much attention to managing it.

- ◊ It began with highlighting the central role that change plays in both organisational and societal contexts. Noting how **change has been a pervasive force** for centuries, it emphasised how businesses, industries, and environments are in a state of continuous transformation, making adaptability essential.
- ◊ We then examined **why organisations should, at all, be preoccupied with change**. Whether driven by competition, technological advancements, regulatory shifts, or internal pressures, organisations often perceive change as both an opportunity and a challenge. The discussion delved into how change can be a source of innovation and growth, but also a source of disruption and uncertainty.
- ◊ Next, we delved deeper into the question of **what change really is**. Here, we considered change according to different dimensions, classifications, and levels. These distinctions lay the groundwork for a more nuanced understanding of change throughout the book.
- ◊ Finally, we set the stage for **making sense of the perspectives that are yet to come**. These perspectives are not competing answers but complementary tools, each offering insight into specific dynamics of change, and together enabling a more adaptive, reflective, and context-sensitive approach.

Together, these building blocks lay the groundwork for what's to come. In the chapters ahead, we won't be chasing a single 'right' way to understand change; instead, we'll embrace the richness and nuance that different perspectives reveal, allowing a more layered and insightful view to emerge.

## REFERENCES

[1] Armenakis, A. A., & Bedeian, A. G. (1999). Organizational change: A review of theory and research in the 1990s. *Journal of Management*, *25*(3), 293–315.

[2] Burke, W. W. (2017). *Organization change: Theory and practice*. Thousand Oaks, CA: Sage.

[3] Cawsey, T. F., Deszca, G., & Ingols, C. (2011). *Organizational change: An action-oriented toolkit*. Thousand Oaks, CA: Sage.

[4] De Wit, B., & Meyer, R. (2010). *Strategy synthesis: Resolving strategy paradoxes to create competitive advantage*. Boston, MA: Cengage Learning.

[5] Hayes, J. (2018). *The theory and practice of change management*. Basingstoke: Palgrave MacMillan.

[6] Pettigrew, A. M., Woodman, R. W., & Cameron, K. S. (2001). Studying organizational change and development: Challenges for future research. *Academy of Management Journal*, *44*(4), 697–713.

[7] Senior, B., & Swailes, S. (2016). *Organizational change*. Harlow: Pearson Education.

[8] Todnem By, R. (2005). Organisational change management: A critical review. *Journal of Change Management*, *5*(4), 369–380.

# Part II

# Perspectives on Change

**IN THIS PART, YOU WILL LEARN TO . . .**

- define and identify change in different ways, recognising various approaches to understanding and managing it;
- explain how perspectives vary in shaping change and decision-making;
- apply perspectives to assess real-world change scenarios and their implications;
- evaluate the benefits and challenges of different perspectives on change.

If anything, organisational change is far from straightforward. It isn't simply something that 'is'; nor can it be approached in 'one true way'. It is complex, nuanced, and deeply influenced by the assumptions of those who engage with it. Much like everything else in life, really. Consider yourself for a moment, as you read this book. Even if you believe yourself to be the most straightforward person on Earth, there is no singular or absolute way to understand you. To some, you may appear outgoing, while others might perceive you as overwhelming. Some may find you quiet and reserved, while others see you as shy. To some, you're a parent; to others, a child. The point is that there's no definitive 'you' – only various interpretations of who you are. Each perception highlights certain facets of your identity while inevitably overlooking others.

Organisational change operates in much the same way. Different people approach it with different perspectives, each emphasising certain aspects and leaving others out. Some may view change as a highly logical and structured process, while others might see it as something that defies rationality. Some believe that change happens despite resistance, while others think that it occurs precisely because resistance exists. For some, change is a one-time event, a project to complete; for others, it's an ongoing, continuous process. Just as there are countless ways to interpret a person, there are multiple pathways to understanding and navigating change.

In this part, we will explore seven distinct approaches to organisational change. Each offers a unique lens through which to view and engage with change, and none is inherently superior to the others. Instead, each perspective adds a layer of insight, providing a richer, more multifaceted understanding of the complexity and fluidity of change in organisations.

# 2 A Managerial Perspective on Change

**PERSPECTIVE IN BRIEF**

- **Concepts related to the perspective** – planned change, change management, and organisational development
- **Keep reading to learn more about** – diagnosing and implementing change, change leadership, communication, and evaluation
- **Prime contributors** – C. Argyris, R. Beckhard, W. Burnes, R. Blake, J. Kotter, K. Lewin, and H. Shepard
- **Guiding metaphor** – change as a game of chess

## Introduction

In Chapter 1, we set the stage for developing a multi-angled understanding of organisational change. In this chapter, we embark on the first real leg of that journey.

Think for a moment about the big decisions in your life: choosing a university, taking a new job, buying a house – or even deciding whether to have a child. Chances are, you approached those moments with a sense of deliberation. You paused. Reflected. Weighed pros and cons. Made plans. Consulted experts. Googled. Maybe even drafted a spreadsheet or two.

In moments like these, change is often framed as something that can – and should – be managed. It is treated as a disruption to an otherwise stable status quo, one that requires clear thinking, rational analysis, and intentional action. The goal, after all, is to get it right. And getting it right, we assume, means making informed choices, exercising control, and following a well-structured path towards a desired outcome.

This way of thinking is not limited to our personal lives. It is deeply embedded in how many people (especially in organisational contexts) approach transformation. They visualise change like a chess game: success hinges on having the right strategy, anticipating future moves, and executing plans with precision. From this angle, the challenge is not just to respond to change but to control it – to lead it, structure it, and ensure that it delivers results.

This, in essence, is the **managerial perspective** we'll explore in this chapter – a way of seeing change as something orderly, technical, and tractable. It's a perspective that values planning over improvisation, expertise over intuition, and logic over ambiguity. It is so widely shared, so culturally reinforced, that it can easily feel like the default way to think about change. This chapter will explore the intricacies and implications of adopting such a managerial view – examining its structured models, its emphasis on expert-driven interventions, and its potential benefits and limitations.

So, let us position our pieces on the board, study the layout, and prepare to make our first move. Because understanding this perspective isn't just about observing from the sidelines – it's about getting into the game.

## 2.1 The Genesis of Thought

As perspectives go, a managerial perspective can be thought of as one of the more elderly chaps: it is an angle that has been around for almost a century. But what developments caused it to be conceived in the first place?

### 2.1.1 The Turn from Neutral to Normative

By the end of World War II, many scientists felt that their traditional stance of impartiality had to be revised: given the state that large parts of the world were in – that is, destroyed – many believed that remaining neutral and distant was no longer appropriate. Consequently, researchers dealing with organisations started to express an urge to actively help reconceive where to go – developing an interest in what should be, rather than what currently existed.[7]

This led to the development of several new practices, all aimed at improving organisations and managerial work.[23] Examples include precursors of team-building and leadership training (helping managers become more knowledgeable about themselves and their behaviour towards others) and survey assessments in an organisational context (assisting managers in coming to terms with what was happening).[20] In this way, instead of observing and theorising while standing idly by, researchers gradually entered a stage in which 'interventions' were increasingly put forward – with researchers rolling up their sleeves, getting 'down and dirty', and helping organisations move from their current outlooks towards potentially better ones.[12]

### 2.1.2 Increasing Knowledge Opened Pathways to Intervention

Of course, intervention requires more than intent – it also requires insight. By the end of the 1940s, organisational research had evolved into a reasonably established field. While most of this knowledge concerned organisations' current state of affairs – that is, those things that do not necessarily concern change, such as insights on structure, leadership, or motivation – the combination of such static insights did cultivate a sense of something going on 'in between': what if organisations wanted to *replace* their way of structuring; or what if they wanted to *revise* the way they were leading or motivating people? Metamorphically speaking, while having a clear set of organisational pictures did not yet render the film in motion, it did help to gradually build towards that kind of knowledge: as organisational research became increasingly developed, a managerial perspective on change emerged because it *could*. In earlier decades, coming to terms with change had been considered impossible without first understanding the basics of organising in stasis; now, that knowledge had become increasingly available.[7, 12, 23]

### 2.1.3 The Growing Entanglement of Research and Action

Finally, the rise of action research proved pivotal in sustaining the momentum of the managerial perspective.[34] As many advocates of a managerial perspective on change were heavily engaged with the practical side of doing business, a virtuous cycle of theory and practice was gradually nurtured. In simple terms, this can be visualised as organisational thinkers walking into companies with elaborate theories, which they then tried to put into practice. If theories were found useful, they were retained and further improved upon; if not, they went into the bin and new models were developed. In this sense, by focusing on writing what could be used in practice and sharpening in practice what had been written, organisational change became a topic fuelled by a passionate community of both managerial practitioners and scholarly theorists – ultimately leading to insights being continuously developed and reconceived on account of new experiences.[1, 20, 39]

**Box 2.1 The Point?**

The establishment of a managerial perspective was certainly not a random event: it resulted from a perfect storm that checked the boxes of intention, feasibility, and iteration. It was the puzzle, falling together; or the chess game, moving forward.

## 2.2 Unpacking the Heart

Just as a game of chess has a couple of ground rules that you would do well to remember if you want to get into the game properly – and want to avoid pieces flying across the room – thinking managerially about change involves abiding by a few key tenets. In this section, I'll unpack what can be understood as the heart of the managerial perspective (see Figure 2.1), looking into: how it thinks about the capacity of change; how it develops; how it is driven; and what the perspective states that change should ultimately be aiming for.

### 2.2.1 Capacity of Change: Change as a Deviation from the Status Quo

The first fundamental tenet underscoring thinking managerially about change is that **transformation is considered a deviation from the norm**. When a company is purring in production, your manager is having their daily coffee, or you are swearing at the printing machine, all is well – or at least 'normal', according to the managerial perspective. Yet when you are sitting slightly anxiously in a town hall meeting and are listening to your CEO's burning of the figurative company platform, that norm is considered breached. In this sense, thinking about change in a managerial

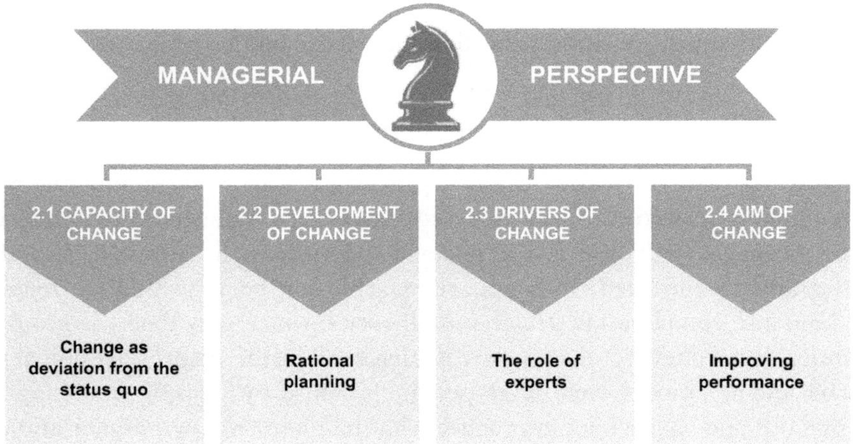


**Figure 2.1** Unpacking the heart of the managerial perspective.

way positions the organisation as a stable entity that operates consistently: its workings considered normal when uninterrupted. To change involves deliberately breaking up that normal procedure, crossing the borders of what is known, and pulling away from the standard of stability.[23, 38] By interrupting its normal functioning, changing an organisation involves forcing it into an uncomfortable, somewhat tumultuous state: change, as such, is considered the odd duckling in a family of status quo.[37]

Now, if you remember the story of that odd duckling, you'll recall that the poor guy did not have an easy time: if not managed carefully by poppa and momma duck, it was bound for rejection. From a managerial view, such rejection is thought to loom equally large over change. Practically speaking, this means that organisations are considered not to change of their own accord; rather, they should be directed – they must be jolted into movement lest they remain rigid. The challenge, then, is to manage change in a way that minimises disruption to the stability of the organisation, while still allowing for necessary modifications to be made. This requires a careful balancing act, as leaders must assess the potential consequences of change and weigh them against the benefits. In some cases, change may involve a complete overhaul of established procedures and processes; in other cases, it may simply involve making minor adjustments to existing systems.[25]

An important implication of this understanding of change as a directed deviation is that change requires motive and intention: without a clear idea of *why* to change, organisations would simply remain in their natural steady states, and our odd little change duckling would be kicked out faster than they could quack. Change thus requires a form of intervention, or an action in which people enter into an ongoing system of relationships, and come between or among persons, groups, or objects for the purpose of helping them.[3] Working through individual, team, and organisational interventions, the people directing change must intentionally lead the organisation away from its normal conduct – and, in doing so, overcome the friction and resistance such disruption is bound to cause.[25]

### Box 2.2 The Point?

Talking about organisational change from a managerial perspective always implicates considering change as something of an anomaly: an activity that – almost forcefully – redirects the organisation onto new paths, breaking up the status quo in which the firm would otherwise still be dwelling.[8, 12]

## 2.2.2 Development of Change: Rational Planning

So, if change is considered a deviation from the norm, how do we best tackle it? The answer: with **rational planning**. From a managerial view, change is thought of as best approached in a highly structured and logical fashion: just as in our game of chess, change is considered to be something that managers must intentionally plan out, preferably in highly ordered phases.[21, 41] While the content and the order of these phases may differ, they must collectively represent a highly systematic approach, conceptualised as a 'best practice' or a recipe for success. The following stages can typically be noted.[42]

First, the **diagnosis phase** involves establishing a decent understanding of what is precisely going wrong with the organisation's current state of affairs: what external or internal circumstances necessitate change? To establish a fair diagnosis, change agents are required to establish a neutral outlook on the organisation's current directions either through the use of qualitative means – such as observations, interviews, and surveys – or by resorting to more quantitative tools – such as spotting trends in key performance indicators.[25] During the diagnosis stage, solutions are not yet advanced: instead, agents focus on clearly defining the problem that the change programme will need to address.[12] Often, this phase is complemented by raising awareness of the issue at hand – creating a readiness for change among those who will eventually be subject to it.[26]

### Box 2.3 Practical Advice?

Useful questions to consider during *diagnosis*:

- What specific internal or external factors are creating the need for change?
- How can we gather unbiased data to accurately diagnose the problem?
- How can we ensure that stakeholders understand and acknowledge the need for change?

Next, during **analysis**, a plan must be generated to tackle the identified problem(s). Here, the change agent is expected to draw from the data gathered during diagnosis to anticipate any human, technical, or organisational issues – think of resource allocations, lead times, interdependencies, resistance by workers, and so on.[20] Various techniques and approaches have been developed to help change agents devise such an informed plan, such as the managerial grid,[10] techniques encapsulated in total quality management,[40] or various approaches related to goal setting.[30] What is essential is that the change agent does not go lightly about the efforts called for during analysis: for those approaching change in a managerial fashion, the analytical stage is often considered the most important one, with this stage thought to require more time than any of the others.[25]

### Box 2.4 Practical Advice?

Useful questions to consider during *analysis*:

- Which frameworks or methodologies will best support our planning efforts?
- How can we ensure that our plan aligns with both short-term needs and long-term goals?

Once the plan has been developed and reviewed, it's time to put it into practice. **Implementation** is often considered a somewhat irksome undertaking, with the change progress requiring close monitoring to avoid it being hindered by several potential barriers.[38] One of the most common obstacles is the 'people issue',[26] or resistance to change displayed by organisational members who, as individuals, may have interests that diverge significantly from the organisation's goals. To align organisational members with developed change plans, the managerial perspective advises using a broad set of tools, such as communication plans, incentives, and sanctions.[1, 45]

### Box 2.5 Practical Advice?

Useful questions to consider during *implementation*:

- How can we effectively communicate the change plan to all stakeholders?
- How will we monitor the implementation process to ensure that it stays on track?

Finally, during the **feedback phase**, the change programme's outcomes need to be reviewed and evaluated to ensure sustainability and identify areas for improvement in future change initiatives. Feedback can be qualitative or quantitative but should always be directed at establishing better outlooks on the change put forward. This phase is considered vital for the performance of the change programme taken up in the present as well as the programmes pushed for in the future.[26, 36, 38]

### Box 2.6 Practical Advice?

Useful questions to consider during *feedback*:

- What metrics will we use to evaluate the success of the change?
- How can we gather feedback from all levels of the organisation to gain a comprehensive view?
- What lessons can we learn from this change initiative to improve future efforts?

By structuring change as a series of well-defined stages, a managerial perspective on change highlights the significance of rationalisation. The approach enables a conscious and methodical development of the change programme, emphasising the importance of maintaining order and logical progression throughout its process.

### 2.2.3 Drivers of Change: The Role of Experts

So far, we have established a managerial sense of how change should be understood and how it should be developed. But who is to take care of these things? When approaching change in a managerial way, change is thought to be best handled by those with specific skills in the matter: **experts or change agents** are considered best equipped, capable of managing change in a way that 'ordinary' employees cannot. While the most general reference to the change agent's position would be that of the 'helping professional',[28] several more-specific references have over time been developed. What to think, for example, of the change agent as a 'doctor', meant to cure the sick organisational patient; or of the agent representing a 'technician', charged to fix all things bust in the organisational machine?[1] Regardless of the analogy, the crucial point to understand is that these people, from a managerial view, constitute the leaders without whose skills, techniques, and knowledge no change can really be successful.[8, 11, 37]

That these skills, techniques, and knowledge requirements can be rather extensive is to be well appreciated. In fact, looking into the expectations a managerial perspective may put on those leading transformation, one might wonder what kind of superhuman is capable of all the benevolences listed. Stimulating new intra-organisational connections, providing expert knowledge, giving continuous support, mobilising human energy, teaching opportunities … From a managerial angle, the change expert is viewed as a highly skilled individual whose capabilities are considered to far exceed those of others.[6, 36] Even Superman hero Clark Kent might find the challenge daunting – after all, battling villains might be the easier task.

Yet while expertise is emphasised as a key driver of change, this does not preclude change agents from originating within the organisation. When thinking about change in a managerial way, people typically recognise the value of *external* advisors – such as consultants or academics[25] – but also acknowledge the potential of *internal* experts to contribute effectively to change initiatives. Yet such internal expertise is often assumed to reside primarily within the human resources department[12] or the upper organisational echelons.[24] While a change programme can impact someone severely, this does not mean that this individual necessarily deserves a say in the matter: from a managerial perspective, those undergoing change are often thought to lack the know-how for assessing such changes effectively. Training, knowledge, and experience are the qualities that the managerial perspective validates for putting anyone at the steering wheel – not the level of involvement.[28, 45] In this sense, a managerial perspective on change puts stark distinctions between those 'leading' the change and those 'receiving' it – or, put differently, between the initiators of change and those expected to adapt to it.

### 2.2.4 Aim of Change: Improving Organisational Performance

Leaders, usually, are meant to lead others *somewhere*. In the managerial view, that destination is relatively clear: when thinking managerially about change, the aim is to enhance **performance**.[6] If anything, this means that change should tick at least some of the following boxes:

- Does the change help an individual within our firm do their job?
- Does the change help a team or a group within our firm do their job?
- Does the change help the organisation deliver the value that customers are asking for?
- Does the change help the organisational network that the firm is a part of?

While seemingly strict in its evaluation of change, mark that this notion of effectiveness can be interpreted broadly. Examples include the extent to which the organisation succeeds in attaining the goals it has set out; the degree to which it can improve its safeguarding of needed resources; the retention of strategic fit with the external environment; or the extent to which all stakeholders find themselves satisfied with outcomes.[12, 33] The central idea is that all change programmes must result in tangible and measurable outcomes. From a managerial perspective, change is not conducted just for fun; instead, it is being consciously advanced for the sake of improving the organisation's current reality towards a more beneficial state of play.

**Box 2.7 The Point?**

When upholding a managerial view, the outcome of a change programme is deemed to be strongly related to the state of the organisation as a performant entity: if anything, it is measurable performance that needs to benefit from the change in order for the transformation to be considered any good.[9, 23]

## 2.3 Extending Your Toolkit

Now that we have established a basic understanding of the core assumptions on which a managerial perspective is built, it's useful to look into different ways in which the perspective can be put into practice. While a managerial way of thinking represents one of the oldest approaches to organisational change, many models relating to the perspective still enjoy large numbers of enthusiastic supporters. The following are among the most popular tools in the perspective's toolbox. Use them to extend your own.

### 2.3.1 Lewin's Three-Stage Model

Originated by Kurt Lewin, the **three-stage model of change** is without a doubt one of the most foundational frameworks for understanding organisational transformation.[4, 15, 35] At its core, the model emphasises the importance of creating awareness and readiness for change by challenging established norms and behaviours. As momentum builds, new practices and strategies are introduced, compelling individuals and teams to adapt to an evolving environment. Finally, the focus shifts to reinforcing and stabilising these changes, ensuring that they become the new standard over time. By addressing both the psychological and the structural aspects of change, the three-stage model offers a practical framework for guiding organisations through successful transitions. In what follows, we'll delve deeper into each of the three stages.

#### 2.3.1.1 Unfreezing

First, making any change happen within an organisation starts with 'unfreezing' – that is, nurturing a context in which the change will be allowed to take hold. To do this, existing 'quasi-stationary' equilibria need to be explicitly destabilised, with organisational members candidly assessing whether their daily activities necessitate a change. Put simply: what are the forces that *call* for change – and what are the forces that *obstruct* such change from happening? Ultimately, change can only be realised if the urge to retain organisational relevance tops the anxiety over abandoning established practices. By explicitly addressing extant mindsets and modes of operation, psychological defence mechanisms may be lowered, with motivation and understanding setting the stage for change and reducing potential resistance.[4, 15, 35]

For example, consider a traditional manufacturing company that has been producing the same product line for decades. Despite declining sales and increasing competition, the company's employees continue with the same production processes because 'it's always been done this way'. The management team, recognising the need for innovation, could start the unfreezing stage by presenting data showing market trends, customer feedback, and financial projections that highlight the urgency of change. They might bring in external experts to discuss industry shifts or even visit companies that have successfully adapted to similar challenges.

To further destabilise the status quo, the company could organise workshops where employees assess their daily tasks and identify inefficiencies or outdated practices. This candid assessment might help them realise that their current activities no longer align with market demands, fostering a collective recognition that change is necessary. By addressing these mindsets, the company begins to lower psychological defences, making employees more open to change. For instance, if employees fear losing their jobs due to automation, management can reassure them by offering training programmes to help them adapt to new roles, thus reducing resistance.

#### 2.3.1.2 Changing

Second, it is during the change phase that the organisation makes whatever alterations it deems necessary. To devise what shifts are needed, the firm will need to analyse its current and desired situations; then, having identified the precise gap between these different states of play, it can push to make such a shift happen effectively. To do so, the organisation will need to involve the right individuals in the process, providing adequate resources and support to tackle any challenges that may arise. Essential to mark is that the act of moving is seldom straightforward: iteration and trial and error are key.[4, 15, 35]

In our manufacturing company, after recognising the need for more modern production techniques, management may decide to implement lean manufacturing practices. To make this shift, they begin by conducting a thorough analysis of their current production process, identifying bottlenecks, waste, and areas where automation could improve efficiency.

The company might then pilot the new process in one department, involving key employees who are open to innovation and providing them with the necessary training and resources. This pilot programme allows the organisation to test the new methods, gather feedback, and make adjustments before rolling them out company-wide. During this stage, the organisation communicates openly with all employees, addressing concerns and ensuring that they have the support they need to adapt. If the new process doesn't work as expected, the company revises it based on employee feedback and tries again.

#### 2.3.1.3 (Re)Freezing

In the third and final phase, having made the necessary adaptations to the organisation, an effort of '(re)freezing' is required. In this stage, the change is to be consolidated and made permanent; without such explicit efforts, change can often be remarkably short-lived. Here, the organisation is urged to solidify the change in new routines, norms, values, and policies; to work through feedback and continuous evaluation; and to explicitly recognise achievements. Put differently, how can we make sure that we don't quickly relapse into our former habits, but remain committed to our new ways? This stage highlights that change is inherently a collective effort, as changes in individual behaviour cannot be sustained unless group norms and routines are also transformed.[14]

Continuing with the manufacturing company example, after successfully implementing lean manufacturing practices across the organisation, management will need to focus on making these changes permanent. They might do so by updating the company's standard operating procedures to reflect the new processes, ensuring that every employee understands and follows the new guidelines. Regular training sessions and workshops can be held to reinforce the new practices and ensure that everyone is on the same page. Additionally, the company might introduce new performance metrics aligned with the lean manufacturing principles, such as reducing waste or improving production time, and recognise employees who excel in these areas. Feedback mechanisms, such as regular team meetings or suggestion boxes, can help management continuously monitor how well the changes are being integrated and make further adjustments if needed. In this way, the organisation ensures that the change is not just a temporary fix but a lasting transformation, fully integrated into the fabric of the company's operations and culture.

**Box 2.8 The Point?**

Overall, Lewin's three-stage model is a powerful starting framework that emphasises the importance of preparing for and consolidating change in a structured way. Although this model seems simple at first glance, its impact on organisations dealing with change can hardly be overstated: for beneath almost any discussion of change management, the notion of a three-stage process is often deeply embedded.[27]

## 2.3.2 Kotter's Eight-Step Model

While Lewin's model can be considered a common 'gateway drug' to the managerial view on change, most people only get hooked after going for something with a bit more bite: **Kotter's eight-step model**.[31] Recognising that change is often met with resistance, the eight-step model provides quite a detailed process to build momentum, align stakeholders, and embed lasting improvements. It emphasises the importance of leadership, clear communication, and sustained effort to ensure that change is not only implemented but also maintained over time. In what follows, I'll distil the essence of this well-trodden path for change.

### 2.3.2.1 Establish a Sense of Urgency

In the first step of Kotter's model, you need to establish a sense of urgency, often by identifying what threatens the organisation and what provides opportunities for change.[31] What are the reasons for the organisation to transform itself – and why are those reasons pressing? Think about a retail company facing declining sales due to the rise of e-commerce. To establish a sense of urgency, the management team could present data that shows how online shopping is rapidly gaining market share while the company's bricks-and-mortar sales are stagnating. They might share customer feedback highlighting dissatisfaction with the in-store experience compared to the convenience of online shopping. Additionally, management could emphasise that competitors are already investing heavily in digital platforms, and failing to act could lead to a significant loss of market share.

### 2.3.2.2 Build a Guiding Coalition

Next, Kotter's model stipulates the need to build a guiding coalition, this by identifying which people are considered influential in the different organisational substructures and hierarchical levels.[31] This coalition should include key stakeholders, influencers, and decision-makers who can help build momentum and overcome resistance to change. Important here are the presence of (i) position power, (ii) expertise, and (iii) credibility. In the retail company example, the guiding coalition may include senior executives, department heads, and key employees from different divisions such as marketing, IT, and customer services. The coalition could also involve influential store managers who have strong relationships with front-line staff. By including a diverse group of stakeholders, the company ensures that different perspectives are considered and that the change effort gains widespread support.

### 2.3.2.3 Develop a Change Vision

With your guiding coalition in place, Kotter's model stresses the need to develop a change vision and set out what the organisation will look like after the change has been implemented.[31] Decide how to reach opportunities and avoid any noted threats. Decide how to frame the change in terms of values and beliefs. In the retail company, the change vision might involve transforming the business into a leading omnichannel retailer that offers a seamless shopping experience both online and in-store. The vision could include specific goals such as launching a user-friendly e-commerce platform, integrating inventory management across channels, and enhancing the in-store experience with digital tools.

#### 2.3.2.4 Communicate the Vision

After having developed your vision, communicate it to all people involved in the change in a convincing and easily understandable manner.[31] Use various communication channels to reach everyone in the organisation. The retail company might use a combination of town-hall meetings, email newsletters, and internal social media platforms to communicate the change vision. Senior leaders could host question-and-answer sessions where employees can ask questions and voice concerns. The company could also create a series of videos or infographics that illustrate the benefits of the change and how it aligns with the company's mission. To further reinforce the message, the company could encourage managers to discuss the vision with their teams, thus disseminating information in a more personalised way.

#### 2.3.2.5 Empower Broad-Based Action

In the fifth step, Kotter calls to empower broad-based action by providing people with the tools, resources, and support they need to turn the vision into a reality.[31] Continuously scan for barriers, the most common being structure barriers (or the obstruction of change by the presence of formal structures), information barriers (or the obstruction of change by the absence of knowledge or skills), systems barriers (or the obstruction of change by the presence of undermining performance reward mechanisms), and boss barriers (or the obstruction of change by political games or the absence of top-level endorsement). In the retail company, empowering action might involve providing training programmes to help employees develop the digital skills needed to operate the new e-commerce platform. The company could also invest in new technology, such as point-of-sale systems that integrate with online orders, to streamline operations. To further support the change, the company might adjust its performance management system to include metrics related to digital sales and customer satisfaction across channels. This ensures that employees are incentivised to adopt new practices and contribute to the success of the change effort. Additionally, the company should identify and address any resistance to change. For instance, if some employees are reluctant to adopt new technology, management could provide additional training or one-on-one coaching to build their confidence and skills. By removing barriers and providing the necessary support, the company empowers employees to take ownership of the change and contribute to its success.

#### 2.3.2.6 Generate Short-Term Wins

With barriers having been removed, it's time to try to generate short-term wins, thus demonstrating the benefits of the change as you go along and sustaining momentum for the effort.[31] Allow people to achieve preliminary successes and reward the contributions of those involved. For the retail company, a short-term win might involve successfully launching a new mobile app that allows customers to shop online and pick up orders in-store. The company could measure the success of this initiative by tracking the number of app downloads, customer satisfaction ratings, and in-store-pick-up orders.

#### 2.3.2.7 Consolidate and Build on the Gains

Then, consolidate and build on the gains: analyse success stories and tap from these experiences to achieve continuous improvement.[31] After the successful launch of the mobile app, the retail company might analyse customer feedback to identify areas for improvement. Based on this analysis, the company could roll out additional features, such as personalised product recommendations or a loyalty programme integrated into the app. The company could also use the momentum from the short-term wins to tackle more complex challenges, such as overhauling its supply chain to better support omnichannel fulfilment. By continually building on the initial successes, the company can maintain the momentum of the change effort and ensure that the transformation continues to progress.

#### 2.3.2.8 Institutionalise the Change

Finally, institutionalise the change by making it part of the routines and culture of the organisation.[31] Continue leadership support and frequently discuss the change's success stories. For the retail company, institutionalising the change might involve embedding digital practices into the company's standard operating procedures, such as requiring all new product launches to be accompanied by online marketing campaigns. The company could also integrate digital metrics into its performance reviews, ensuring that employees are consistently evaluated on their contributions to the omnichannel strategy. To reinforce the change, leadership could also continue to share success stories and celebrate milestones, such as achieving a significant increase in online sales or customer satisfaction. By keeping the change top of mind and aligning it with the company's values, the organisation can ensure that the new practices become ingrained in its culture and that employees remain committed to the ongoing transformation.

**Box 2.9 Be Aware!**

Kotter's eight-step model provides a straightforward and seemingly easy-to-follow approach to change management: it offers a structured approach to change that helps organisations stay focused and on track. That said, the model can sometimes oversimplify organisational change's complex and dynamic nature: some organisations have found the model too rigid and unable to adapt to their unique needs and circumstances. Additionally, implementing the eight steps can be time-consuming, which may slow down change initiatives. Still, with Kotter's eight-step model being one of the most widely used frameworks for managing organisational change, it's an invaluable addition to the toolbox of any change enthusiast.[2]

### 2.3.3 McKinsey's Influence Model

While Kotter's model provides a clear sequential roadmap for managing change, the final model I'll discuss here shifts the focus more towards managing the setting in which behaviour takes place. Rooted in psychology and behavioural science, **McKinsey's influence model** highlights four essential 'building blocks' for effective transformation – asserting that lasting change occurs only when individuals are motivated, empowered, and supported in adapting their behaviours over time.[32] Sounds useful? Let's take a closer look.

#### 2.3.3.1 Understanding and Conviction

First, if you want people to change their thinking and behaviour, McKinsey's model states that you need them to understand why such a change is necessary at all – with building block one thus focusing on understanding and conviction. Change agents must start by creating a compelling narrative that communicates the facts and the thinking behind it. Such a narrative must tap into five sources of meaning, namely, why does this matter for (i) society, (ii) the company, (iii) the customer, (iv) the working team, and (v) the individual? By using clear and direct language, good narratives address employees' key concerns, such as: where are we now; where are we going; how will we get there; what does it mean for our team and me; how will we be supported; and how will we know that we are succeeding?[32]

Often, managers neglect to share critical pieces of a change narrative because they have already been dealing with it for a considerable time – making it hard to remember what those new to a change will experience as startling or scary. In other words, they fall prey to a knowledge curse, where they assume that others have the background required to understand what is being said. Good narratives are simple, relatable, and authentic, and are shared over multiple channels and moments. To improve ownership, executives can choose to disseminate a story by utilising an interactive cascade process, where each layer of managers can reformulate the narrative in their own words and pass it on to the next.

#### 2.3.3.2 Reinforcing with Formal Mechanisms

Next, while understanding the narrative behind change is an important first step, it will fall flat if people don't feel adequately supported by the organisational system – reflected in building block two relating to the reinforcement of behaviour with formal mechanisms. To truly shift behaviour, employees need to see that the system around them actively enables and reinforces the changes being asked of them.[32]

This begins with the reward system: what behaviours are recognised, valued, and rewarded? It is essential that individuals have the authority to influence the decisions for which they are held accountable. At the same time, organisations should not rely solely on financial incentives. Non-financial motivators – such as public recognition, increased autonomy, access to learning opportunities, or time to pursue personally meaningful projects – can be equally powerful. Crucially, the broader organisational architecture must also align with the desired change. This includes revisiting processes, structures, and systems – such as administrative routines, IT platforms, planning and budgeting cycles, and talent management practices – to ensure that they actively support the new behaviours. Across all three levers – financial, non-financial, and systemic – the guiding principle is coherence: each element must consistently reinforce the behavioural change the organisation seeks to embed.[32]

#### 2.3.3.3 Role Modelling

Furthermore, as social creatures, humans are known to model their behaviour quite strongly to those they consider 'significant'. Therefore, in the McKinsey model, role modelling is a critical third component for stimulating change. Unlike promoting the desired behaviour in the occasional town-hall meeting, role modelling concerns displaying what is expected through everyday activities.[32]

Here, two types of individual matter most: (i) senior leaders and (ii) influence leaders. The former group has a disproportionate impact on change and should live by the creed of being the change that they want to see in others. They are the captains of the organisational boat and are responsible for acting in the way they desire from others. The latter group, on the other hand, are people who have a wide circle of personal contacts, regardless of their official title or status. They can be factory workers or middle managers as long as they are respected by others in the organisation. Having both these types of people displaying the behaviour you want to see in your employee group is critical.

#### 2.3.3.4 Developing Talent and Skills

Finally, if you want people to change, the McKinsey model emphasises that you must allow them to develop the necessary talent and skills. Equip them with the necessary skills, which may include new technical skills but can also involve developing better 'soft skills' such as relational or emotional skills.[32]

Sometimes, skills can be developed by training your existing workforce. In such cases, it has been argued that it's best to opt for a 'field and forum approach', emphasising experiential learning. In this approach, people learn new skills in a classroom setting but are stimulated to immediately put such skills into practice through fieldwork assignments linked with coaching. Yet, sometimes, skills cannot be developed by training your existing workforce and should be brought in from outside the company. Here, practices include hiring new staff, partnering with external contractors, shrinking permanent roles, and rotating jobs. The bottom line across both approaches is that it offers the company the necessary skills to tackle the change.

## 2.4 Impact on the Ground

If you've reached this section of the chapter, you've already accumulated quite some knowledge on thinking managerially about change. But how will this likely benefit you in practice? As thinking managerially is one of the oldest ways of approaching organisational change, it has left quite a mark on how we cope with the phenomenon. Here, I'll consider the most noteworthy ways in which the perspective matters for our dealings with change.

### 2.4.1 A Managerial Perspective Validates Change as a Topic

First, approaching change in a managerial fashion does much to validate the issue as being worthy of explicit thought and consideration. By conceptualising rational models and structured reasoning, people can turn a rather abstract and fleeting notion into a phenomenon that can be observed, understood, and potentially channelled: in a sense, thinking managerially about change marks organisational transformation as a thing that can be rigorously planned, and implemented accordingly.

To understand the importance of coming to terms with a phenomenon in order to act on it, think of the development of young children. While toddlers experience a wide range of emotions, they initially have little control over them. However, as they grow into youngsters and learn to differentiate a little between emotions – such as anger versus jealousy or joy versus love – their ability to manage these feelings gradually improves. Though they may still struggle from time to time, their increasing awareness and understanding provide a foundation for greater emotional regulation.

Similarly, organisations that approach change through a structured, managerial lens may develop a stronger capacity to anticipate, navigate, and shape transformation. Note that this is a remarkable achievement because, by doing this, our focus shies away from the status quo and starts to be laid on what is happening in between stable states. As such, approaching change from a managerial angle may serve a role similar to what cinematography has done for the art of imagery: it brings movement and depth to what might otherwise appear static, drawing attention to the dynamic forces shaping the picture.[23]

### 2.4.2 A Managerial Perspective Makes Change Actionable

Next, by empowering people to 'work with' change rather than merely acknowledge its existence, thinking about change in a managerial way does more than putting change on the agenda: it sets the topic on the to-do list. By providing frameworks for the mind to relate to, a managerial perspective transforms change from an abstract and distant idea into a tangible and controllable process. With the appropriate skillset, change can be moulded and steered in the right direction, allowing individuals to take control and manage the change process effectively.[6, 45]

To better understand why this is important, consider the act of being creative. While brilliant ideas can occasionally emerge seemingly out of nowhere, relying on such spontaneous bursts of inspiration feels precarious, especially when creative output is required consistently. This is where frameworks and theories become essential. Creative processes, when guided by structured methodologies – such as brainstorming techniques, design thinking, or lateral thinking frameworks – shift from being unpredictable flashes of genius to deliberate and repeatable exercises.

In much the same way, approaching change with a managerial lens transforms it from an overwhelming, amorphous force into a navigable journey. It equips individuals and organisations with the mental tools to anticipate, adapt to, and even capitalise on change, rather than being passively shaped by it. Whether the guidelines and intervention strategies that come with this kind of thinking are always effective may even be beside the point. What's important is that upholding a managerial view may transform change into a verb: that is, an almost tangible activity that people can try to wrap their heads (and organisations) around. By breaking down the components of change into understandable and actionable parts, the managerial perspective helps turn the inevitable into the achievable – an angle that is as empowering as it is essential.

### 2.4.3 A Managerial Perspective Elevates Expertise

Finally, as thinking managerially about change has brought forth a wide array of techniques, models, and theories on how to go about change, it increases the prominence of those with the proper knowledge and training. Expertise, as such, gains a vital role in the organisation's successful coming to terms with change.

In many cases, this heightened recognition of expertise is something to be genuinely grateful for. Picture yourself working in a vast multinational organisation that abruptly moves forward with a sweeping global restructuring, without relying on any expertise. No rationale is provided, no urgent need explained. Worse yet, there's no clear roadmap for how this transformation will unfold. Each day, you arrive at work uncertain whether your role, your team, or even your chair will still be there. Frustrating? Very much so. This kind of disorientation is often the most glaring symptom of change executed on impulse – an approach that risks chaos rather than progress.

The recognition of expertise as a vital source for managing a change process also makes organisations more open to external parties: as in-company leaders are often industry experts rather than change experts, thinking managerially nudges organisations to tap into knowledge beyond corporate boundaries. Not only does a managerial perspective acknowledge external hiring as an effective option but it also typically marks such approach as the most efficient option. Given these clear inclinations towards consultants, it seems fair to say that much of consultancy's sustained success rests on managers retaining a perspective that emphasises change as a controllable endeavour – an endeavour that can be successfully tackled, if only approached with the right set of knowledge and skills.[1, 12, 24, 37]

## 2.5 Drawbacks and Pitfalls

For all the traction that a managerial perspective on change can boast, there are also a fair number of drawbacks and pitfalls to keep in mind. This section covers the thorniest controversies to be aware of.

### 2.5.1 A Managerial Perspective Can Be Overly Linear

If you've worked your way through this chapter in section order, you'll understand by now how a managerial perspective can offer a very comforting sense of structure: it provides clear direction in uncertain times and simplifies complex processes into clearly delineated phases. However, this linear approach also comes with a significant downside, namely, it risks over-simplifying the unpredictable and often chaotic nature of real-world change.[16, 17, 44]

Think about a major life decision – relocating to a new city or switching careers. Do you follow a perfectly rational sequence of steps, one after the other? More often than not, while we may aspire to do that, the actual process is far messier: decisions are made based on intuition, reconsidered multiple times, or shaped by unforeseen circumstances. Change, in reality, is rarely as tidy as managerial models suggest. Phases blend, overlap, or even reverse, making the textbook approach feel more like an illusion of control than control itself.

This illusion becomes even more problematic when older models are applied to today's rapidly changing environment. While structured approaches to change may have sufficed in more stable times, critics argue that many managerial frameworks were designed for contexts that no longer exist. In a world defined by constant disruption and complexity, rigid adherence to linear models can be more of a hindrance than a help.[19]

To be fair, the oversimplification of managerial models is not always the fault of their creators. Many of the most well-known models – such as Lewin's three-stage model – were originally filled with nuances, caveats, and flexibility. Over time, however, managers seeking quick, actionable insights stripped away these subtleties, leaving behind an overly rigid interpretation.[4, 14] At their core, these models were never intended as strict blueprints; rather, they were intended as tools to help structure thinking about change. Instead of prescribing a fixed sequence of steps, they aimed to bring clarity to an otherwise ambiguous process. When used in this way – as flexible guides rather than rigid checklists – managerial perspectives on change can still be valuable.[5]

#### Box 2.10 Practical Advice?

Instead of rigidly adhering to predefined phases, leaders should be prepared to revisit and adjust their strategies as new information emerges. This might involve implementing feedback loops, where ongoing assessments of the change process inform adjustments to the plan. Additionally, it's important to communicate to all stakeholders that the change process is not a one-size-fits-all journey. Encourage teams to view the change plan as a living document that evolves over time. This mindset can help mitigate the risks associated with overly rigid models and promote a culture of adaptability, ensuring that the organisation can navigate unexpected challenges more effectively.

### 2.5.2 A Managerial Perspective Marginalises the Human Side of Change

Furthermore, when looking into the core ideas that come with a managerial perspective, some organisational members might start to feel somewhat uncanny: for while a managerial view can validate a sense of logic and reasoning, it can also lead to a deliberate overlooking or denouncing of the human experience in transformation. By focusing on rationalisation, performance, and optimisation, managerial thinking can detach organisational change from the deeply personal and emotional realities in which it unfolds.

One key issue here is how resistance to change is framed. Early managerial thinkers, in their efforts to understand why change initiatives fail, helped cement the idea that resistance comes primarily from operational staff. Over time, this narrative has painted employees as obstacles rather than as key contributors to transformation. When a change effort encounters difficulties, blame often falls on front-line workers – the ones tasked with implementing the plan – rather than on decision-makers who may have underestimated the complexities of execution.[18, 37]

For instance, consider a company undergoing a digital transformation. From a managerial perspective, if the rollout of a new software system encounters difficulties – perhaps due to inadequate training or unforeseen technical issues – the blame often falls on the operational staff who struggle to adapt, rather than on the decision-makers who may have misread the complexities of the change. This reinforces the notion that there is a divide between those who 'get' the change (the managers or change agents) and those who don't (the operational personnel).

In this way, change is perceived as creating a stark division between the promoting 'agents' and the obstructing 'receivers'. While thinking about change in a managerial fashion may be very effective for legitimising change initiatives, it can also impose a significant toll on employees.[22] Those at the top – executives and managers – are in charge of the change, setting the direction and pace, while those at the bottom – operational workers – are expected to comply without question. This top-down approach can create a significant divide within the organisation, where employees feel disenfranchised and less invested in the change, which ultimately undermines its success.[1, 5, 37]

### Box 2.11 Practical Advice?

To help ensure that the human aspect is not neglected, leaders could prioritise open communication and employee involvement throughout the change process. Regular check-ins and feedback sessions can help identify potential sources of resistance early on, allowing leaders to address them. Moreover, it's crucial to acknowledge and validate the emotional responses that change can evoke. Providing support, such as training, counselling, or mentorship programmes, can help employees navigate a transition more smoothly.

## 2.5.3 A Managerial Perspective Is Inconsiderate of Context

Next, a managerial perspective on change often prioritises efficiency, standardisation, and replicability. The appeal is clear – universal techniques and best practices offer managers a sense of control and predictability. However, the managerial perspective also comes with a critical flaw: it can overlook the unique complexities of each organisation's context. By relying on templates and one-size-fits-all solutions, managers risk sidelining the very factors that often make change successful – culture, history, and situational nuances.[13, 20, 37, 39]

Imagine a multinational corporation rolling out a new leadership framework across its global offices. A standardised approach may work well in one region but clash with deeply ingrained work norms in another. Yet, the managerial mindset, in its pursuit of broadly applicable solutions, often neglects these contextual subtleties.

This over-reliance on generic models can reduce change management to little more than a checklist exercise. Organisations become so fixated on following so-called best practices that they fail to recognise how those practices need to be adapted to fit their specific circumstances. Hollow corporate phrases replace meaningful, context-driven strategies, leaving employees disengaged and sceptical of yet another top-down initiative.

In a way, this is the fundamental pitfall of managerial models: in trying to be universally applicable, they often become so generalised that they fail to serve anyone effectively. A framework designed to fit all may, in practice, fit no one particularly well.

### Box 2.12 Practical Advice?

To avoid the pitfalls of a context-insensitive approach, organisations should invest time in understanding the organisation's culture, the external environment, and the specific challenges and opportunities that may affect the change process. One effective way to do this may be through stakeholder analysis, where the needs, expectations, and influence of various internal and external stakeholders are mapped out. This can help identify potential barriers and enablers of change, allowing for a more tailored and context-sensitive approach. Additionally, conducting pilot tests or small-scale implementations can provide valuable insights into how well a change initiative will fit within the organisation's specific context, enabling leaders to make necessary adjustments before a full rollout.

## 2.5.4 A Managerial Perspective Remains Largely Unproven

Finally, although approaching change from a managerial angle may keep organisations focused on improving performance, it is necessary to remain aware that the approaches advocated by the perspective often feed on little empirical evidence. In fact, does using managerial models really help to change your company?

Ultimately, few can really tell for sure: although there is an increasing amount of literature that highlights the significance of change and provides recommendations for managing it, surprisingly little proof has been presented to support the various theories and approaches proposed.[43] For this reason, when approaching change from a managerial angle, be aware that some will argue that such an approach may not so much serve you as it will the internal and external experts that find their legitimacy based on the array of techniques and methods set out.[19, 29]

## SUMMARY

Chapter 2 examined a **managerial perspective** on change, emphasising strategic planning, expert-driven interventions, and a structured approach to change (see Table 2.1 for an overview).

**Table 2.1 A managerial perspective on change: overview**

| | |
|---|---|
| **Guiding metaphor** | Change as a game of chess |
| **The Genesis of thought** | |
| Development 1 | The turn from neutral to normative |
| Development 2 | Increasing knowledge opening pathways to intervention |
| Development 3 | The growing entanglement of research and action |
| **Unpacking the heart** | |
| Capacity of change | Change as a deviation from the status quo |
| Development of change | Rational planning |
| Drivers of change | The role of experts |
| Aim of change | Improving performance |
| **Extending your toolkit** | |
| Tool #1 | Lewin's three-stage model |
| Tool #2 | Kotter's eight-step model |
| Tool #3 | McKinsey's influence model |
| **Impact on the ground** | |
| (+) | A managerial perspective validates change as a topic. |
| (+) | A managerial perspective turns change actionable. |
| (+) | A managerial perspective elevates expertise. |
| **Drawbacks and pitfalls** | |
| (−) | A managerial perspective can be overly linear. |
| (−) | A managerial perspective marginalises the human side of change. |
| (−) | A managerial perspective is inconsiderate of context. |
| (−) | The managerial perspective remains largely unproven. |
| **Related concepts** | |
| ► | Planned change |
| ► | Change management |
| ► | Organisational development |

- ◊ We started by tracing the **evolution of thought** in this domain, beginning with a shift from neutral to normative research, where studies moved from merely observing change to prescribing how it should be managed. As research progressed, knowledge became more readily available, enabling organisations to take a proactive role in implementing change. Over time, the distinction between studying change and actively shaping it blurred, leading to the increasing entanglement of research and action.
- ◊ At its **core**, a managerial perspective was noted as seeing change as a deviation from the status quo. It is developed through rational planning, where structured processes and expertise guide interventions. Experts play a crucial role in diagnosing challenges and designing solutions, reinforcing a view that change is something that can be engineered and managed. The ultimate aim of change within this perspective is improving performance, with a focus on efficiency and effectiveness.
- ◊ To support this structured approach, we explored **three key models** that are commonly used: Lewin's three-stage model, which provides a fairly high-level framework for planned change; Kotter's eight-step model, which offers a more step-by-step guide to leading organisational transformations; and McKinsey's influence model, which emphasises behavioural and mindset shifts as drivers of change.
- ◊ Drawing on these and other insights, we marked the managerial perspective as **contributing to change** by making it seem more structured and manageable, validating change as an important managerial discipline and increasing the prominence of expert-driven approaches.
- ◊ However, for all its benefits, we also noted that this perspective is not without its **limitations**. Importantly, by assuming that change follows a predictable, linear sequence, it often overlooks the complexities and unpredictability of real-world organisational dynamics. The structured nature of managerial approaches may also downplay the human and emotional dimensions of change, treating it as a purely technical process. Finally, there is a risk of neglecting broader contextual factors, such as culture, power dynamics, and external influences, which can significantly impact how change unfolds in practice.

The managerial perspective is closely linked to broader concepts such as planned change, change management, and organisational development, all of which contribute to the structured efforts organisations undertake to navigate transitions. While the managerial approach has played a crucial role in shaping modern change management practices, it also raises important questions about flexibility, adaptability, and the role of human dynamics in achieving meaningful and lasting transformation.

## CASE: MICROSOFT'S LEAP INTO A NEW AGE

### The Managerial Perspective in Practice

In 2014, Microsoft was known to be a troubled company. Despite having long been one of the most groundbreaking firms in corporate history, Microsoft had not found the new millennium treating it well. It had become infamous for its toxic corporate culture, with people drawing cartoons that depicted the company as made up of warring factions. Its approval ratings on employee review fora were abysmal and were dwarfed by the ratings at other major tech companies: in 2011, Microsoft CEO Steve Ballmer got the approval of barely a third of his employees, compared to the more than 90 per cent approval rating at Google. Innovation and creativity were crippled by management systems that pushed employees to prioritise politics over organisational performance. As a result, talent was jumping ship faster than it could be replaced. Microsoft was outpaced by competitors on multiple fronts, including in search engines and smartphones. From all angles, it had become a company that seemed destined to fade towards irrelevance.

Yet only a decade later Microsoft's share price had risen more than sevenfold. Its Azure service had become a leading product in cloud computing, with a large share of Fortune 500 companies choosing it. Its Teams platform had developed into one of the most popular business communication platforms worldwide. The company was generally considered to be one of the leading experts in artificial intelligence (AI) – also owing to a number of strategic partnerships, such as with OpenAI – making Microsoft one of the first to unlock the new era of technology-driven solutions.

How to make sense of this drastic turnaround? In this case study, we will look into a rather spectacular example of consciously devised change. It concerns a change that was spear-headed by a number of central figures, the most prominent being an India-born cricket enthusiast: Microsoft's newly appointed CEO Satya Nadella.

## A New Wind at Microsoft

Nadella, an organisational insider, developed his career within the Microsoft founded by Gates and continued by Ballmer. He joined the company in 1992 as a computer scientist. Throughout his tenure, he held various leadership positions and was ultimately named CEO on 4 February 2014. On that day, he wrote a letter to all employees emphasising how he had joined Microsoft to contribute to making the world a better place, and how he had admired the firm's creative prowess in tech. Later, however, he also acknowledged that this prowess was increasingly under threat, noting that Microsoft's culture had become inflexible. Execution and punctual delivery eclipsed collaboration and experimentation; meetings were steeped in formality; and any effort by senior leaders to engage with ideas from lower-level employees required navigating a maze of bureaucratic layers. A premium was placed on intellectual dominance – employees often felt compelled to demonstrate they were the sharpest in any room, creating an environment where status outshone substance. In this environment, passion and commitment struggled to breathe, and creativity was quietly sidelined.

During his first year as CEO, Nadella spent most of his time listening to others. By allowing people to speak up – without them having to fear repercussions – he learnt that employees were hoping for necessary changes, but also wanted to preserve the core values of Microsoft. Engineers desired to take the lead again instead of following competitors. What employees really requested was a clear plan to overcome inaction.

To drive this transformation, Nadella gathered a senior leadership team that he believed would collaborate on each other's challenges, encourage open conversation, and work effectively together. Among others, this included Peggy Johnson, a former Qualcomm executive; Kurt Delbene, former lead manager of Microsoft's Office division; and Kathleen Hogan, a former member of McKinsey and Oracle and now serving as Microsoft's chief people officer. Additionally, some other executives were let go. For Nadella, this move was crucial to ensure a cohesive team with a shared perspective.

In 2015, Nadella revealed the company's new mission statement: 'To empower every person and every organisation on the planet to achieve more.' To achieve this new mission, he stated that each employee within the company would have to let go of their 'fixed mindset' and work towards a 'growth mindset' instead – or a way of approaching things as opportunities for learning, rather than showing off current performance.

Most of this message was based on the book *Mindset: The New Psychology of Success* by Carol Dweck. In this book, Dweck claims that individuals with a fixed mindset are more likely to stick to familiar activities and current capabilities, while those with a growth mindset are driven to learn new things and ultimately improve themselves – despite initial struggles. Drawn to these ideas because of the value they had for his private situation – raising a child who was born with cerebral palsy – Nadella saw their potential to guide Microsoft's culture change. He concluded that the company's culture would revolve around the idea that everyone can change their mindset and become a 'learn-it-all' instead of a 'know-it-all'.

At an off-site gathering with a large group of executives, a discussion was initiated on refining the desired culture. The leaders of this group became known as the 'culture cabinet' and were tasked with defining the concept of a growth mindset for Microsoft. After extensive debate and input from experts, the group arrived at three defining pillars: a focus on the customer; an emphasis on diversity and inclusion; and promoting a united approach as One Microsoft.

During the years that followed, Nadella modelled a culture of curiosity and a desire to learn, embracing new ideas and information as they were presented to him. He also exemplified what this meant in practice. After causing controversy at a conference when he suggested that women should not ask for a raise but instead trust the system to address the gender pay gap, Nadella sent an email to all Microsoft employees acknowledging that he had given the completely wrong advice. He acknowledged that this was an area where he had much to learn, setting the tone for the culture of empathy and growth that he had asked others for. A few years later, Microsoft achieved equal pay for women and men.

To turn his ideas on a growth mindset into reality, Nadella and his 'culture cabinet' got to work. This included doing seemingly minor things such as assigning the leadership team to read a book on developing healthy relationships, or stimulating individuals to choose one of ten behaviours that promote inclusiveness and engage in a discussion about it. It also included more sweeping changes. For example, to embody the value of customer obsession, Microsoft employees were encouraged to interact directly with customers: teams were nudged to engage in immersive experiences to speak with customers on their own turf. This allowed executives to better understand the challenges faced by their customers, leading to meaningful discussions and improved problem-solving.

Furthermore, to stimulate a diverse and inclusive environment at Microsoft, Nadella changed the annual executive retreat to include founders of newly acquired companies – a thing that was formerly unheard of. These new leaders provided a fresh, innovative outlook and helped push the company to be better. Moreover, to promote the collective ethos of One Microsoft, a much-hated stack-ranking performance system (which scored employees as either better or worse than their peers) was eliminated. Instead, it was replaced with ongoing feedback, coaching, and a system that emphasises both short-term and long-term development. 'Performance metrics' referred to revenue and profit in the current year, while 'power metrics' indicated future performance, focusing on factors such as customer usage and satisfaction.

### Results Were Coming but Challenges Remained

After several years of focusing on cultural transformation, small, positive results were noticed. For instance, while executives had long considered the idea of doing customer visits during retreats preposterous, many eventually ranted for days about what they had seen and how this would impact Microsoft as a company. Passion and enthusiasm for the program started to load the air.

Yet, despite employees highlighting their belief that the company was moving in the right direction, there were some areas of concern. A survey showed that employees felt that their middle management was not prioritising talent development, which led to discouragement even among the most optimistic workers. Furthermore, in 2016, Microsoft launched an AI-based chatbot named Tay. The experiment failed when Twitter trolls targeted the bot with hateful and offensive language, causing it to spew similar messages back; the press criticised the experiment as a humiliation for Microsoft. However, Nadella encouraged the creators of Tay to continue pushing and to learn from their mistakes, reminding them to be humble and to lead with purpose. Nadella had set a clear mission and had aimed to create an empowering culture – but implementation was not yet complete.

To further solidify the new culture, Nadella and his team started to implement numerous thoughtful and subtle references to empathy, inclusion, and accessibility – hidden in plain sight like Easter eggs for those who took notice. In the cafeteria, a napkin holder reminded employees of the value of lifelong learning; on one of the elevator doors, the Chinese symbol for 'listen' was incorporated, serving as a quiet reminder of the importance of attentive communication and understanding. Tucked away amid the outdoor greenery, a small placard was installed that drew attention to a computer science co-teaching programme, subtly promoting collaboration and accessibility in education. These and many other initiatives were meant to advance and solidify the company's culture – emphasising to all who worked there that the change was here to stay. Here, Nadella stressed that discussing culture change and customer focus without connecting them to core performance metrics could lead to failure. He explained that their own tools had all become key instruments for driving cultural change, as they now tracked metrics like consumption growth alongside traditional measures such as end-quarter revenue and profit by segment.

### An Exciting Future Ahead

At the time of writing, Microsoft was once again considered one of the top destinations for engineering talent. More than 90 per cent of employees mentioned that they would recommend the company to a friend, with approval ratings of Satya Nadella soaring at 96 per cent. The company has risen to become a major player in the gaming industry, and its investments in AI have positioned the firm as a force to be reckoned with for years to come. Microsoft, once again, looks like a company that has it all: the success to dazzle and the humbleness to endure.

### Reflect

1. How does the Microsoft case illustrate the core ideas of a managerial perspective on change?
2. How can you make sense of the case based on (i) Lewin's three-stage model; (ii) Kotter's eight-step model; and (iii) McKinsey's influence model?
3. Reflect critically on the drawbacks of Microsoft's approach. What could be improved? What could be revised?

### Case Study Sources

Carucci, R. (2019, 14 October). Microsoft's Chief People Officer: What I've learned about leading culture change. *Forbes*, www.forbes.com/sites/roncarucci/2019/10/14/microsofts-chief-people-officer-what-ive-learned-about-leading-culture-change/.

The Economist. (2017, 16 March). What Satya Nadella did at Microsoft. www.economist.com/business/2017/03/16/what-satya-nadella-did-at-microsoft.

The Economist. (2020, 22 October). How Satya Nadella turned Microsoft around. www.economist.com/briefing/2020/10/22/how-satya-nadella-turned-microsoft-around.

Joly, H. (2022, 10 June). Does your company's culture reinforce its strategy and purpose? *Harvard Business Review*, https://hbr.org/2022/06/does-your-companys-culture-reinforce-its-strategy-and-purpose.

London, S., & Nadella, S. (2018, 3 April). Microsoft's next act [podcast transcript]. *McKinsey Quarterly*, www.mckinsey.com/industries/technology-media-and-telecommunications/our-insights/microsofts-next-act.

McCracken, H. (2018, 1 June). Transforming culture at Microsoft: Satya Nadella sets a new tone. *In the Black*, https://intheblack.cpaaustralia.com.au/people/satya-nadella-transforming-culture-microsoft.

Microsoft Corporation. (2015). Annual report 2015. https://www.microsoft.com/investor/reports/ar15/index.html.

Nadella, S. (2017, 21 September). Satya Nadella: The C in CEO stands for culture. *Fast Company*, www.fastcompany.com/40457741/satya-nadella-the-c-in-ceo-stands-for-culture.

Nadella, S., Shaw, G., & Nichols, J. T. (2017). *Hit refresh: The quest to rediscover Microsoft's soul and imagine a better future for everyone*. New York: Harper Business.

Tabrizi, B. (2023, 20 February). How Microsoft became innovative again. *Harvard Business Review*, https://hbr.org/2023/02/how-microsoft-became-innovative-again.

## REFERENCES

[1] Anderson, D. (2010). *Organization development: The process of leading organizational change*. Thousand Oaks, CA: Sage.

[2] Appelbaum, S. H., Habashy, S., Malo, J.-L., & Shafiq, H. (2012). Back to the future: Revisiting Kotter's 1996 change model. *Journal of Management Development*, *31*(8), 764–782.

[3] Argyris, C. (1970). *Intervention theory and method: A behavioral science view*. Reading, MA: Addison-Wesley.

[4] Bargal, D. (2012). Kurt Lewin's vision of organizational and social change. In D. Boje, B. Burnes, & J. Hassard (eds.), *The Routledge companion to organizational change* (pp. 31–46). Abingdon: Routledge.

[5] Bartunek, J. M., Balogun, J., & Do, B. (2011). Considering planned change anew: Stretching large group interventions strategically, emotionally, and meaningfully. *Academy of Management Annals*, *5*(1), 1–52.

[6] Beckhard, R. (1969). *Organization development: Strategies and models*. Reading, MA: Addison-Wesley.

[7] Bennis, W. G. (1963). A new role for the behavioral sciences: Effecting organizational change. *Administrative Science Quarterly*, *8*(2), 125–165.

[8] Bennis, W. G., Benne, K. D., Chin, R., & Corey, K. E. (1976). *The planning of change*. Boston, MA: Holt, Rinehart and Winston.

[9] Bennis, W. G., & Shepard, H. A. (1956). A theory of group development. *Human Relations*, *9*(4), 415–437.

[10] Blake, R. R., & Mouton, J. (1964). *The managerial grid: The key to leadership excellence*. Houston, TX: Gulf.

[11] Blake, R. R., Mouton, J. S., & McCanse, A. A. (1989). *Change by design*. Upper Saddle River, NJ: Prentice-Hall.

[12] Burke, W. W. (1992). *Organization development: A process of learning and changing*. Reading, MA: Addison-Wesley.

[13] Burnes, B. (1996). No such thing as … a 'one best way' to manage organizational change. *Management Decision*, *34*(10), 11–18.

[14] Burnes, B. (2004). Kurt Lewin and the planned approach to change: A re-appraisal. *Journal of Management Studies*, *41*(6), 977–1002.

[15] Burnes, B. (2012). Kurt Lewin and the origins of OD. In D. Boje, B. Burnes, & J. Hassard (eds.), *The Routledge companion to organizational change* (pp. 15–30). Abingdon: Routledge.

[16] Child, J. (1977). *Organization: Contemporary principles and practice*. Hoboken, NJ: John Wiley and Sons.

[17] Clegg, S. R., Kornberger, M., & Pitsis, T. (2015). *Managing and organizations: An introduction to theory and practice*. Thousand Oaks, CA: Sage.

[18] Coch, L., & French Jr, J. R. P. (1948). Overcoming resistance to change. *Human Relations*, *1*(4), 512–532.

[19] Cummings, S., Bridgman, T., & Brown, K. G. (2016). Unfreezing change as three steps: Rethinking Kurt Lewin's legacy for change management. *Human Relations*, *69*(1), 33–60.
[20] Cummings, T. G., & Worley, C. G. (2014). *Organization development and change*. Boston, MA: Cengage Learning.
[21] Dunn, W. N., & Swierczek, F. W. (1977). Planned organizational change: Toward grounded theory. *Journal of Applied Behavioral Science*, *13*(2), 135–157.
[22] Ford, J. D., Ford, L. W., & D'Amelio, A. (2008). Resistance to change: The rest of the story. *Academy of Management Review*, *33*(2), 362–377.
[23] French, W., Bell, C., & Zawacki, R. A. (1994). *Organization development and transformation: Managing effective change*. Boston, MA: Irwin.
[24] Hambrick, D. C., Nadler, D., & Tushman, M. (1998). *Navigating change: How CEOs, top teams, and boards steer transformation*. Boston, MA: Harvard Business School Press.
[25] Harvey, D., & Brown, D. (2001). *An experiential approach to organization development*. Upper Saddle River, NJ: Prentice-Hall.
[26] Hayes, J. (2002). *The theory and practice of change management*. Basingstoke: Palgrave MacMillan.
[27] Hendry, C. (1996). Understanding and creating whole organizational change through learning theory. *Human Relations*, *49*(5), 621–641.
[28] Jones, G. N. (1969). *Planned organizational change: A study of change dynamics*. London: Routledge and Kegan Paul.
[29] Kanter, R. M. (1992). *Challenge of organizational change: How companies experience it and leaders guide it*. New York: Free Press.
[30] Kaplan, R. S., & Norton, D. P. (1992). *The balanced scorecard: Measures that drive performance*. Boston, MA: Harvard Business School Press.
[31] Kotter, J. P. (1996). *Leading change*. Boston, MA: Harvard Business School Press.
[32] Lawson, E., & Price, C. (2003). The psychology of change management. *McKinsey Quarterly, Special edition: The value in organization*, 30–41.
[33] Levinthal, D. (1991). Organizational adaptation and environmental selection-interrelated processes of change. *Organization Science*, *2*(1), 140–145.
[34] Lewin, K. (1946). Action research and minority problems. *Journal of Social Issues*, *2*(4), 34–46.
[35] Lewin, K. (1947). Frontiers in group dynamics: Concept, method and reality in social science; social equilibria and social change. *Human Relations*, *1*(1), 5–41.
[36] Lippitt, R. (1958). *Dynamics of planned change*. New York: Harcourt, Brace and Company.
[37] Parker, C. A. (1980). The literature on planned organizational change: A review and analysis. *Higher Education*, *9*(4), 429–442.
[38] Paton, R. A., & McCalman, J. (1992). *Change management: A guide to effective implementation*. Thousand Oaks, CA: Sage.
[39] Porras, J. I., & Berg, P. O. (1978). The impact of organization development. *Academy of Management Review*, *3*(2), 249–266.
[40] Powell, T. C. (1995). Total quality management as competitive advantage: A review and empirical study. *Strategic Management Journal*, *16*(1), 15–37.
[41] Robertson, P. J., Roberts, D. R., & Porras, J. I. (1993). Dynamics of planned organizational change: Assessing empirical support for a theoretical model. *Academy of Management Journal*, *36*(3), 619–634.

[42] Stouten, J., Rousseau, D. M., & De Cremer, D. (2018). Successful organizational change: Integrating the management practice and scholarly literatures. *Academy of Management Annals*, *12*(2), 752–788.

[43] Todnem By, R. (2005). Organisational change management: A critical review. *Journal of Change Management*, *5*(4), 369–380.

[44] Tsoukas, H., & Chia, R. (2002). On organizational becoming: Rethinking organizational change. *Organization Science*, *13*(5), 567–582.

[45] Zaltman, G., & Duncan, R. (1977). *Strategies for planned change*. Hoboken, NJ: John Wiley and Sons.

# 3 An Organic Perspective on Change

## PERSPECTIVE IN BRIEF

- **Concepts related to the perspective** – emergent change, evolutionary change, contextual change, complexity in change, and a process-based view on change
- **Keep reading to learn more about** – continuous improvement and innovation, and collaboration in change
- **Prime contributors** – R. Chia, A. Langley, A. Pettigrew, M. Poole, R. Stacey, H. Tsoukas, A. Van de Ven, and K. E. Weick
- **Guiding metaphor** – change as a running stream

## Introduction

While many of us prefer change to be structured and intentional – as Chapter 2 portrayed it – there are numerous instances where such logic is notably absent. A simple stroll to a nearby river, for example, reveals a form of change that unfolds naturally and without a predetermined plan. As each water droplet reacts to curves and obstacles in the riverbank as well as to the trajectory of other droplets, it moves forward. Collectively, these movements escalate into a running river, continuously changing its flow according to the elements of its environment – torrential rains, a fallen branch, you standing in with your feet – but also impacting that same environment in return. There is no 'manager of rivers' directing the droplets which way to go; yet, despite such absence, transformation is continuously occurring.

Even the way you are sitting here, reading this book, reflects how change can unfold without deliberate orchestration. For one, I feel quite certain that the clothes you are wearing right now are distinctly different from the ones your great-great-grandmother was wearing when going about her day. While she may have been dressed in clogs and a bonnet, you're much more likely to be wearing a pair of trainers and a cap. Such changes in fashion have not come about because a globally appointed 'leader of apparel transformation' wanted it so, but because of ordinary people's everyday decisions linking together over time. In most cases, such decisions happened unconsciously, based on chance, but they nonetheless added up to a global sense of fashion that is decidedly different from the one that reigned at the time of your great-great-grandmother.

In this chapter, we will delve deeper into the **organic perspective** on change – a view that challenges the notion of structured, top-down transformation as discussed in Chapter 2. Unlike the carefully orchestrated plans that often still dominate organisational strategies, thinking organically about change invites consideration of the interactions, adaptations, and (sometimes unconscious) decisions of individuals within a system. Just as a river's path is shaped not by a single directive force but by the collective movements of countless water droplets, so too can organisations, societies, and even personal habits evolve without a predetermined blueprint.

This perspective encourages us to consider change as fluid, responsive, and often unexpectedly impactful, shaped by the complex interplay of small actions rather than grand strategies. In this chapter, we will examine how adopting an organic view of change can lead to more resilient and adaptive outcomes in both organisational and everyday contexts. At the same time, we will reflect on the potential limitations of this approach – particularly the challenges it presents for those seeking concrete strategies to guide transformation. With that in mind, let's dive into the rushing streams of chance, emergence, and interactivity and find out what the organic perspective is all about.

## 3.1 The Genesis of Thought

To make any sense of an organic perspective on change, we first need to trace its roots. Here, two pivotal developments stand out: a growing scepticism towards established change theories, and a surge of new ideas in related fields.

### 3.1.1 A New Order Rises

By the late 1970s, Western industries faced an unprecedented shift. For the first time since the Industrial Revolution, a non-Western competitor – Japan – was setting the pace in business and management. Japanese firms, driven by principles like 'kaizen' (continuous improvement), 'kanban' (visual workflow management), and 'poka-yoke' (error-proofing), were outperforming their American and European counterparts. This forced many organisational thinkers to ask whether Western management theories were still relevant or had outlived their usefulness.[8, 29]

From this wave of doubt, a clear challenge emerged against the then dominant managerial perspective on change. While structured, step-by-step models had been the gold standard for years, their limitations were becoming increasingly impossible to ignore. Most importantly, critics argued that the overly rigid nature of these models failed to capture the messy, unpredictable reality of organisational change – that is, why would organisational reality be anything like an ice cube, unfreezing, changing, and refreezing?[19]

Thinking managerially was thus increasingly challenged as leading to gross oversimplifications of organisational reality, breaking down change until all its distinguishing characteristics were no longer visible.[46] While the models of the managerial perspective had done much to popularise organisational change in theory and practice, critics expressed being increasingly uncomfortable with how well these conceptions fitted a real-life setting.[32]

### 3.1.2 Fresh Directions Opened in Adjacent Fields

Criticism alone doesn't spark progress; it needs to be met with new ideas. Fortunately, the intellectual climate of the time provided exactly that. Across management and organisational studies, scholars were shifting their focus, exploring alternative ways of understanding businesses and their transformation processes.

One of the key breakthroughs came from strategy research, where scholars began questioning the idea of 'best practices'. They noticed that, often, organisations were succeeding not because they followed widely accepted management techniques but because they tailored their strategies to their unique circumstances. This insight led to the rise of contingency theory,[21, 40] contextualism,[10, 33] and complexity theory,[13, 41] all of which emphasised that organisational change should be approached with a case-by-case mindset rather than a rigid managerial blueprint. By moving away from theoretical ideals, organisations began to be viewed in the context of their unique business settings: which characteristics or environmental quirks define us as an organisation? And how do we define our outside world in return?

At the same time, a similar transformation was unfolding in organisational decision-making. For decades, rational decision-making had been a cornerstone of management theory. The assumption was simple: people analyse options logically and make choices based on objective reasoning. However, researchers increasingly began exposing the flaws in this belief, demonstrating how human decisions are riddled with biases, emotions, and irrational shortcuts. For example, when you walk into a job interview wearing flip-flops, the person making the hiring decision will probably be prone to reject you, not because flip-flops are considered a liability in their rational calculus but because they believe, based on your flip-flops, that you'll be a careless worker overall. While that may be far from the truth – you may be the most diligent worker they've ever met – that initial impression could still cost you the role.

This growing recognition of human irrationality led scholars to explore alternative decision-making models such as political behaviour in organisations,[31] the role of chance and randomness,[11] and the trial-and-error approach of 'muddling through'.[23, 39] These perspectives moved away from the idea of managers as rational, all-knowing decision-makers and instead formed the basis for a view on change that emphasises it as an evolving, uncertain, and sometimes chaotic process.

#### Box 3.1 The Point?

From these two intellectual shifts – the critique of rigid change models and the rise of contextual and behavioural insights – a new way of thinking about organisational transformation began to take shape. This emerging perspective, which we are referring to as the organic perspective on change, stood in direct contrast to managerial approaches.

But what exactly does it mean to think about change organically? And how does this differ from the traditional managerial mindset? In Section 3.2, we'll explore the perspective's core tenets.

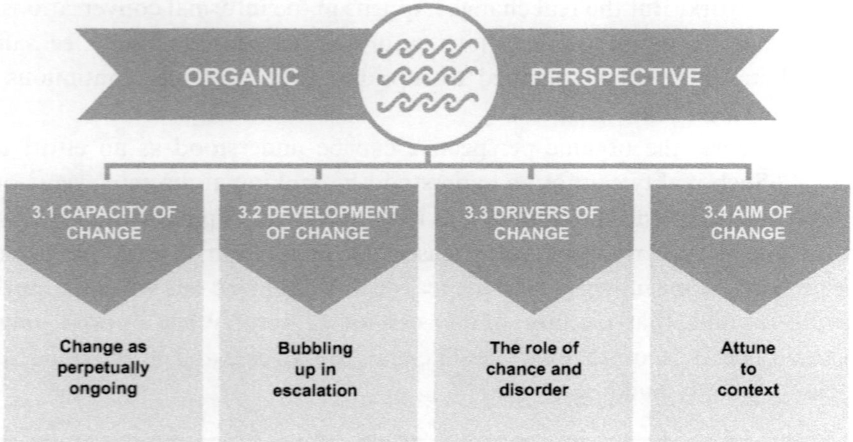


**Figure 3.1** Unpacking the heart of the organic perspective.

## 3.2 Unpacking the Heart

To make sense of an organic perspective on change, it pays to again pay a visit to four main elements (see Figure 3.1): how does thinking organically about change relate to the capacity of change; the development of change; its drivers; and its ultimate aims and goals?

### 3.2.1 Capacity of Change: Change as Perpetually Ongoing

If you have been an attentive reader so far, you will remember how thinking managerially involved framing change as something of an organisational oddity: a deliberate disruption, that is, interrupting the firm's stable state. When approaching change from a managerial angle, change was believed to stay restricted to a clear time frame, which could be planned and phased to its eventual dissolution and success. This view saw change as a confined deviation from the ever-present norm – a sudden crack, so to speak, breaking up the smooth glazing of the organisational cake.

However, when approaching change from an organic angle, understanding change as a deliberate disruption is considered to be deeply troublesome[27] – for if change is seen as an anomaly, an infrequent event in organisational life, we fail to recognise how widespread change already is.[46] When thinking organically, **change isn't a rare disturbance that interrupts an otherwise stable status quo; it *is* the status quo**. Change, in this view, is not something that happens to things; it is framed as the way in which reality is brought into being in every instant.[20]

Let's think about organisational culture and practices. The way people work doesn't usually shift because a leader announces a new set of values or rolls out a bold vision statement. Instead, it evolves through countless small moments – how meetings are run, how conflict is handled, who gets promoted, which jokes land and which don't. Imagine a company trying to become more collaborative. The official initiative might include workshops, new tools, and slogans about teamwork. But the real change happens in the informal conversations after meetings, in how managers respond to suggestions, or in whether people actually feel safe disagreeing with each other. These aren't planned disruptions; they're subtle, continuous adjustments that accumulate over time.

In this sense, the organic perspective can be understood as an effort to catch reality in flight.[36] Such reality cannot be understood by looking at discrete events or phases but must be lived and experienced. Think of it as looking at a set of pictures depicting someone you love: while those pictures may give you a reasonable impression of what that person looks like, they will probably come nowhere near the real deal. Your loved one will have quirks, habits, ways of moving around, that pictures simply cannot capture. When approaching change from an organic angle, it becomes somewhat like that, too. Events and chronologies are crucial building blocks – but only building blocks.[36]

### Box 3.2 The Point?

When approaching change from an organic angle, organisations and their changes are best understood as indivisible: continuously churning on without being defined by particular beginnings or endings.[10] Organisations are believed to not merely be but perpetually occur.[36] In other words, what truly exists is not completed things but things that are in the process of being created.[38]

## 3.2.2 Development of Change: Bubbling Up in Escalation

This understanding of organisations as always being in flux carries important implications for how we think about the way in which change occurs. For decades, taking care of change was considered an explicitly rational and intentional activity: organisations changed because the people managing them thought it appropriate for them to do so. Yet, from an organic perspective, this portrayal of change as a rational and intentional process poorly reflects how things actually unfold: in this view, organisational change doesn't follow neatly structured plans – it emerges as **everyday interactions evolve, intersect, and gradually gain momentum**.

Imagine that you are working for a marketing company. One day, you read in your local newspaper that people are going wild over AI-driven language models. Tech savvy as you are, you go online and check out what all the fuss is about. While you first have a good laugh by making the model write a Shakespearian rant about your mother-in-law, you quickly realise that this model could really help you with your marketing work. First, you start by asking for inspiration for marketing slogans; then, you ask the system to help you construct blog articles, social media posts, and email newsletters. As your enthusiasm grows, the co-workers you meet for lunch are becoming increasingly intrigued as well. They also pick up on the technology and start altering their practices accordingly. At the end of the year, your marketing organisation is working in a completely different way than it used to – without a single executive change plan having been issued.

Or imagine that you're working on a high-pressure project with a tight deadline. One day, feeling particularly stressed and frustrated, you snap at a co-worker during a meeting, making a cutting remark about their work. At first, this incident seems minor, perhaps just a blip in the day's interactions. However, this small moment begins to ripple through the organisation in unexpected ways. Your co-worker, feeling slighted, starts to withdraw from the team, contributing less and becoming more isolated in their work. Other team members notice this change in behaviour and begin to speculate, leading to a subtle shift in the team's dynamics. Trust within the team starts to erode, making collaboration more strained. Over time, these changes affect the project's progress, with delays and miscommunications becoming more frequent. As productivity falters, management steps in, noticing the decline in team performance, and decides to restructure the team to address the issues. What started as a single rude remark has now sparked a host of changes across the organisation, leading to new policies on communication, a reorganisation of team roles, and even the eventual departure of a valued team member who no longer feels comfortable in the environment.

What led to change in these examples? Being embedded in an inherently connected social setting,[42] it is the natural interplay between employees' individual decisions that caused fundamental changes on the organisational level – irrespective of any explicit intentions. In this sense, organisational change can be understood not as the outcome of a deliberate plan but rather as the continuous escalation of small-scale choices into a somewhat consistent whole.[20, 37, 47] It happens not because of some grand scheme but because people continually act on and interact with the world they live in.[26]

### 3.2.3 Drivers of Change: The Role of Chance and Disorder

Closely tied to this idea of change emerging from small-scale occurrences is the notion that **chaos and disorder** play a fundamental role. Thinking organically about change means recognising it as a complex and chaotic process that involves unexpected consequences, ambiguities, and misunderstandings.[2] From this view, order and logic are mere derivatives of organisational reality, by which people try to draw sensible interpretations of what is far less structured and arranged: they are ways in which we try to distil something easily digestible from the original, formless state of constant change.[9]

As a result, organisational change may be driven not by leaders' intent and expertise but by people coping with uncertainty, complexity, and unpredictability – all emphasising the significance of the unknown in a future that cannot yet be predicted.[12] By explicitly acknowledging the role of chaos, surprise, and ambiguity, thinking organically may help revalue organisational reality according to its social nature. While assumptions about reality being orderly may be beneficial for the sake of structure and communication, they may be inherently misguided.[25] Chance and the incidental may trump choice and the deliberate.

Take, for example, an office move. A company might plan a seamless transition to a new location, carefully scheduling logistics and anticipating challenges. However, an overlooked detail – like an underestimated commute time for key employees – might unexpectedly trigger dissatisfaction. Frustrated by the longer travel, some employees start leaving for competitors, causing knowledge gaps and decreased productivity. As new hires struggle to fill the void, morale takes a hit, and the company's culture shifts in unforeseen ways. What began as a seemingly minor logistical decision ends up reshaping the organisation's identity and long-term trajectory – without anyone ever intending it.

> **Box 3.3 The Point?**
>
> Although somewhat dramatic in its outcome, the move example illustrates how the accidental and seemingly trivial can form organisational change, irrespective of any intricate schemes designed in advance.[37] Rather than being steadfast in planning and rational analysis, thinking organically about change involves marking these qualities as being largely inadequate. From this view, chance and random events represent the drivers of organisational transformation, stacking individual events – almost by accident – towards a larger whole.[1] Achieving successful change may thus have little to do with leaders' deliberate guidance and more to do with attaining an understanding of the intricacy of social issues at hand[8] – including coming to terms with a stupid logistical oversight.

### 3.2.4 Aim of Change: Incrementally Attune to Context

Finally, if change is believed to emerge through seemingly random events and unintended consequences, then its purpose, too, must be reimagined. From an organic perspective, change is not about executing a grand vision; it is about gradually **attuning to context** – adjusting, reacting, and evolving in step with the environment. Rather than isolating change from everyday activities, thinking organically about change involves framing organisational developments as step-by-step adjustments to the environments in which they occur. These environments can be understood in two ways.

First, as every organisation is embedded within a setting that exists beyond organisational boundaries, change finds itself defined by uncertainties developing in the external context.[22, 28, 34] Such external context includes customers, suppliers, government agencies, educational institutions, and so on. As a result, it is believed that organisational change cannot be fully understood or acted upon in isolation. As change is fundamentally moulded by the organisation's links to things happening beyond corporate walls – such as developments in markets, the shifting nature of company relationships, or geopolitical evolutions[8] – it must be dealt with in clear contact with that environment. In this respect, development and change directly serve the interaction a company keeps up with its context: they are contextually inspired.[14, 18]

Moreover, organisations don't only find themselves embedded in external contexts; they also find themselves snugly tucked within systems of deeply interwoven social interrelations they, themselves, represent – internal contexts, so to speak, laced with history, values and norms, and a plethora of relationships.[7] From the organic perspective, organisational change cannot be understood separately from this company-specific background: to make sense of why things are happening as they are, it is necessary to delve deep into the interpretation, subjectivity, and experience of those involved. Coming to terms with change should not merely be about laying bare the facts; it should also be concerned with developing an understanding of the essence that binds these facts together. As such, a comprehensive understanding of change requires an exploration of the logics that give events meaning and significance.[35]

Imagine an organisation that operates in the rapidly evolving technology sector. Traditionally, the organisation has relied on a hierarchical structure with clear, top-down directives to manage its operations. However, as the external environment shifts due to advancements in artificial intelligence, the company finds that its existing strategies and workflows are increasingly inadequate. Concurrently, internal changes are taking place: a new generation of employees, who value collaboration and flexibility over rigid structures, is gradually taking up key roles within the organisation. These employees bring with them a different set of expectations and a desire to work in a more interconnected, less hierarchical manner. As a result, departments are starting to collaborate more fluidly, cross-functional teams are emerging to tackle AI-related projects, and decision-making is becoming more decentralised. Rather than being consciously aimed at success, this change is largely driven by the need to adapt to both the external technological advancements and the internal shift in workforce dynamics. Ultimately, the result is a gradual, step-by-step transformation that aligns the organisation more closely with its environment.

**Box 3.4 The Point?**

When approaching organisational change from an organic angle, transformation is understood not as a deliberate exercise in optimisation but as moulded by the broader context in which that organisation sits. To change may not mean that the organisation is consciously redirecting itself to a new course as given; rather, it may relate to how the social structure of the organisation develops said new course largely by itself, churning through the everyday wants and needs of all parties involved.

## 3.3 Extending Your Toolkit

Having unpacked the core ideas of organic thinking, one might reasonably wonder: if change is always unfolding, non-linear, and hard to pin down – then how on earth can we work with it? From an organic perspective, the notion of managing change can feel as elusive as herding cats.

Yet that doesn't mean we're powerless. Rather than trying to force or steer change directly, the organic approach invites us to shape the conditions in which change unfolds. By altering the context of interaction – the patterns, relationships, and cues that guide behaviour – change can be enabled to emerge almost by and of itself.

This section explores three key tools for doing so: (i) complex adaptive systems theory, (ii) network analysis, and (iii) nudging. Each offers a practical way to work with the grain of emergent change, rather than against it.

### 3.3.1 Complex Adaptive Systems Theory

Imagine a forest. In forest management, attempts to control every aspect of the ecosystem – such as determining the exact location and species of trees, deciding which animals should inhabit the area, and regulating the water flow – are not only impractical but also often counterproductive. For instance, we may introduce more rabbits, only to find that they soon overpopulate the space. Instead, effective forest management focuses on creating conditions that allow the forest to thrive and adapt naturally. By understanding the dynamics of the forest ecosystem, managers can facilitate conditions that enable self-organisation, allowing the forest to evolve and sustain itself over time. Here, change is not imposed from above but emerges from within the system itself, driven by the interactions and relationships among its components.

This approach mirrors the principles of **complex adaptive systems (CAS) theory**, which proposes treating organisations as systems that evolve through the interactions of their parts.[3, 17, 42] At the heart of CAS theory are five major building blocks that need to be guaranteed.

The first, **self-organisation**, refers to the ability of a system to develop patterns, structures, and behaviours without central control.[3, 17, 42] In a self-organising system, the components interact in ways that lead to the spontaneous emergence of order or patterns. In the context of forest management, self-organisation might be observed in how different species of plants and animals find their niches, interact, and establish a balanced ecosystem. Without a central authority dictating the behaviour of each species, the forest achieves a form of order through the autonomous actions of its components. Similarly, in organisations, self-organisation occurs when teams or departments are free to develop their own processes, cultures, and practices without direct top-down intervention.

#### Box 3.5 Practical Advice?

- Encourage decentralised decision-making – empower teams to make decisions within their scope, reducing reliance on hierarchical approvals.
- Create flexible team structures – allow teams to form and dissolve dynamically based on projects, rather than rigid, predefined roles.
- Promote a culture of experimentation – provide resources for employees to test new ideas and solutions without fear of failure.

The second building block, **emergence**, concerns the process by which larger, more complex properties or patterns arise from the interactions and relationships among simpler components.[3, 17, 42] These emergent properties cannot be predicted simply by analysing components in isolation. For example, in forests, the health and the biodiversity of the ecosystem are emergent properties that arise from the interactions among plants, animals, soil, and climate. No single element dictates the overall health of the forest; rather, it is the collective interaction that leads to the emergence of a thriving ecosystem. In organisations, emergence can be observed when new ideas, innovations, or solutions are allowed to arise from collaborative efforts, often in ways that were not anticipated by individual members.

### Box 3.6 Practical Advice?

- Encourage cross-functional collaboration – facilitate knowledge-sharing across departments to generate unexpected synergies.
- Host innovation labs or hackathons – create spaces where employees can explore and prototype new ideas without immediate constraints.
- Leverage collective intelligence – use crowdsourcing or open forums where employees can contribute insights and spot trends in real time.

The third, **non-linearity**, refers to the principle that small changes in a system can lead to large effects, and vice versa.[3, 17, 42] This means that the relationship between cause and effect in a CAS is not proportional or predictable. In forest management, a small change, such as the introduction of a new species or a slight variation in water availability, can have significant impacts on the entire ecosystem. Conversely, large-scale interventions might result in minimal changes. Similarly, in organisations, a minor shift in policy, culture, or leadership must have the leeway to lead to substantial transformations, while major initiatives must be accepted as possibly having only limited impact.

### Box 3.7 Practical Advice?

- Pilot small-scale changes before full implementation – test new initiatives in select teams or markets to observe their broader impact.
- Encourage bottom-up influence – allow small employee-led initiatives to gain traction organically, rather than enforcing top-down change.
- Remain open to unintended consequences – monitor and adapt strategies based on unexpected ripple effects rather than rigidly adhering to initial plans.

The fourth building block, **adaptation**, refers to the ability of individual components within a system to adjust to changes in their environment, enabling the system to better fit prevailing conditions.[3, 17, 42] In forests, plants and animals continuously adapt to changes in climate, soil conditions, and the presence of other species. These adaptations allow the ecosystem to survive and thrive despite environmental fluctuations. In organisations, adaptation occurs when employees, teams, or departments are able to adjust their behaviours, strategies, or processes in response to changing market conditions, technological advancements, or customer demands.

### Box 3.8 Practical Advice?

- Develop a flexible mindset – train employees in methodologies that encourage rapid iteration and responsiveness to change.
- Invest in continuous learning – offer upskilling programmes to help employees stay ahead of industry shifts and technological advancements.
- Use scenario planning – regularly anticipate different future possibilities to prepare for uncertainty rather than reacting in crisis mode.

Finally, **feedback loops** are processes in which the output of a system is returned as input, influencing subsequent behaviour.[3, 17, 42] Feedback can be positive (reinforcing change) or negative (stabilising the system). In a forest, feedback loops are evident in processes such as nutrient cycling, where the decomposition of organic matter returns nutrients to the soil, promoting new growth. Positive feedback might occur when a successful species proliferates, while negative feedback might stabilise the ecosystem by preventing any one species from dominating. In organisations, feedback loops are seen when information, results, or outcomes are led back to influence future decisions, behaviours, and strategies.

### Box 3.9 Practical Advice?

- Encourage continuous employee feedback – create open channels for feedback, such as pulse surveys or retrospective meetings.
- Establish real-time data tracking – use analytics and performance metrics to quickly identify trends and adjust strategies accordingly.
- Reward responsiveness to feedback – recognise and incentivise teams that actively implement learnings from feedback rather than just collecting it.

One of the most compelling aspects of CASs is their inherent self-preservation. Because CASs are built on principles of self-organisation, emergence, non-linearity, adaptation, and feedback, they are better equipped to change when needed. In the same way that a forest can recover from a wildfire through the natural processes of regeneration, organisations structured as CASs can bounce back from setbacks, adapt to new circumstances, and continue to evolve. Without relying on a rigid hierarchy, companies can respond fluidly to new opportunities or threats, making them more resilient in the face of uncertainty. This robustness is the result not of meticulous planning or control but, rather, of the natural outcome of allowing the system to evolve organically.

## 3.3.2 Network Analysis

If complex systems thrive through informal patterns of interaction and adaptation, then understanding those patterns becomes crucial. This is where **network analysis** comes in.

Suppose that I hand you two versions of the same organisational chart. The first is the typical hierarchy: neat boxes and lines, listing names and job titles. The second takes a different approach. Instead of focusing on official roles, it maps out real relationships – who collaborates closely, who avoids each other, who secretly mentors whom, and who shares rides to work. Which one would be more useful in predicting how the group will function?

For most of us, the answer is clear: the relationship-based map. Humans are social creatures and our actions are deeply shaped by our connections with others. Titles may tell us who reports to whom, but relationships reveal who truly influences whom.

Network analysis maps out how individuals, teams, and departments connect and influence each other, offering a visual representation of the social fabric that drives decision-making, collaboration, and – most importantly – change.[5, 44, 45] By uncovering these hidden networks, network analysis helps leaders identify key influencers, potential bottlenecks, and pathways through which change can spread organically. Instead of relying solely on top-down mandates, organisations can use these insights to leverage natural connections, amplify engagement, and make transformation efforts far more effective.

To support this, network analysis measures the role of individuals and groups through several metrics, the following three of which are particularly central:[5, 44, 45]

- Connection – the number of direct links an individual has with others in the network. The more connections someone has, the more avenues they have for sharing and receiving information. In short, their influence grows with every additional link.
- Betweenness – how much someone acts as a bridge between different parts of the network. Think of it like a connector who links up separate clusters or groups within the organisation. A high betweenness score indicates that this person holds the key to connecting people who wouldn't otherwise interact. They're central in enabling communication flow.
- Closeness – how easily someone can reach everyone else in the network, either directly or through a few steps. The closer someone is to everyone, the faster they can access critical information and pass it along. This metric reveals a person's ability to quickly access and share knowledge.

By analysing these metrics (often with the help of software tools), we can uncover key informal roles that don't appear on the official organisational chart.[5, 44, 45] Let's look at some of the most important roles, based on Figure 3.2.

**Hubs** have a significant impact on the network. A network with a centralised hub is vulnerable to failure if the hub is disabled or removed. On the other hand, hubs are often suitable candidates for being change champions or superusers due to their ability to efficiently distribute knowledge.

**Gatekeepers** bridge boundaries and connect different groups. They serve as links between departments, functions, and groups and act as information catalysts, mediating knowledge exchange between crucial parts of the organisation.

**Pulse-takers** have a maximum impact using the minimum number of direct and indirect contacts (typically fewer than three steps away). They are in a prime position to monitor information flow and have the best view of what is happening within the network.

These roles can significantly influence how change happens within an organisation.[5, 44, 45] Consider a company undergoing a digital transformation. By mapping out the network, leaders

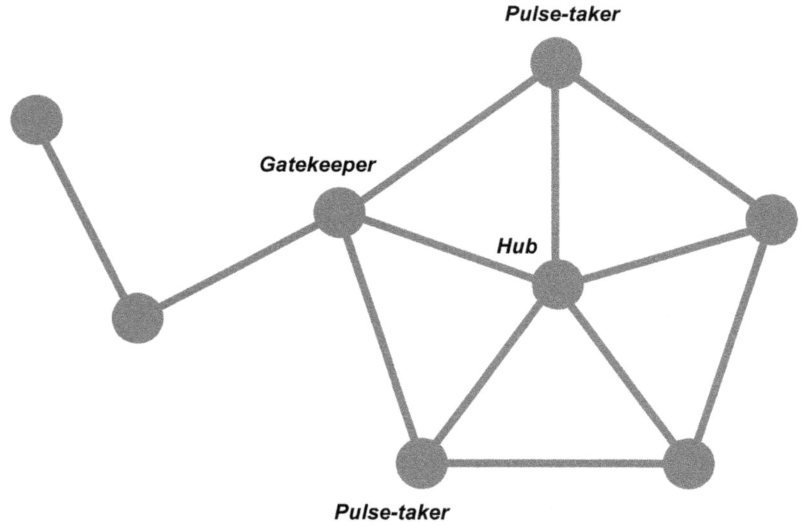


**Figure 3.2** Simple illustration of a network analysis graph.

might discover that a mid-level manager, previously unnoticed, serves as a gatekeeper between the IT department and the rest of the organisation. Recognising this role, the company can engage this manager as a key player in driving the transformation, ensuring that the right information and support flows between teams. Similarly, identifying hubs can help the company select change champions who can effectively disseminate new practices and ideas throughout the organisation.

**Box 3.10 The Point?**

By understanding the organisation's social network, leaders can anticipate where resistance might arise, identify key influencers, and tailor their strategies accordingly. If a particular node is known for being resistant to change, efforts can be made to engage them early in the process, turning a potential obstacle into an ally.

### 3.3.3 Nudging

Building on this attention to informal influence and behavioural dynamics, a final powerful way to guide change through context is the concept of **nudging**.[43] Initially conceived as a way to encourage better decision-making through positive reinforcement and subtle cues, nudging has evolved into a highly effective strategy for shaping behaviour without imposing rules or restrictions. Rather than dictating actions, nudging gently steers individuals towards desired choices by subtly altering the environment in which decisions are made.

Take, for example, the now-famous fly sticker in men's urinals. By placing a small image of a fly inside the urinal, restroom designers found a clever way to improve cleanliness. Without any written instructions or imposed rules, the fly provides a subtle but effective target, reducing spillage and improving hygiene – simply by tapping into human instinct.

Another playful example comes from a subway station where stairs were transformed into a giant piano. Each step was outfitted with sensors that produced musical notes when stepped on, turning the mundane act of climbing stairs into an interactive and enjoyable experience. The result? A significant increase in stair use, as commuters actively chose the healthier option simply because it was more engaging.

In office settings, nudging can encourage more sustainable habits. For instance, placing the only office printer at the end of a long hallway makes printing slightly less convenient, nudging employees to reconsider whether they truly need a physical copy. Over time, this small tweak may lead to a noticeable reduction in paper waste – without enforcing any strict printing limits.

Nudging can also be used to reinforce company values. Imagine walking into a company cafeteria and seeing a large painting of Mahatma Gandhi – a figure synonymous with integrity, ethical leadership, and non-violence. While no one is directly told to embody these principles, the constant visual reminder subtly reinforces a culture of ethical decision-making and peaceful conflict resolution.

**Box 3.11 Practical Advice?**

These examples should give you a basic idea of what nudges often look and feel like. But how to devise successful ways of nudging a change in behaviour altogether? To craft an impactful nudge, it's best to keep three key principles in mind:

- Make it easy – reduce friction and simplify choices to encourage the desired behaviour.
- Make it salient – use visibility, timing, and emotional engagement to capture attention at the right moment.
- Make it social – show that others are making the same choice, to tap into people's natural tendency to follow the crowd.

Nudging represents a subtle yet powerful approach to fostering change within organisations. By focusing on context rather than direct instruction, nudges gently guide individuals towards desired behaviours and outcomes. Whether it's encouraging cleanliness with a fly sticker, promoting health with a piano staircase, reducing waste by positioning a printer strategically, or inspiring ethical behaviour with a painting of Gandhi, nudging demonstrates how small changes in the environment can lead to significant shifts in behaviour.

## 3.4 Impact on the Ground

Taken together, it's clear that organic approaches – whether grounded in networks, complexity, or subtle behavioural cues – offer a fundamentally different lens on change from the managerial view outlined in Chapter 2.[24] But does the perspective really add value? Below are three key reasons why incorporating organic thinking into your mindset can make a meaningful difference.

### 3.4.1 An Organic Perspective Values the Role of Time

First, one of the most important benefits of thinking organically about change is that it values the role of time. Viewed through a managerial lens, time is often seen as a mere backdrop – something to be overcome or managed within a set frame. Usually, change is expected to happen quickly, with any delay labelled as resistance. However, when change is approached organically, this rush against time makes little sense; instead, we're called to see time as an integral component of the transformation itself.

Consider a company wanting to shift its corporate culture to become more collaborative. Instead of mandating an immediate overhaul, the organisation begins by encouraging small changes – teams are given more autonomy, cross-departmental projects are introduced, and leaders model collaborative behaviours over time. The company focuses on fostering trust and communication in organic ways, letting these new practices grow and evolve naturally within teams.

This approach contrasts sharply with the pressure to force change within a set time frame. By giving employees the space to gradually embrace changes, companies can create environments where collaboration becomes embedded in the culture, rather than being a top-down directive that people may resist. Over time, as the company observes and adjusts to the needs and challenges that arise, the shift towards collaboration may be not only smoother but also more authentic and sustainable, with deeper buy-in from employees across all levels.

#### Box 3.12 The Point?

The organic view offers a deeper engagement with the realities of organisational life, one that aligns with its inherent complexity and unpredictability. Rather than rushing through the process, the perspective emphasises the value of allowing changes to unfold naturally, adjusting as needed along the way. By revaluing the role of time – not as a constraint to be managed but as a vital partner in the change journey – it creates space for what is often more thoughtful, lasting change.[9, 15, 46]

### 3.4.2 An Organic Perspective Values the Role of Context

Next, by emphasising the importance, in achieving change, of context – such as history, language, interpretation, and political relationships – an organic perspective pushes beyond mere considerations of content. While such broadening may render accounts of change more complex and harder to grasp, it also allows organisational change to become much more attuned to the needs of the case at hand.

Given that no two organisations are exactly alike, the importance of this kind of rebalancing cannot be overstated: when change is presented as a generic activity, it is often found to be difficult to match it with the particularities of a specific case. This is where the nitty-gritty comes into play, adding both flavour and complexity to the everyday reality of actual organisations. Without addressing these details, change can rarely be effectively implemented. By focusing on context as much as on content, the organic perspective reconnects our sense of change with actual practice and experience – encouraging us to get involved (with or without being aware of it) and see how developments might truly proceed.[3, 33]

### 3.4.3 An Organic Perspective Values the Role of 'Ordinary' Employees

Finally, in the managerial perspective of Chapter 2, the role of the average employee in the change process was minimal. Those without specialised expertise were expected to follow instructions, their involvement reduced to mere execution. In contrast, the organic perspective views change as emerging from the collective actions of all employees, thereby elevating the importance of non-expert positions. This shift redefines employees not as passive recipients of directives but as active participants in the change process.

Rather than seeing transformation as the outcome of top-down decisions – a carefully scripted drama directed by leaders – the organic perspective fosters a more collaborative and inclusive approach. It empowers a broader base of employees to find purpose and meaning in their work, enabling them to drive change from within the organisation. In this way, the organic view acknowledges that bottom-up forces, driven by the employees themselves, are often the true engines of organisational change.[16, 30]

**Box 3.13 The Point?**

All in all, maintaining an organic perspective brings the process of change down from the ivory towers of boardrooms and checklists, placing it back into the hands of those who experience it daily. It recognises that meaningful change often originates from the grassroots level, where employees' insights, creativity, and engagement can collectively shape the organisation's future.

## 3.5 Drawbacks and Pitfalls

Yet, even as the organic perspective brings change closer to the ground, it's important to acknowledge that the approach is not without its complications. Here are the most notable ones, along with advice on how to navigate them.

### 3.5.1 An Organic Perspective Is Difficult to Execute

First, while the core ideas of the organic perspective are intriguing, many struggle with how to translate these complex ideas into actionable steps. While this view of change may feel intellectually stimulating, how does one navigate its ideas in a real-world setting? For example, if the very essence of change resists structure and order, how can one reasonably act on it? Revolving around concepts such as complexity, chaos, and instability, the organic perspective can make taking action surprisingly hard.[6] For many, this leads to frustration and harsh critiques, with some dismissing the organic view as little more than an abstract philosophy with no practical utility.[12, 46]

To bridge the gap between theory and practice, it would be best to encourage teams to observe and reflect on how change naturally unfolds within the organisation, and use these observations to inform larger strategic decisions. By treating the organic perspective as a complementary approach rather than a complete replacement for managerial methods, organisations can reap its benefits without becoming paralysed by its inherent ambiguity.

While the organic perspective may not provide many ready-made tools, it can inspire new ways of thinking that lead to innovative solutions. Instead of rigidly planning every step of a change process, leaders might focus on creating environments where adaptive behaviours can emerge organically. This could involve decentralising decision-making, encouraging cross-functional collaboration, and allowing for more fluid organisational structures that can respond more flexibly to changes in the external environment.

### 3.5.2 An Organic Perspective May Be Only Partially True

Next, while an organic perspective on change may accurately capture how small-scale decisions can escalate into larger organisational shifts, one cannot help but wonder – is this always the case? If you've ever worked in an organisation, you've likely experienced large, top-down change initiatives that don't align with the organic view. So, is it really accurate to claim that all organisational change unfolds in an organic, unpredictable way?

While the organic perspective can certainly illuminate how change happens in certain situations, it's not always the right lens. In fact, there are clear moments when a more structured, managerial approach is necessary.[4] So, organisational change may not be something that can be fully understood by embracing just one perspective; it may require a hybrid approach, blending both organic and managerial viewpoints.[24] By dismissing the managerial perspective outright, the organic view risks becoming a mirror image of what it criticises – just as one-sided and extreme in its own way.

#### Box 3.14 Practical Advice?

Rather than adopting the organic perspective wholesale, consider when and where it is most appropriate to apply its principles. For instance, the organic perspective may be particularly useful in rapidly changing environments where flexibility and adaptability are key. However, in situations that require clear direction and coordination – such as during a merger or major restructuring – a more managerial approach may be necessary. Leaders should aim to develop a nuanced understanding of when to apply organic principles and when to rely on more structured, managerial methods.

## SUMMARY

Chapter 3 explored the **organic perspective** on change, which challenges traditional, structured approaches by emphasising the continuous and emergent nature of change (see Table 3.1 for an overview).

**Table 3.1 An organic perspective on change: overview**

| | |
|---|---|
| **Guiding metaphor** | Change as a running stream |
| **The genesis of thought** | |
| Development 1 | A new order rises |
| Development 2 | Fresh directions open in adjacent fields |
| **Unpacking the heart** | |
| Capacity of change | Change as perpetually ongoing |
| Development of change | Bubbling up in escalation |
| Drivers of change | The role of chance and disorder |
| Aim of change | Attune to context |
| **Extending your toolkit** | |
| Tool #1 | Complex adaptive systems (CAS) theory |
| Tool #2 | Network analysis |
| Tool #3 | Nudging |
| **Impact on the ground** | |
| (+) | An organic perspective values the role of time. |
| (+) | An organic perspective values the role of context. |
| (+) | An organic perspective values the role of 'ordinary' employees. |
| **Drawbacks and pitfalls** | |
| (-) | An organic perspective is difficult to execute. |
| (-) | An organic perspective may only be partially true. |
| **Related concepts** | |
| ► | Emergent change |
| ► | Evolutionary change |
| ► | Contextual change |
| ► | Complexity in change |
| ► | Process-based view on change |

- The **shift towards an organic understanding** of change began with growing scepticism about established change theories, which were often grounded in linear, expert-driven models. As doubts arose, researchers and practitioners started exploring alternative viewpoints, drawing on insights from related fields. This led to a reconceptualisation of change as a process that is always in motion, rather than a temporary deviation from stability.
- At **the heart of this perspective** is the belief that change does not follow a predictable sequence but rather emerges and escalates over time. Instead of being driven by structured interventions, change is believed to be influenced by spontaneous developments, unforeseen circumstances, and interactions between individuals and their environment. The role of chance and disorder is central, as disruptions and unexpected shifts often become catalysts for transformation. Unlike the managerial perspective, which aims to enhance efficiency and performance, the organic view focuses on attuning to the surrounding context, ensuring that organisations remain adaptable and responsive.
- To better understand change from this perspective, we examined three key conceptual **tools**. Complex adaptive systems theory helps explain how organisations evolve through interconnected relationships rather than top-down directives. Network analysis provides a way to identify informal structures and emergent patterns that shape how change actually occurs. Nudging offers a more subtle approach to influencing behaviours in ways that align with how people naturally respond to their environment.
- One of the main **contributions** of an organic perspective is its emphasis on time, acknowledging that change is not an event but an ongoing process that unfolds gradually. It also highlights the importance of context, arguing that effective change cannot be separated from the environment in which it takes place. Additionally, this perspective elevates the role of everyday employees, recognising that change is often driven from within rather than imposed from above.
- Despite its strengths, we noted that this approach also has clear **limitations**. Specifically, it provides relatively little practical guidance for those seeking concrete strategies to manage change, as it prioritises emergence over structured action. Furthermore, while it challenges rigid models, it may not fully account for situations where intentional planning and intervention are necessary.

The organic perspective is closely linked to concepts such as emergent change, evolutionary change, contextual change, complexity in change, and process-based views on change. While it offers a compelling alternative to traditional approaches, it also raises important questions about how organisations can navigate uncertainty while still maintaining a sense of direction.

## CASE: THE CHANGING SPARKLE OF DIAMONDS

### The Organic Perspective in Practice

Few products are as universally coveted as diamonds. They have captivated the human imagination for centuries, evolving from being valued for their hardness and durability to becoming symbols of love and everlasting commitment. Many have spent more than a month's salary on a diamond to propose – believing that, like love, diamonds are 'forever' and can withstand anything.

For a long time, that same sense of endurance also seemed to hold for the organisations trading diamonds: the diamond industry, from miners to retailers, proved highly conservative, with few changes being apparent at all. Miners mined, traders traded, and salespeople sold. It was a highly traditional industry, where respecting and learning the ways of elderly generations was more important than spending idle time on change and innovation.

Yet over the past few years that sense of stability has been drastically challenged, with the diamond industry being in severe turmoil. The cause? Laboratory-grown diamonds – diamonds that are man-made and produced in a controlled environment. Lauded by some and despised by others, laboratory-grown diamonds have changed the industry in ways that few ever thought possible.

In this case, we will focus on how organisations' development towards lab-grown diamonds can be understood as the outcome of various interlocking events that no one ever consciously anticipated or engineered. It's a tale of drama and upheaval, emotion and reason, tradition and disruption – and, most of all, it's a tale of change and emergence. With that said (and expectations being raised), let's delve deep into the story of laboratory-grown diamonds, descending into a story that took over half a century to mature.

## Diamonds and the Diamond Business

Before turning to the changes introduced by lab-grown diamonds, it is essential to establish a clear baseline. How is the traditional diamond business structured in terms of its product characteristics, value chain configuration, sources of market power, prevailing business models, and broader industry context?

Despite their lustre, diamonds are essentially nothing more than crystalline carbon forms, established due to specific combinations of pressure and temperature found deep within the Earth's mantle. Their molecular composition gives them a number of useful physical and optical properties – think of exceptional hardness, high thermal conductivity, and strong light refraction. If growing conditions are optimal – that is, if carbon molecules are exposed to the correct amount of pressure and heat, without other elements interfering – the resulting diamonds gain in terms of clarity, colour, and overall size. These diamonds are typically considered 'gem-quality'. If growing conditions are suboptimal, the resulting diamonds are typically smaller and less visually appealing: while they can still be used in industrial applications (e.g., drills, electronics, etc.), these 'industrial-quality stones' cannot be processed into jewellery.

But how does a diamond travel 'from mine to finger'? In the first stage, diamonds are extracted from diamond deposits. This can either mean big holes in the ground (mines) or alluvial sediment (rivers). Large mining conglomerates like the De Beers Group, Alrosa Mining Company, Dominion Diamond Mines, and the Rio Tinto Mining Group are typically considered to be upstream parties as they provide rough diamonds to agents farther down the value chain. Upstream activities are predominantly concentrated in Africa, Russia,

Australia, and Canada. After the rough diamonds are extracted, they are typically sold to middlemen. Being allowed to purchase diamonds directly from premium vendors is often considered a privilege, and only a selection of middlemen have that option. After being sourced, rough diamonds undergo various midstream activities – such as sorting, scanning, mapping, polishing, and grading. Major midstream hubs are located in Belgium, the United Arab Emirates, India, and Hong Kong. Polished stones, once ready, often go through a series of middlemen again, who direct the right polished stones to the right jewellers – for example, while some will only work with perfect-quality stones, others need diamonds with fancy colours or of specific sizes and shapes. Polished diamonds are subsequently set into jewellery – typically rings, earrings, and necklaces – and marketed to end-customers, with the United States and Europe being the main downstream or consumer markets. Other markets, such as China, are also developing rapidly. Finally, a range of organisations oversee supporting functions to facilitate the efficient execution of diamond-related activities, such as financing, industry representation to governments, logistics, and the provision of networking facilities. If, after a certain time, the customer wants to resell their diamonds, they are typically able to do so.

In terms of market power and margins, this traditional diamond business is highly uneven. As there are few companies that have the capital to mine diamonds, supply is limited to a number of key players. This means that upstream operating margins amount to about 15 per cent to 20 per cent. The middle segment, although concentrated in a select number of hubs, is much more fragmented. As a result, it has severely less market power: typically, middlemen such as polishers, sorters, and traders work on margins between 1 per cent and 4 per cent. The downstream segment, finally, is represented by a very large number of different jewellers and retailers. As they are close to end-consumers and have more leeway to decide their sales prices, their operating margins typically hover between 5 per cent and 15 per cent.

Turning to the business model, the traditional model of diamonds is based on three key features: uniqueness, rarity, and trust. First, no two diamonds are exactly the same: each depends on the specific growing conditions it faced deep within the Earth's mantle. This uniqueness drives the need for expertise and specialisation within the diamond value chain. Second, diamonds are rare. There are few areas where conditions have been precisely right to enable carbon atoms to crystallise into diamonds. This rarity is what propels diamonds' high prices: more than high demand, it is limited supply that dictates the excessive amounts people sometimes pay for what are – essentially – pretty rocks. Finally, diamonds' uniqueness and rarity make them challenging to trade using standard sales practices, which involve exchanging a predetermined amount of money for a predetermined amount of product. To trade diamonds successfully, one must thus trust that the other party will not exploit the situation for short-term profit.

Finally, let's consider industry context. Traditionally, the diamond industry is a very close-knit industry. Geographically, diamond hubs – such as the Antwerp Square Mile or New York's 47th Street – are highly concentrated, with thousands of diamond traders in close proximity to each other. Socially, the diamond industry is dominated by a select number of cultural communities (e.g., Indians, Jews). And, on a group level, diamond traders often belong to larger diamond-trading families, with the occupation regularly dating back several generations. Diamond-trading families are not seldom interlinked by marriage, establishing social interconnections between family groups.

### The Rise of Gem-Quality Lab-Grown Diamonds

With this baseline in place, we can now turn to the emergence of lab-grown diamonds. How can we account for their rise – and, ultimately, their success – within this historically entrenched industry structure?

In the nineteenth century, after it was discovered that diamonds were nothing more than pure carbon, many attempts were made to produce diamonds artificially. While some minor successes were being claimed, none of these experiments resulted in reproducible results. In the 1940s and 1950s, several promising techniques were developed, such as 'high pressure–high temperature' synthesis (HPHT) and 'chemical vapour deposition' (CVD). As results by both the Swedish ASEA (General Swedish Electrical Limited Company) and the American General Electric Group grew more encouraging, technologies were gradually improved.

In 1953, the first laboratory-grown diamond was produced, and the first reproducible one was made one year after. Although these laboratory-grown diamonds had the same chemical and physical composition as their natural counterparts, their quality was poor and their cost was high. For these reasons, while jewellers and gem-quality traders were aware of these developments, most considered them to be only a feat of quirky science – a 'laboratory baby' that, although slightly worrying, was not all that impactful.

Yet, as techniques evolved, production costs decreased significantly, with the yield steadily increasing. While still being unfit for jewellery, laboratory-grown diamonds became increasingly attractive for industrial applications – and were rapidly introduced in applications such as electronics, optics, surgical scalpels, and telecommunication equipment.

By the late 1970s, laboratory-grown diamonds were increasingly used in the industrial segment, gradually displacing natural diamonds. Stimulated by such success, research centres continued their development. In the 1980s, dramatic leaps were made in terms of quality; in the late 1990s, equally dramatic leaps were made in terms of cost. By the end of the decade, several companies claimed that they were close to producing gem-quality lab-growns economically – or at a cost equal to that of extracting a diamond from the Earth.

In the early 2000s, several emerging start-ups, such as Gemesis, Apollo, and New Diamond Technology, began producing gem-quality lab-grown diamonds for commercial use. Their entry into the market came as a shock to many diamond traders, who had previously considered the creation of high-quality lab-grown diamonds unlikely. Publicly, industry professionals expressed outrage and concern about the potential impact on the market. Privately, however, many were intrigued. Some insiders noted that while panel discussions were filled with vocal opposition, traders would later seek discreet conversations to explore the implications. It became clear to many that lab-grown diamonds were here to stay and could not simply be dismissed.

In 2006, the film *Blood Diamond* was released. Starring Leonardo DiCaprio and critically acclaimed, achieving five Academy Award nominations, it told the story of how natural diamonds were sometimes used to fund rebel groups and brutal violence in war-torn Sierra

Leone. For the diamond industry, repercussions were dramatic: for the general consumer, mining diamonds became associated with human rights abuses and vicious conflict. Although certification schemes were developed to guarantee that purchased diamonds were 'conflict free', the damage to the product's image was severe.

In the same year, a batch of undisclosed lab-grown diamonds was discovered, rousing panic that lab-growns would ultimately 'pollute' the product pipeline, obliterate mutual trust, and destroy consumers' perception of value. As a response, several institutions started to invest heavily in developing detection equipment, which would allow traders to tell which stones were natural and which were lab-grown. Observers at the time emphasised the urgency of the situation, noting that the natural diamond industry needed to carefully strategise its approach to this emerging challenge, as the stakes were high.

That much was indeed at stake for the gem-quality traders could also be seen by looking at the impact laboratory-grown diamonds were having on the industrial segment. Due to continuous technological improvements, the industrial segment had become increasingly dominated by lab-growns: in 2008, it was estimated that fewer than 1 per cent of diamonds used for industrial appliances were still naturals. For many, margins just proved to be better with laboratory-grown diamonds.

In the gem-quality segment, such economic considerations were becoming increasingly relevant as well. By the early 2010s, the production of gem-quality lab-grown diamonds broke even. Soon thereafter, many traders reported that they would be making higher margins selling lab-growns compared to naturals. However, for consumers, lab-grown diamonds were still nowhere near the real deal, with many still regarding the product as 'cheap' and 'fake'.

While such negative consumer perception was important, the industry's social context was the main deterrent to engaging with laboratory-grown diamonds. For example, in many diamond bourses – or specialised trade floors – trading laboratory-grown diamonds was explicitly banned, with pictures of offenders publicly blacklisted at the entrance. Major diamond-mining companies launched aggressive marketing campaigns portraying lab-grown diamonds in the most negative light possible. Traders known to engage with lab-grown diamonds faced social ostracisation, with long-time colleagues deliberately avoiding them. Even discussing the topic was often off-limits. One industry executive recalled that merely suggesting a meeting with lab-grown diamond producers led to an uproar in the Antwerp Square Mile, highlighting the strong resistance within the trade community.

At the same time, several regulatory wars were being fought to impede lab-growns from gaining steady footing. For example, due to the activities of several lobbyist organisations, the term 'diamond' was long exclusively reserved for the natural product – with artificial producers being forced to use the pejorative term 'synthetic diamonds' instead. This reflected a broader industry concern: while lab-grown diamonds were chemically identical to mined ones, some traditional players sought to label them as entirely different – if not outright fake. Additionally, efforts to introduce a separate product code for lab-grown diamonds were successfully blocked, making it exceedingly difficult for traders to track supply and demand.

Yet, despite facing obstacles, interest in laboratory-grown diamonds persisted and grew stronger as production costs decreased and quality improved, leading to several new start-up companies offering them in the industry. Perhaps even more critical was that more traditional diamond traders started to display (covert) interest: several diamond organisations established – seemingly unrelated – entities that explored the potential of laboratory-grown diamonds. While many industry figures publicly distanced themselves from synthetics, behind the scenes, financial intermediaries and independent ventures often had direct ties to traditional players, allowing them to sidestep potential reputational risks. These initiatives were typically led by younger, less established individuals who saw lab-grown diamonds as a promising strategic shift, offering higher margins, fewer ethical concerns, and a more predictable supply than natural diamonds.

In 2018, industry leader and mining company De Beers baffled the rest of the sector by announcing that it would launch its own line of laboratory-grown diamonds. To safeguard the value of its inventory of natural diamonds, De Beers drew a clear distinction between its lab-grown and its natural products – pricing the lab-grown diamonds at roughly one-tenth of the cost of equivalent mined diamonds and approximately one-quarter of the price of lab-grown diamonds produced by other companies.

For many, this decision by De Beers proved a veritable milestone. Soon after, many other diamond organisations revealed their ongoing involvement with laboratory-grown diamonds. Additionally, many industry 'veterans' got involved with their own lab-grown start-ups. Large retailers, such as Signet, started to accept laboratory-grown diamonds as part of their portfolio.

Contextually, a lot changed as well. Naming guidelines established by the US Federal Trade Commission were updated, granting significantly greater flexibility for laboratory-grown products. In 2020, the Bharat diamond bourse in Mumbai voted to allow laboratory-grown diamonds on its trade floors. Soon after, the main bourses in Antwerp, New York, and Dubai followed suit. Several celebrities, including Emma Watson, Gwyneth Paltrow, and Leonardo DiCaprio, started openly endorsing lab-grown diamonds for environmental reasons. In 2021, Pope Franciscus II blessed a laboratory-grown diamond, supporting a method of manufacturing that steered clear of 'harmful mining'.

By the end of 2021, two-thirds of US retailers were carrying lab-grown diamonds. In 2022, market share of gem-quality lab-growns had risen to a hefty 10 per cent of total value and 16 per cent of total volume. As the bridal category was increasingly penetrated, many foresaw dramatic changes in the industry's future. Industry experts emphasise that this is just the beginning, with further growth and transformation expected in the years to come.

## Reflect

1. How did diamond organisations change their strategy towards lab-grown diamonds over time?
2. Was such change the result of a premeditated change plan?
3. What contingency factors impacted diamond traders' adoption of lab-grown diamonds? How did traders' behaviour affect these contingency factors in return?
4. Do you think that the adoption of lab-grown diamonds was inevitable? Why (not)?

### Case Study Sources

Bain & Company. (2013). *The global diamond report 2013: Journey through the value chain.* www.bain.com/insights/global-diamond-report-2013/.

Bain & Company. (2018). *The global diamond industry: A resilient industry shines through.* www.bain.com/contentassets/a53a9fa8bf5247a3b7bb0b10561510c2/bain_diamond_report_2018.pdf.

Bates, R. (2018, 5 June). Is De Beers' lab-grown line a Machiavellian masterstroke? *JCK*, www.jckonline.com/editorial-article/de-beers-lab-grown-line/.

De Keyser, B., & Vandenbempt, K. (2025). Persisting under pressure: How organizations coordinate their response to disruptive innovation. *Research Policy*, *54*(8), 105275.

Even-Zohar, C. (2007). *From mine to mistress: Corporate strategies and government policies in the international diamond industry*. London: Mining Communications.

Freedman, J. (2022, 21 June). The economics of lab-grown. *Rapaport*, https://rapaport.com/magazine-article/the-economics-of-lab-grown/.

Golan, E. (2023, March 30). Diamond analytics forecast: When will lab-grown diamond sales be the majority? *Edahn Golan Diamond Research and Data*, www.edahngolan.com/diamond-analytics-when-will-lab-grown-dimaond-sales-be-the-majority/.

Jeffay, J. (2021, 7 December). Pope blesses foundry's lab grown diamond. *IDEX*, www.idexonline.com/FullArticle?Id=47233.

Lee, J. (2025, 3 January). Natural diamonds had a rough year – Some hope to restore their shine. *Wall Street Journal*, https://shorturl.at/I7uH9.

Rapaport, M. (2013, 1 December). Sinthetics. *Rapaport*, https://rapaport.com/post_types/sinthetics/.

Tapper, J. (2025, 25 January). Diamonds lose their sparkle as prices come crashing down. *The Guardian*, www.theguardian.com/business/2025/jan/25/diamonds-lose-their-sparkle-as-prices-come-crashing-down.

## REFERENCES

[1] Aldrich, H. (1979). *Organizations and environments*. Englewood Cliffs, NJ: Prentice-Hall.

[2] Alvesson, M., & Sveningsson, S. (2015). *Changing organizational culture: Cultural change work in progress*. Abingdon: Routledge.

[3] Anderson, P. (1999). Perspective: Complexity theory and organization science. *Organization Science*, *10*(3), 216–232.

[4] Beer, M., & Nohria, N. (2000). Cracking the code of change. *Harvard Business Review*, *78*(3), 133–141.

[5] Borgatti, S. P., Mehra, A., Brass, D. J., & Labianca, G. (2009). Network analysis in the social sciences. *Science*, *323*(5916), 892–895.

[6] Buchanan, D. A., & Boddy, D. (1992). *The expertise of the change agent: Public performance and backstage activity*. Upper Saddle River, NJ: Prentice-Hall.

[7] Burgelman, R. A. (1991). Intraorganizational ecology of strategy making and organizational adaptation: Theory and field research. *Organization Science*, *2*(3), 239–262.

[8] Burnes, B. (2011). Understanding the emergent approach to change. In D. Boje, B. Burnes, & J. Hassard (eds.), *The Routledge companion to organizational change* (pp. 133–145). Abingdon: Routledge.

[9] Chia, R. (2002). Essai – Time, duration and simultaneity: Rethinking process and change in organizational analysis. *Organization Studies*, *23*(6), 863–868.

[10] Child, J., & Smith, C. (1987). The context and process of organizational transformation. *Journal of Management Studies*, *24*(6), 565–593.

[11] Cohen, M. D., March, J. G., & Olsen, J. P. (1972). A garbage can model of organizational choice. *Administrative Science Quarterly*, *17*(1), 1–25.

[12] Dawson, P., & Andriopoulos, C. (2014). *Managing change, creativity and innovation*. London: Sage.

[13] Dubinskas, F. A. (1994). On the edge of chaos: A metaphor for transformative change. *Journal of Management Inquiry*, *3*(4), 355–366.

[14] Dunphy, D., & Stace, D. (1993). The strategic management of corporate change. *Human Relations*, *46*(8), 905–920.

[15] Hernes, T. (2008). *Understanding organization as process: Theory for a tangled world*. Abingdon: Routledge.

[16] Hernes, T., Hendrup, E., & Schaffner, B. (2015). Sensing the momentum: A process view of change in a multinational corporation. *Journal of Change Management*, *15*(2), 117–141.

[17] Houchin, K., & MacLean, D. (2005). Complexity theory and strategic change: An empirically informed critique. *British Journal of Management*, *16*(2), 149–166.

[18] Hrebiniak, L. G., & Joyce, W. F. (1985). Organizational adaptation: Strategic choice and environmental determinism. *Administrative Science Quarterly*, *30*(3), 336–349.

[19] Kanter, R. M. (1992). *Challenge of organizational change: How companies experience it and leaders guide it*. New York: Free Press.

[20] Langley, A., Smallman, C., Tsoukas, H., & Van de Ven, A. H. (2013). Process studies of change in organization and management: Unveiling temporality, activity, and flow. *Academy of Management Journal*, *56*(1), 1–13.

[21] Lawrence, P. R., & Lorsch, J. W. (1969). *Organization and environment*. Cambridge, MA: Harvard University Press.

[22] Levinthal, D. (1991). Organizational adaptation and environmental selection-interrelated processes of change. *Organization Science*, *2*(1), 140–145.

[23] Lindblom, C. E. (1959). The science of muddling through. *Public Administration Review*, *19*(2), 79–88.

[24] Livne-Tarandach, R., & Bartunek, J. M. (2009). A new horizon for organizational change and development scholarship: Connecting planned and emergent change. In R. W. Woodman, W. A. Pasmore, & A. B. (R.) Shani (eds.), *Research in organizational change and development* (vol. 17, pp. 1–35). Bingley: Emerald.

[25] MacKay, B., & Chia, R. (2013). Choice, chance, and unintended consequences in strategic change: A process understanding of the rise and fall of NorthCo Automotive. *Academy of Management Journal*, *56*(1), 208–230.

[26] March, J. G. (1981). Footnotes to organizational change. *Administrative Science Quarterly*, *26*, 563–577.

[27] Meyer, A. D., Gaba, V., & Colwell, K. A. (2005). Organizing far from equilibrium: Nonlinear change in organizational fields. *Organization Science*, *16*(5), 456–473.

[28] Miles, R. H. (1982). *Coffin nails and corporate strategies*. Englewood Cliffs, NJ: Prentice-Hall.

[29] Nelson, R. R., & Winter, S. G. (1982). *An evolutionary theory of economic change*. Cambridge, MA: Belknap Press.

[30] Orlikowski, W. J. (1996). Improvising organizational transformation over time: A situated change perspective. *Information Systems Research*, *7*(1), 63–92.
[31] Pettigrew, A. M. (1973). *The politics of organizational decision making*. London: Tavistock.
[32] Pettigrew, A. M. (1985). *The awakening giant: Continuity and change in imperial chemical industries*. London: Routledge.
[33] Pettigrew, A. M. (1985). Contextualist research and the study of organizational change processes. In E. Lawler (ed.), *Doing research that is useful in theory and practice* (pp. 53–72). San Francisco, CA: Jossey-Bass.
[34] Pettigrew, A. M. (1987). Context and action in the transformation of the firm. *Journal of Management Studies*, *24*(6), 649–670.
[35] Pettigrew, A. M. (1990). Longitudinal field research on change: Theory and practice. *Organization Science*, *1*(3), 267–292.
[36] Pettigrew, A. M. (1997). What is a processual analysis? *Scandinavian Journal of Management*, *13*(4), 337–348.
[37] Plowman, D. A., Baker, L. T., Beck, T. E., Kulkarni, M., Solansky, S. T., & Travis, D. V. (2007). Radical change accidentally: The emergence and amplification of small change. *Academy of Management Journal*, *50*(3), 515–543.
[38] Poole, M. S., & Van de Ven, A. H. (2004). *Handbook of organizational change and innovation*. Oxford: Oxford University Press.
[39] Quinn, J. B. (1980). *Strategies for change: Logical incrementalism*. Toronto: Irwin Professional.
[40] Scherer, F. M. (1980). *Industrial market structure and economic performance*. Boston, MA: Houghton Mifflin.
[41] Stacey, R. (1992). *Managing chaos: Dynamic business strategies in an unpredictable world*. London: Kogan Page.
[42] Stacey, R. (1995). The science of complexity: An alternative perspective for strategic change processes. *Strategic Management Journal*, *16*(6), 477–495.
[43] Thaler, R., & Sunstein, C. (2008). *Nudge: Improving decisions about health, wealth, and happiness*. New York: Penguin.
[44] Tichy, N., & Fombrun, C. (1979). Network analysis in organizational settings. *Human Relations*, *32*(11), 923–965.
[45] Tichy, N. M., Tushman, M. L., & Fombrun, C. (1979). Social network analysis for organizations. *Academy of Management Review*, *4*(4), 507–519.
[46] Tsoukas, H., & Chia, R. (2002). On organizational becoming: Rethinking organizational change. *Organization Science*, *13*(5), 567–582.
[47] Weick, K. E. (2000). Emergent change as a universal in organizations. In M. Beer & N. Nohria (eds.), *Breaking the code of change* (pp. 223–241). Boston, MA: Harvard Business School Press.

# 4 A Tension Perspective on Change

## PERSPECTIVE IN BRIEF

- **Concepts related to the perspective** – dialectics in change, dialogue in change, and tensions in change
- **Keep reading to learn more about** – power and politics in change, and stakeholder diversity and inclusion
- **Prime contributors** – J. K. Benson, J. Ford, L. Ford, M. S. Poole, S. Piderit, R. Quinn, and A. Van de Ven
- **Guiding metaphor** – change as a thunderstorm

## Introduction

In Chapter 2, we explored the managerial perspective, where change is seen as something to be planned, structured, and managed. Chapter 3 introduced the organic perspective, in which change emerges from the dynamic, often unpredictable interactions between people. Now, we turn to a third way of thinking – one that places tension and disagreement at the very core.

Working with organisations is fundamentally about working with people. In essence, organisations are nothing more – and nothing less – than groups of people collaborating to achieve a common goal. Sometimes these people see eye to eye, agreeing on how to approach the tasks they've set for themselves. Other times, they disagree, holding significantly different views on the direction to take, the steps to move forward, and who should be involved. Like any social setting, bringing people together in an organisation can foster strong kinship and flourishing connections, but it can also generate considerable tension.

While many of us often perceive tension as something uncomfortable, it's crucial to recognise that tension can also be the very catalyst for organisational change. Consider the following questions:

- What organisation(s) have you been part of so far? This could be a for-profit company, a sports group, a youth association, a volunteering community . . .
- Within that organisation, what aspects have been widely agreed upon over the last few years?
- What aspects have been contested during this period?

- Where has your organisation experienced the most change?
- Where do you hope or anticipate that the organisation will undergo the most change in the future?

Without knowing the specifics of your situation, I'd wager that the areas where change has occurred or is expected to occur are those that have been most contested. Perhaps it's a promotion system viewed as unfair by newer recruits. Maybe it's a branding strategy that some groups find discriminatory. Or perhaps it's an IT system that less digitally savvy members have struggled with repeatedly. Whatever the case, tension often acts as an accelerant, and it may only take a spark for it to ignite change.

This chapter introduces the **tension perspective on change**, which emphasises conflict, contradiction, and power struggles as central forces in transformation. Unlike views that frame change as a structured process (Chapter 2) or a natural evolution (Chapter 3), this perspective considers organisations as arenas of competing interests – where resistance is not just an obstacle to be overcome but a productive force that shapes new possibilities.

## 4.1 The Genesis of Thought

To understand how the tension perspective took shape, we need to explore the ideas and conditions that set the stage for its emergence – because, just like lightning doesn't strike on a clear and sunny day, the tension perspective didn't just appear out of nowhere. What sparked its development and what allowed it to gain momentum?

### 4.1.1 From Neutral Systems to Political Arenas

Between the 1970s and 1980s, the field of strategic management began to back away from the idea that firms were made up of a single, uniform type of individual. As societal shifts such as the cultural upheavals of May 1968 in France encouraged people to break free from traditional norms, organisations were increasingly seen as diverse collectives rather than homogeneous units. This growing recognition of social and ideological plurality led to a reconceptualisation of the firm: it was seen no longer as a gathering of like-minded individuals but as a melting pot of varied perspectives, interests, and needs. Rather than assembling 'birds of a feather', organisations came to be understood as spaces where diverse voices coexist – and often collide.[3, 7, 24, 29, 38]

As a result of these observations, organisations came to be seen as political arenas, where interactions between individuals or groups with conflicting interests played a central role in shaping everyday life. This raised critical questions: How did members of a firm engage with one another? And how did these interactions influence the organisation's overall direction?[18, 43] While such dynamics could sometimes disrupt the smooth functioning of the firm, they were also viewed as a source of vitality, making the organisation more robust and responsive. In this light, managing an organisation came to mean managing potential sources of opposition,[21] and researchers started paying closer attention to dissent – not to suppress it but to expose and question the assumptions underpinning prevailing decisions.[29]

### 4.1.2 Revisiting Resistance

Due to this reconceptualisation, researchers of the 1990s and early 2000s started to increasingly question the long-standing idea of resistance to change. After all, if organisations are composed of diverse and often competing interests, why should the preferences of those in positions of authority be considered any more legitimate than those of others within the same firm? For many authors, the concept of resistance appeared increasingly problematic,[32] as it often dismissed the genuine and principled motives of those who oppose change.[12] Rather than viewing resistance as a straightforward barrier, scholars began to see it as a complex, ambivalent force – one that could disrupt but also enrich the change process. In this spirit, managers were urged not to suppress resistance but to engage with it, recognising how it might surface alternative perspectives and contribute to more meaningful and inclusive forms of organisational transformation.

To better grasp the increasing diversity within organisations, organisational theorists argued that alternative conceptual frameworks were needed. These frameworks offered tools not only for identifying sources of conflict and underlying tensions but also for navigating them in ways that could foster growth, learning, and mutual understanding.[22] Many of the resulting models drew on rich philosophical traditions, including Socratic and Aristotelian notions of *dialektike* or dialogue, Hegelian dialectics, Bakhtin's theory of relational dialectics, and Marx's analysis of class struggle.[2, 21, 30, 31] They provided a foundation for thinking about organisations not as unified entities but as contested spaces shaped by ongoing negotiation among differing – and sometimes opposing – voices.

## 4.2 Unpacking the Heart

Having traced the historical roots of the tension perspective, it's time to get closer to its core. Understanding where these ideas come from is one thing, but learning what they mean is quite another.

When thunder strikes, my dog never concerns himself with the tension behind it: he would much rather just crawl into my lap and wait it out. Now, if you want to become more adept at managing change in your organisation through tension, I suggest you resist the urge to find a metaphorical lap to crawl into – and instead delve into the following pages. Figure 4.1 offers a helpful overview of the core tenets to explore.

### 4.2.1 Capacity of Change: Change as Conflict-Based

The first cornerstone of approaching change from a tension perspective is recognising **conflict** as an inherently dynamic force. From this angle, conflict isn't just a nuisance; it's potentially constructive,[21] productive,[9] and often even necessary for change to occur.[15]

In most cases, conflict is not something that we plan for as much as it is a natural outcome of an organisation being a social group, comprising a wide range of different points of view.[15, 18] For instance, while some individuals will look favourably upon the notion of bonuses being

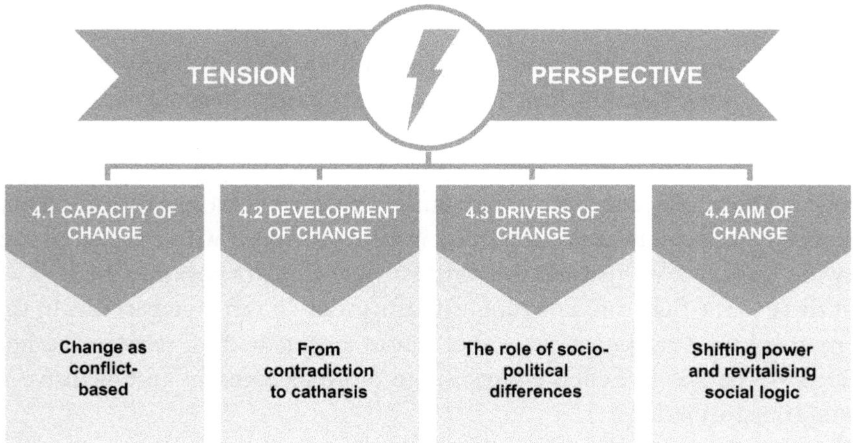


**Figure 4.1** Unpacking the heart of the tension perspective.

extended to managers for organisational performance, other people will probably look at such a policy much more disapprovingly. While some employees will support their organisation producing products in a way that maximises profits, others will consider such an approach to be inconsiderate of the environment in which the organisation operates. Differences like these have little to do with resentful individuals being intentionally malicious; rather, they boil down to the natural varieties that are always present when different people come together under the same roof.[3, 46] It is the natural outcome of organisations being complex entities, made up of many goal-directed individuals with diverging purposes.[9]

Or, think about a large multinational corporation. Here, tensions might arise between regional offices when the headquarters in one country imposes policies that don't align with local practices. A marketing strategy that works perfectly in the Australian market might face resistance in the European branches due to cultural differences. Employees in these regions might feel that their unique market insights are being ignored, leading to conflict over the direction of the company's branding efforts. This conflict can be a catalyst for change, prompting the organisation to adopt a more localised approach that balances global brand consistency with regional nuances.

## Box 4.1 Be Aware!

While no organisation can eradicate differences among their employees, some grounds prove less fertile than others for various opinions to take hold – allowing managers some control over the level of conflict they consider appropriate. An organisation employing only three individuals might have a somewhat less conflict-prone environment than the multinational employing thousands across the globe. Thus, size matters. Similarly, while the organisation that employs only senior Caucasian men might find it easy to reach consensus, it will lack the variety in opinions that other, more diverse competitors might be boasting. In this respect, while all organisations – by their very nature – set the stage for conflict and change to occur, they can differ in the extent to which they do. Social actors will inevitably compete with opposing groups to defend their interests – and, in so doing, transform the platform on which they are based.[13, 27, 30]

### 4.2.2 Development of Change: From Contradiction to Catharsis

If you've ever been outside on a hot, summer day, you'll know how a storm comes on: clouds start packing, the air gets denser, the wind picks up – you feel the world holding its breath until lightning comes crashing down. From a tension perspective, the process of organisational change is not all that different. The following four stages are most commonly referred to.

The first stage involves **contradictions becoming apparent within the social system**. In this stage, latent differences among individuals and groups begin to surface, often triggered by diverging views on organisational policies or strategic decisions.[39, 45] These tensions may manifest as deeply opposing positions – for example, between headquarters and regional branches – or as more nuanced, partial disagreements, such as those between American, European, Asian, or African offices. Regardless of intensity, such emerging contradictions mark a shift from implicit dissonance to explicit contestation. In the thunderstorm analogy, this stage would compare with a cold and warm mass of air making first contact.

For example, imagine that you are in a meeting and your boss expresses an opinion that clearly prioritises those who have been in the organisation for a considerable amount of time (unlike you). This statement highlights how you and your boss have different interests and beliefs driving your actions. As the conversation progresses, you notice other colleagues silently nodding in agreement with your boss's perspective, while a few others exchange concerned glances, signalling their discomfort. At this moment, you realise that what initially seemed like a straightforward discussion about company policy is, in fact, surfacing deeper, underlying contradictions within the team.

In the second stage, **recognised contradictions start fostering the build-up of tensions**. As organisational members become aware of their contradicting views, they begin reflecting on the system's relative sociality: how do individuals within the entity relate to each other; and how do I, as an individual, relate to the organisation? This relative reflection makes people increasingly aware of the social subgroup they belong to, and of the limitations and opportunities that this subgroup is currently bestowed with. You may begin to exchange views with other fresh hires, sharing experiences and stories. From this outset, individuals may start exploring new possibilities, often in subtle ways, and gradually gather support from others to reshape alternative social structures.[39] Referring to our thunderstorm analogy, this stage compares to the accumulation of electric charges on clouds as they are formed.

Let's go back to our meeting example. After the meeting, you and your fellow new hires start having informal discussions over coffee breaks and in group chats. You share your frustrations about the evident preference given to long-term employees, recounting moments when you felt sidelined or undervalued. These conversations spark a sense of solidarity among you, and soon you are collectively brainstorming ideas on how to voice your concerns. Perhaps you come up with the idea of forming a committee to represent the interests of newer employees, or of drafting a proposal to suggest more inclusive decision-making processes. Slowly but surely, a sense of shared purpose begins to grow, along with a realisation that change may be necessary.

In the third stage, **accumulated tensions discharge**: once those challenging the dominant vision have amassed sufficient influence, they may confront and disrupt the existing social order – often introducing radical changes in the process.[45, 46] This kind of organisational catharsis can emerge gradually, as tensions accumulate and surpass a critical threshold, or it can be triggered suddenly by a specific event. Triggering events may take many forms – a performance crisis, a damning employee engagement survey, or a public scandal – but are typically seized upon by insurgent actors as compelling evidence that the dominant vision has failed.[10, 14, 17, 39] In our thunderstorm analogy, this is when lightning hits.

In our company example, you may ultimately decide to strike and boycott your organisation on social media, together with other new hires: it is the catharsis coming out of your collective frustrations and misgivings. This action might be precipitated by a specific incident, such as the release of a company-wide memo that further entrenches the unequal treatment of employees based on tenure. Fuelled by this trigger, you and your colleagues may organise a virtual walkout, where you refuse to log into work and flood social media with your stories and grievances. The momentum builds as your posts go viral, attracting attention from both within and outside the company. The company's leadership is forced to take notice, leading to a series of emergency meetings and, eventually, the initiation of a formal review of the policies that sparked the conflict in the first place.

### Box 4.2 Be Aware!

A triggering event alone is rarely enough to drive change; rather, it serves as a catalyst, releasing tensions that have long been building beneath the surface. Here, external factors, such as shifts in the environment, may seem to initiate change, but it is the underlying internal contradictions that determine whether and how change unfolds. Without these internal tensions, the same external pressures might have little to no effect. This dynamic helps explain why organisations vary in their responses to certain challenges – some adapt and transform, while others remain unaffected.[15]

Finally, after tensions have climaxed, a (partially) **new social system will emerge** – one that inevitably gives rise to fresh contradictions. While these contradictions may differ from those of the original system, variations between individuals' goals and aims will inevitably still be around: as the organisation remains a social group, it will still bring together individuals of diverse priorities and needs. Furthermore, although the catharsis and the change it brought forth might have been beneficial for some, it might also have been detrimental for others. In this sense, while catharsis might have cleared the air for a while, it will inevitably set the stage for new contradictions to accumulate, eventually leading to new conflicts and organisational alterations. It is a cyclical and recurring process in which the outcome always sets the stage for a new change revolution to take place.[18]

In our example, while the newly hired employees might have successfully lobbied for their rights in a stand-off with management, such changes might not be equally beneficial for those who are approaching the end of their careers: the policy changes that you and your peers advocated for – such as increased flexibility, more diverse representation in leadership, and equitable project allocation – might inadvertently marginalise older employees who have long been accustomed to a different way of working. Some of them may feel that their experience is no longer valued or that they are being edged out in favour of younger, more dynamic hires. This, in turn, creates new tensions within the organisation, as these seasoned employees begin to voice their concerns, setting the stage for the next cycle of conflict and change.

**Box 4.3 The Point?**

From a tension perspective, organisational change follows a process like a brewing thunderstorm, progressing through four key stages. First, underlying contradictions within the system become explicit. As these contradictions are surfacing, tensions build, prompting individuals to form subgroups and seek change. This culminates in catharsis, where accumulated tensions are forcefully discharged (often triggered by a significant event). Finally, a new social system emerges – but as contradictions persist, they set the stage for future conflicts and continuous cycles of organisational transformation.

### 4.2.3 Drivers of Change: The Role of Socio-political Differences

But what exactly fuels the storm? At the heart of escalating tensions lie deep-seated **socio-political differences** – not deliberate obstruction but structural disparities that shape how people experience the organisation. While some people may be senior and well-established within your firm, others may have only just entered; while some are close to headquarters and speak its language, others are more distant and speak another tongue; while some are very well represented by management, others may be overlooked. In all these cases, it is not a matter of some people 'getting it' and others not; it is underlying differences in status, proximity, and representation that generate tension and, ultimately, change.

Importantly, organisations rarely operate with a single, shared reality; instead, they contain a multitude of views, each shaped by individual experiences and positions within the system. While socio-political differences are seen as a fundamental driver of change, their impact depends on three key factors: the presence of diversity and pluralism, the degree of interaction between perspectives, and the handling of opposition.

First, the organisation requires **some degree of diversity** to sustain a plurality of ideas. While pluralism can be sparked by variation in demographical characteristics – such as age, gender, or ethnicity – it can also draw on more implicit group characteristics, such as differences in educational levels or personal interests. Should the organisation choose to employ a very homogenous group, its diversity in opinions will plummet, leading to a firm that, although tightly consolidated, will display little to no impetus for change.[8, 12, 36]

Think about an organisation that primarily hires from a narrow pool of candidates, focusing on individuals from a specific educational background or geographic region. While this may result in a cohesive work culture, it also limits the range of perspectives brought to the table. When faced with a complex problem, the lack of diversity in thought can stifle creativity and hinder the development of innovative solutions. On the other hand, an organisation that embraces diversity – whether in terms of gender, ethnicity, or educational background – will likely see a broader array of ideas and approaches, sparking healthier debate and driving the organisation towards more meaningful change.

Next, while organisational diversity may generate a wide range of opinions, such differences will not produce change unless they are allowed to **interact**. Dialogue or communication between those upholding different mindsets is critical.[6, 26, 42, 44] In this way, change is not driven by communication but rather occurs and is sustained *within* communication. The change process is not a matter of using communication as a means to an end but instead results from the natural interaction between different perspectives and ideals.[15]

Imagine a company where departments operate in silos, with little to no interaction between teams. The marketing team, focused on brand image, and the product development team, focused on technical specifications, might have vastly different views on a new product launch. Yet, without open channels of communication, these differing viewpoints remain isolated, and potential synergies are lost. In contrast, if teams are encouraged to collaborate and engage in regular discussions, they can challenge each other's assumptions, leading to a more robust and well-rounded product that better meets market demands. The interaction between these diverse perspectives becomes the engine for innovation and change.

Finally, as differing viewpoints interact, they should be allowed to give rise to **opposing positions**. While reaching agreement can be beneficial when both parties are willing, it should not be viewed as the primary objective of social interactions; instead, opposition should be offered the space to emerge. In this context, change can be understood as one position challenging another, where the process of implementation involves overcoming the opposing stance.[15]

Consider a scenario where a company's leadership is pushing for rapid digital transformation, while a significant portion of the workforce resists, fearing job displacement and loss of traditional roles. This opposition may initially seem like a barrier to progress, but it is essential to the change process. The resistance forces leadership to confront and address the concerns of the workforce, perhaps by offering retraining programmes or finding ways to integrate new technologies without completely erasing existing jobs. Through this adversarial process, the company can achieve a more balanced and sustainable transformation, one that takes into account the needs and fears of all stakeholders. The opposition does not hinder change; it refines and strengthens it.

**Box 4.4 The Point?**

From a tension angle, it's socio-political differences that spark organisational change. Up to a certain degree, such differences can be actively controlled – this by working on the degree of diversity and pluralism, the amount of interaction, and the level to which opposition is accepted.

### 4.2.4 Aim of Change: Shifting Power and Revitalising Social Logic

Finally, if socio-political differences are what ignite change from a tension view, then the aim of that change is rarely impartial – it's about **shifting power** and redefining whose logic prevails. As dominant social classes within the organisation emphasise and solidify particular sets of values, policies, and directions, they define comprehensive rules of the game within the firm's social and economic life.[20] This creates an environment that is ripe for potential challengers, with change arising from the mismatch between the current social arrangement and those who aim to reconfigure.[39] In this way, tensions rarely spark into organisational change without some kind of goal: typically, it revolves around the socio-political realignment of subgroups within the larger whole.

Let's say that your organisation's management team has long been dominated by engineers who prioritise product innovation above all else. As the company grows, a new cohort of marketing professionals emerges, arguing that the organisation's focus should shift towards understanding customer needs and market trends. The engineers' values and policies have shaped the company's direction for years, but now the marketers, feeling under-represented, begin to challenge this dominance. The tension between these two groups sets the stage for potential change – a reconfiguration of the organisation's priorities that could lead to either a more balanced approach or, alternatively, a period of internal strife and confusion.

**Box 4.5 Be Aware!**

Whether a revitalisation of the existing order is necessarily better for the organisation at large remains to be seen. While revised rules can benefit one group within the organisation, they may also harm other groups or the organisation as a whole. For instance, although the company might benefit from the dominance of the engineering mindset being challenged, it could also emerge more chaotic or confused, struggling to find a new identity. Thus, there is no guarantee that socio-political conflict will produce benevolent outcomes. Maintaining the status quo may have its downsides, but its replacement with a new social configuration can be just as problematic.[45]

While the politics underlying organisational progress can make change feel futile – more like a social turf war than meaningful development – the tension perspective argues that each iteration's long-run impact is nonetheless meaningful. Change is not just simple destruction and substitution; it is a process where the negated elements shape and influence the new form that emerges from the conflict, with some of these elements undergoing transformation and being carried forward.[15] In this sense, although change might not always lead to improvements right away, it will provide the organisation with new elements to draw on in future iterations: to tap from what did work, and do away with what did not.[18, 31, 39]

## 4.3 Extending Your Toolkit

While operationalising the tension perspective on change may sound, well, *tense*, there are a few important frameworks that could lighten the load. These are: (i) dialectics; (ii) dialogue theory; and (iii) stakeholder mapping.

### 4.3.1 Dialectics

Initially conceptualised in the philosophical work of Socrates, Hegel, and Marx, the concept of **dialectics** has been aptly used to advance a wide variety of organisational theories, including change.[3, 21, 34] Derived from the Ancient Greek for 'through, across' (διά or diá) and 'to speak' (λέγειν or légein), the essence of dialectics involves contradictory opposites which interact to eventually supersede each other. When this happens, the outcome is not simply a recombination of the previous two but a new 'thing' conditioned and informed by what went before.[15] Perhaps the most well-known conceptualisation of this dialectical idea is Hegel's framing of thesis, antithesis, and synthesis, in which an initial idea or position (thesis) encounters opposition or contradiction (antithesis), leading to a resolution (synthesis) that integrates and transcends both.

Let's try to wrap our heads around this framework by first considering an example of broader societal change – let's say the French Revolution. Before the revolution, France operated under the model of the Ancien Régime, a rigid hierarchical system dominated by absolute monarchy and a stratified social order (i.e., thesis). The king, along with the privileged clergy and nobility, maintained control over the country's resources and political power, while the vast majority – comprising commoners, peasants, and the emerging bourgeoisie – shouldered the tax burden and had little to no political representation. This centralised authority functioned relatively unchallenged for centuries, maintaining stability through tradition and divine right.

Yet as economic hardship deepened, Enlightenment ideas spread, and frustration over inequality grew, a direct challenge to the existing system emerged. Commoners, inspired by thinkers like Rousseau and Voltaire, began demanding representation, fairness, and an end to feudal privileges. The storming of the Bastille followed, symbolising the public's rejection of absolute monarchy and the oppressive status quo. Soon, this struggle between the monarchy and revolutionaries reached a critical breaking point, resulting in a radical abolition of the monarchy and the establishment of the First French Republic (i.e., antithesis).

However, this situation did not create a sustainable alternative but rather another extreme take – highlighted in what became known as the Reign of Terror. Eventually, after years of instability, the revolutionary government collapsed, paving the way for the rise of Napoleon Bonaparte, who synthesised elements of both the old monarchy and the revolution's ideals to create a new, authoritarian yet modernised regime (i.e., synthesis).

While you could nowadays still be living in a societal system that is inspired by the Napoleonic regime, no contemporary system fully aligns with it. In this sense, the synthesis was not a definite be-all-and-end-all, but rather a new stage for conflict to eventually feature on – and, ultimately, change the rules of the game altogether.

Moving from a societal to a company level, the dialectic framework can be equally powerful. Imagine an organisation where workers have historically had little say in the company's direction – maybe a tech company where all major decisions have been made exclusively by the executive leadership team, with little to no input from the broader workforce (i.e., thesis). This centralised decision-making approach has led to several successful product launches, but it has also created a sense of disenfranchisement among employees, particularly those in the engineering and design teams who feel that their on-the-ground insights are being ignored.

Over time, the frustration among workers may grow, leading them to challenge the status quo and propose a more democratic approach, with people arguing that those who are directly involved in product development should have a say in the strategic direction of the company (i.e., antithesis). This antithesis, driven by the workers' desire for greater involvement, directly opposes the original thesis and creates tension within the organisation.

Leadership initially resists this push, viewing it as a threat to its authority and a potential bottleneck in the decision-making process. However, as the debate intensifies and both sides present their arguments – workers highlighting the benefits of incorporating diverse perspectives and leaders stressing the importance of streamlined decision-making – a new solution begins to take shape. The company decides to establish a council made up of representatives from different departments, including both management and rank-and-file employees, to discuss and advise on key strategic initiatives before final decisions are made by the leadership team.

As these two opposing forces interact, a new organisational ground thus begins to form. Rather than either extreme prevailing (workers being entirely excluded from decision-making or holding ultimate decision-making power), the organisation reaches a compromise by agreeing to consult with employee representatives on significant issues (i.e., synthesis). This synthesis incorporates elements of both the original thesis and the antithesis, blending the need for worker input with the practicalities of efficient decision-making. However, it is not a mere addition of the two but a genuinely new reality that emerges from their interaction.

Over time, this synthesis might lead to further refinements as the company continues to evolve. For instance, the council's role could expand or contract based on its effectiveness, giving rise to new tensions and the next stage of development. In this sense, the synthesis represents not the end but rather a new beginning – a new thesis that will face its own challenges and contradictions, prompting further cycles of change. The dialectical process, therefore, is continuous, driving the organisation forward through a series of conflicts and resolutions that each leave their mark on the evolving organisational structure.

**Box 4.6 The Point?**

Dialectical theory offers a holistic and dynamic perspective on the world and its processes of change, providing a useful tool for analysing complex phenomena and finding solutions to complex problems. It can be understood as being progressive in retrospect – as building continuously towards the future, while drawing simultaneously on the past.[10, 21, 45]

### 4.3.2 Dialogic Theory

If dialectical theory helps us see change as a dynamic interplay of past and future, **dialogic theory** brings that interplay into the present – through conversation. Dialogic theory, rooted in the work of thinkers such as Mikhail Bakhtin[1] and David Bohm,[4] emphasises the importance of open-ended, meaning-making conversations where multiple voices coexist. In contrast to debate, where different points of view often don't interact much, dialogic theory invites participants to collectively explore differences, acknowledging that tensions are not problems to be solved but conditions to be engaged with.[16, 23, 44]

In the context of organisational change, dialogic theory suggests that transformation is not just about implementing a new strategy or structure; it is about fostering conversations that allow diverse viewpoints to interact. Rather than suppressing contradictions, organisations practising dialogic theory recognise them as sources of creativity and learning. Tensions, in this sense, are considered persistent and must be continuously navigated rather than eliminated.

Applying dialogic theory in organisational change requires fostering spaces where employees, leaders, and stakeholders can openly discuss divergent views without the pressure to immediately converge on a solution. This entails:

- Suspending judgment – creating an environment where participants listen actively and refrain from immediately defending their positions. For example, in a strategy realignment initiative, managers might hold sessions where employees articulate concerns about market repositioning without fear of retribution.[16, 23, 44]
- Encouraging reflexivity – enabling individuals to question their assumptions and recognise how their perspectives shape their understanding of change. For instance, a healthcare organisation undergoing digital transformation could encourage doctors, nurses, and administrators to reflect on how their professional identities and routines shape their attitudes towards electronic health records.[16, 23, 44]
- Embracing tensions as productive – acknowledging that opposing views may hold value and that their coexistence can lead to more innovative outcomes. In a merger between two firms with differing corporate cultures, for example, recognising and working through contrasting values could lead to the development of a more resilient and inclusive hybrid culture rather than enforcing one dominant model.[16, 23, 44]
- Facilitating multi-voiced engagement – ensuring that different voices within the organisation, including those at the periphery, are heard and considered in shaping the change process. This might involve front-line workers in decision-making processes about workflow automation rather than solely relying on executives and consultants.[16, 23, 44]

**Box 4.7 Be Aware!**

Dialogue does not mean consensus. Instead, it stresses that organisations aim to work through tensions constructively, ensuring that multiple perspectives inform change rather than being overridden or ignored.

Think about a multinational company undergoing digital transformation. A dialogue-based approach would facilitate structured conversations where employees across hierarchical levels discuss their concerns, aspirations, and ideas for adaptation. The firm could introduce 'dialogue forums' where engineers, production workers, and executives could openly discuss the impact of automation. These conversations may reveal not only fears of job loss but also employee insights into how technology could be integrated in ways that may improve both efficiency and job satisfaction. By embracing these tensions rather than dismissing them, the company could co-develop strategies that combine automation with upskilling initiatives, creating a more sustainable and inclusive transformation.

**Box 4.8 The Point?**

Dialogic theory provides a way to systematically engage with tensions, ensuring that change efforts are informed by the richness of diverse perspectives rather than constrained by the need for immediate resolution.

## 4.3.3 Stakeholder Mapping and Conflict Management

While dialogic theory invites us to explore tensions through conversation, **stakeholder mapping** takes a more pragmatic turn, helping us navigate those tensions when change is already underway. Although not strictly embodying all of the tenets of the tension perspective, the framework of stakeholder mapping and conflict management aligns closely with its core concerns. Both recognise that change unfolds in contested terrain – where different actors hold divergent interests, values, and levels of power. If you're looking for a more directly actionable approach, particularly when a change initiative is already in motion, stakeholder mapping can offer practical guidance.

Whether the change is subtle or sweeping, it inevitably affects a network of people with varying stakes and influence. That's why it's often useful to systematically identify stakeholders and explore structured ways of managing conflict. What follows distils the essence of this approach.[5, 28, 37, 40]

First, start by **identifying who's in the room – and who's just outside the door**. Begin by listing all individuals, groups, or entities who are either affected by a change or have the power to influence it.[5, 28, 37, 40] To surface these stakeholders, you could draw on brainstorming, interviews, organisational charts, and a technique called stakeholder snowballing, where each interviewee is asked who else might have a stake in the change (this helps reveal those quiet influencers you might otherwise miss). Some stakeholders will be obvious; others will be less visible but no less important. Include:

- internal actors – employees, team leaders, department heads, executives, unions, and HR;
- external stakeholders – customers, suppliers, regulators, industry associations, community partners;
- informal or hidden influencers – trusted insiders, unofficial gatekeepers, long-tenured staff, or informal leaders whose opinions carry weight despite their title.

Next, start **mapping what matters to them** in terms of a few key attributes.[5, 28, 37, 40] Mapping certain attributes helps you anticipate reactions, identify allies and blockers, and prepare for the social dynamics that may shape change outcomes. For each stakeholder (or group), you could consider the following questions:

- Interests – what do they care about? What are they hoping to gain – or are afraid to lose?
- Power – how much influence do they have over the change process or its outcome?
- Attitude – are they likely to support, resist, or remain neutral?

Moreover, you could **plot what you've learnt visually**. A simple and widely used tool is the power–interest grid,[11] which categorises stakeholders along two axes: their level of power and their degree of interest in the change. However, alternative mappings can be built around dimensions such as supportiveness versus influence, internal versus external, or engagement required versus current engagement. What matters most is that the format helps you see the field at a glance and make smart choices about where to invest energy.

Then, try to **anticipate where conflict may emerge and what would be the preferred resolution styles**.[40] Preferably, a stakeholder map is not just a lens for identifying potential sources of tension but also a tool for alignment. For each stakeholder, consider:

- Type of conflict – if conflict emerges, will it most likely be about goals (task), processes, or personal dynamics?
- Intensity – how significant will the disagreement or tension be?
- Preferred conflict style – does this stakeholder tend to compete, collaborate, avoid, accommodate, or compromise?
- History – is there unresolved conflict or past tension that might flare up again?

Finally, **feed your map back into your change**: here, your stakeholder map becomes a tool for guiding action.[5, 28, 37, 40] Use it to design:

- Risk mitigation tactics – where are the flashpoints of resistance? Who needs to be brought in early? Who must be won over?
- Tailored communication plans – what messages matter most to each stakeholder group?
- Targeted engagement strategies – what tailored approach could we use? With people who act as collaborators, co-design often works well. With people who act as competitors, you may prefer setting clear boundaries and using data to anchor discussions. With avoiders, providing safe spaces or low-pressure entry points into conversations can help.

For a simplified example of what such a mapping exercise could look like, I've included Table 4.1.

**Table 4.1 A sample stakeholder/conflict mapping**

| Stakeholder | Role/ group | Interests | Power | Support level | Conflict type | Conflict style | Engagement strategy | Notes |
|---|---|---|---|---|---|---|---|---|
| John (head of IT) | Internal sponsor | Wants tech autonomy | High | Mixed | Task conflict | Competing | Involve early, ask to co-design sessions | Possible ally |
| Staff union | External | Wants job security | Medium–high | Low | Relational conflict | Compromising | Share information, negotiate terms | Can delay change |
| Department X | Internal team | Wants clarity | Low | Neutral | Process conflict | Avoiding | Keep informed | Likely passive |

Stakeholder mapping offers not just a snapshot of who matters but also a dynamic playbook for how to engage, intervene, and navigate tensions productively. Done well, it turns change from a static checklist into a living terrain – where influence, alliances, and power dynamics are actively acknowledged and shaped.

## 4.4 Impact on the Ground

As you may have deduced by now, the tension perspective doesn't just help you see the change landscape – it helps you move through it. By recognising change as a contested, political, and evolving process, this approach brings several practical advantages. The following three are the most noteworthy.

### 4.4.1 A Tension Perspective Reframes Conflict as Catalytic

First, it is crucial to recognise how different the role of friction and contradiction becomes when thinking about change from a tension perspective: rather than branding internal differences as things that inhibit the changes an organisation may want to undertake, a tension perspective explicitly values differences and conflict as being fundamentally generative to change taking place at all.[27, 31, 32, 41, 42]

A critical consequence of such rethinking is that tensions no longer come to be viewed as conflicts to be eliminated,[19] but rather as catalysts for creativity and development. Managers are encouraged to embrace and even capitalise on the tensions and anxieties they provoke, as these challenges can play a crucial role in fostering creative insights and driving meaningful developments.[22] As a result, rather than focusing on change directly, this means that managers may want to look into how their organisations are equipped to deal and cope with frictions as they develop over time.

**Box 4.9 Practical Advice?**

- Foster open communication – create an environment where diverse perspectives and dissenting opinions are welcomed and discussed openly.
- Form cross-functional teams – establish teams with diverse expertise to integrate various viewpoints and turn conflicts into opportunities for innovation.
- Encourage constructive debate – set up forums and regular meetings where employees can express differing views and explore them productively.
- Reframe tensions as opportunities – educate and guide teams to view tensions not as obstacles but as valuable sources of insight and creativity.

### 4.4.2 A Tension Perspective Kindles Plurality

Next, viewing change through a tension lens underscores the importance of diverse perspectives within an organisation and the expression of those differences through communication. Change, in this sense, emerges from individuals holding varying opinions about organisational reality. Pluralism and diversity thus become essential sources of organisational change, without which the organisation risks stagnation. Change occurs within the context of human social interactions, which are shaped by communication. These interactions create and perpetuate the social structures people recognise as reality. Therefore, producing intentional change involves deliberately shaping a new reality or set of social structures through communication.[6, 21, 31, 33, 35, 44] In this way, the tension perspective highlights change in organisations as being inherently social and driven by individual interpretation, with individuals who wrestle with what success truly means ultimately reshaping the organisation's core principles in the process.[20]

### 4.4.3 A Tension Perspective Highlights the Importance of Politics

Finally, the tension perspective offers a clearer understanding of the political dimension in organisational development. For change to occur, it is crucial that the various stakeholders within the organisation are allowed to engage, negotiate, and even clash.[3, 9, 18, 39] Change is fundamentally seen as a process of shifting power dynamics between opposing forces, with actors reshaping existing practices, technologies, and institutions to serve their own specific and often competing interests.[18]

In this sense, although change can be somewhat steered towards, it often lies beyond any one party's full control: while top teams can try to push organisations forward all they like, every plan will be interpreted and regurgitated differently according to individual interests. All plans and efforts aside, organisational change is inherently unpredictable and will result in unexpected outcomes as it interacts with existing forces. As such, change is believed to be highly political, requiring an understanding of the social dynamics at work within organisations.[21]

## 4.5 Drawbacks and Pitfalls

Still, for all its generative potential, the tension perspective is not without complications. Here are three major concerns to be aware of when adopting this perspective, along with practical advice for navigating them.

### 4.5.1 A Tension Perspective Deprives Change of Purpose and Finality

First, by framing change as an ongoing process fuelled by contradictions within an organisation's social fabric, the tension perspective can struggle to offer a sense of closure or clear direction. Critics argue that it promotes change for change's sake, portraying organisations as locked in an endless cycle of tension and transformation, where new developments merely create fresh contradictions that spark further change.[15] This can leave leaders and employees feeling adrift, uncertain about where the organisation is headed or what success looks like.[31]

While the arguments in this chapter do suggest that the tension perspective views change as an ongoing process, it is unclear whether the perspective should be criticised for lacking a sense of intentionality. If anything, the tension perspective claims that change arises from the conflict between individual goals and the existing social order – thus implying that change does have a purpose. Such purpose may be individual or group-based, but it's purpose nonetheless: to improve the relative situation of a certain collection of people. In this way, organisational change may not be without purpose, but this purpose may be more fragmented than it is typically understood as being in other perspectives.

### Box 4.10 Practical Advice?

It often helps when leaders and teams are explicitly trained to be more comfortable with ambiguity and uncertainty: rather than seeking definitive answers or rigid plans, it is usually a better idea to focus on building the capacity to cope with different points of view. Provide context to help everyone understand that ongoing discussions are part of a broader process of organisational evolution. This can help reduce the anxiety that often accompanies the lack of clear outcomes and foster a culture of flexibility and innovation.

## 4.5.2 A Tension Perspective Centres Too Much on Conflict as a Driver

Next, thinking about change from a tension point of view may push managers to focus too single-mindedly on conflict as a driver for change. While friction can certainly spur transformation, change also arises from collaboration, inspiration, and strategic planning. By focusing too narrowly on contradictions, organisations risk overlooking other crucial factors, such as employee engagement, technological advancements, and external market forces.[15]

### Box 4.11 Practical Advice?

As with all perspectives, it's usually a good idea to foster a holistic view of change, encouraging teams to consider how various elements within the organisation are interconnected. This can involve examining how tensions interact with other factors, such as employee engagement, market trends, or regulatory changes. By understanding the broader context, teams can better anticipate ripple effects and respond more effectively to emerging challenges. This approach also helps prevent the tunnel vision that can result from focusing too narrowly on conflict.

### 4.5.3 A Tension Perspective May Be Overly Romantic or Optimistic

Finally, some critics argue that the tension perspective can paint an overly idealistic picture of conflict as a natural and even beneficial force within organisations. For some, the weakness of the perspective lies in its idealistic view of the potential for successfully and smoothly integrating opposing forces.[21] That such a combination of opposing tendencies is often anything but straightforward – and even carries clear risk – is to be well understood: in many cases, what is presented as civil discourse may lead to career-damaging actions and even moments where intervention is needed to prevent serious confrontations.[25]

Here, it's important to remember that the tension perspective does not make any strict inferences on whether change sprouting from conflict is at all beneficial or detrimental to the organisation. In this sense, the tension perspective does not claim that all conflict is beneficial – only that contradiction is an inherent part of organisational life. Whether tension results in positive transformation or destructive fallout depends on how it is managed.

#### Box 4.12 Practical Advice?

It's important to approach conflict with a realistic understanding of its potential risks and benefits. To do this sensibly, it may be a good idea to encourage open communication and create safe spaces for expressing differing viewpoints, but also be prepared to manage conflicts that escalate. Developing strong conflict resolution skills within the organisation can help ensure that tensions lead to constructive change rather than destructive outcomes. Moreover, it might help to emphasise the importance of courage and resilience when navigating conflicts, as these qualities can help individuals and teams overcome challenges and achieve positive results.

## SUMMARY

Chapter 4 explored the **tension perspective** on change, which emphasises the role of conflict, contradictions, and power struggles in shaping organisational transformation. Unlike perspectives that view change as a structured process or a natural evolution, this approach frames change as an ongoing dynamic of competing interests, negotiations, and socio-political tensions (see Table 4.2 for an overview).

- ◊ The **origins of this perspective** can be traced back to a shift in how organisations were conceptualised – not as neutral systems striving for efficiency but as political arenas where competing agendas and power struggles play a defining role. This led to a reconsideration of the idea of 'resistance to change', shifting from seeing it as an obstacle to recognising it as an inherent and potentially productive aspect of change.
- ◊ We noted how, at its **core**, the tension perspective sees change as conflict-based, emerging from frictions among different stakeholders, perspectives, and interests. Rather than being a linear progression, change is considered to unfold through cycles of contradiction and

**Table 4.2 A tension perspective on change: overview**

| | |
|---|---|
| **Guiding metaphor** | Change as a thunderstorm |
| **The genesis of thought** | |
| Development 1 | From neutral systems to political arenas |
| Development 2 | Revisiting resistance |
| **Unpacking the heart** | |
| Capacity of change | Change as conflict-based |
| Development of change | Contradiction to catharsis |
| Drivers of change | The role of socio-political differences |
| Aim of change | Shifting power and revitalising social logic |
| **Extending your toolkit** | |
| Tool #1 | Dialectics |
| Tool #2 | Dialogic theory |
| Tool #2 | Stakeholder mapping and conflict management |
| **Impact on the ground** | |
| (+) | A tension perspective reframes tensions as catalytic. |
| (+) | A tension perspective kindles plurality. |
| (+) | A tension perspective highlights the importance of politics. |
| **Drawbacks and pitfalls** | |
| (−) | A tension perspective deprives change of purpose and finality. |
| (−) | A tension perspective centres too much on conflict as driver. |
| (−) | A tension perspective may be overly romantic or optimistic. |
| **Related concepts** | |
| ► | Dialectics in change |
| ► | Dialogue in change |
| ► | Tensions in change |

catharsis, where clashes give rise to new possibilities and shifts in organisational logic. Socio-political differences are viewed as key drivers of change, challenging the notion that change is always a deliberate, expert-driven process. The ultimate aim of change, within this perspective, is not just efficiency or adaptation but the redistribution of power and the revitalisation of social structures.

◊ To better understand change through this lens, we examined three **key tools**. Dialectics provide a framework for understanding how opposing forces interact to create new forms of organisation and meaning. Dialogic theory emphasises the role of conversations, narratives, and meaning-making in navigating tensions and shaping change. Stakeholder mapping, in turn, offers a way of crystallising the divergent interests and potential tensions of different stakeholders involved in an initiative.

◊ One of the key **contributions** of the tension perspective is that it reframes tensions not as barriers to change but as catalysts that drive transformation. It acknowledges the role of plurality and sensemaking, emphasising that different viewpoints and competing narratives shape the change process. It also highlights the deeply political nature of change, recognising that shifts in organisations are often struggles over power, identity, and control.

◊ However, the perspective is not without its **challenges**. By emphasising ongoing tensions, it risks depriving change of a clear purpose or finality, making it difficult to determine when a change effort has 'succeeded'. It may also overstate the role of conflict, treating it as the sole driver of change rather than one of many contributing factors. Additionally, there is a risk of romanticising struggle and contradiction, assuming that they will always lead to productive outcomes.

The tension perspective connects to broader concepts such as dialectics and dialogue in change. While it offers a powerful critique of overly rational and mechanistic views, it also raises important questions about how organisations can navigate conflict constructively and avoid becoming trapped in cycles of endless struggle.

## CASE: UNEQUAL FOOTING AT NIKE

### The Tension Perspective in Practice

'Just Do It.' Ever since 1988, this slogan has motivated people to engage in various sports – running, football, basketball, tennis, and more – changing many people's lives for the better by pushing them towards a healthier lifestyle.

For Nike, 'Just Do It' also characterised the company's epic ascent into the business stratosphere. Founded in 1964 as Blue Ribbon Sports by Bill Bowerman and Phil Knight, the company that became known as Nike has risen to be one of the largest producers of sports apparel worldwide. Its 'swoosh' logo has been frequently ranked as one of the most recognisable company logos ever. In 2022, the company reported a revenue of almost US$50 billion – meaning that in every second of that year, Nike sold sports apparel worth about US$1,500. In the same year, it was announced as the world's most valuable apparel brand by Brand Finance, and the most valuable sports brand by Forbes.

Yet, in 2017, it turned out that the 'Just Do It' slogan could also be understood in a far less benign way. At Nike, 'Just Do It' proved as much a wry description of how female workers were treated as it was a motivational slogan. In this case, we consider a story of oppressors and oppressed, and of the change that ultimately sprouted forth from it.

### Nike's Public Image Concerning Women

For much of the early twenty-first century, Nike cultivated a carefully managed reputation as a corporate leader in diversity. Its branding did more than market sneakers – it sold values. Under the leadership of CEO Mark Parker, who took the helm in 2006, Nike publicly positioned itself as a company deeply committed to inclusivity and social progress. This narrative gained traction with media and analysts alike. Parker's leadership earnt him glowing recognition, including being named Fortune's Businessperson of the Year in 2015 – an accolade attributed, in part, to his championing of workplace diversity.

Nike's messaging was both internal and external. Externally, its official diversity statement underscored the need to reflect the rich demographics of its global customer base, and promoted the idea that creative excellence was rooted in diversity of thought and experience. The company broadcast its commitment to serving 'every athlete individually and completely', presenting itself as a brand that understood – and respected – the plurality of its audiences.

Internally, Parker spoke out on many polarising issues, from racial violence to systemic inequality. He reassured employees that Nike stood with marginalised communities and sought to act as a corporate agent of social good. Rankings followed. Mogul, a platform focused on female empowerment, placed Nike among its top ten companies for millennial women in 2017. Feedback-based awards rolled in from well-known HR platforms, adding further shine to Nike's image as a modern, inclusive employer.

But awards and statements alone cannot guarantee an equitable culture. Beneath the polished exterior, a very different reality played out – one that would eventually force the company into one of its most significant internal reckonings.

### A Pyramid with Crumbling Steps

While Nike's outward-facing language was steeped in inclusion, many women inside the organisation described an altogether different experience – one marked by persistent exclusion, unequal treatment, and stagnated progression. The organisational structure at Nike, they said, mirrored a steep pyramid: broad at the base, but with diminishing opportunity the higher one climbed. Women, in particular, found themselves trapped at the lower levels, disproportionately under-represented in senior roles and frequently passed over for advancement.

Francesca Krane, who had spent half a decade working in Nike's retail brand design team, eventually walked away – not because of dissatisfaction with her work but because she no longer believed that advancement was possible for women like her. The pattern was painfully familiar: men promoted quickly, women overlooked, regardless of merit or performance. Her story resonated with others, many of whom voiced similar experiences of being professionally sidelined.

Beyond promotions, access to influence and high-visibility workstreams was often gated. Female employees were reportedly excluded from key product categories – basketball being a notable example – where brand prestige and executive visibility were especially high. In meetings, women's ideas were routinely dismissed or ignored. The workplace, some said, operated on invisible rules that favoured familiarity over fairness, and favoured men over everyone else. What unfolded was not just inequality in outcomes but a systemic culture in which many women felt invisible.

### Toxicity in the Everyday

Workplace culture, however, was not merely exclusionary – it was frequently described as demeaning and, at times, overtly abusive. Many female employees reported a pattern of behaviour that echoed the norms of a 'frat house' more than a professional environment. Casual misogyny was rampant. Derogatory language was used freely, and stories surfaced of executives making crude sexual remarks about women's bodies – sometimes even in written correspondence.

There were reports of company events ending in strip clubs. Supervisors allegedly pressured women to 'dress sexier'. One male manager reportedly hurled his car keys at a female colleague and called her a 'stupid b***h'. Senior executives were accused of engaging in inappropriate relationships with junior staff, sometimes at company-sponsored gatherings. Several employees described intoxicated male colleagues embracing women at work functions or inviting them to 'private dinners' under the guise of mentorship. According to one anonymous Glassdoor reviewer, success at Nike was less about performance than about who you knew – and whether you fitted the mould.

Human Resources, the very mechanism meant to address workplace grievances, often served as a dead-end. Complaints about inappropriate behaviour were met with indifference or downplayed altogether. Women who spoke up about misconduct were sometimes advised to handle it directly with the offender. Others saw their complaints result in no meaningful consequences – or, worse, found themselves punished for raising the issue. Some were dismissed from their roles following reports to HR, despite previously strong performance evaluations. As trust in HR evaporated, many women simply stopped reporting.

### A New Power Rises

In 2017, tensions that had long simmered beneath the surface at Nike finally began to crystallise, when a consequential exodus of senior female leaders sent shockwaves through the company's headquarters. Among those departing were Patty Ross, who had overseen Workplace Design, and Nikki Neuberger, formerly at the helm of Global Brand Marketing. Neuberger didn't leave in silence. In a direct communication to CEO Mark Parker, she outlined serious concerns – from the routine sidelining of women in strategic conversations to incidents of inappropriate workplace behaviour.

Their exits did more than create leadership vacancies; they catalysed a wave of internal reflection. In the weeks that followed, a network of women within the company began compiling their own evidence, not through formal HR channels but via a discreet and independently initiated survey that invited female employees to share stories of exclusion, bias, and harassment – many of which had gone unreported until then.

Just months later, a seismic cultural shift was underway worldwide. The #MeToo movement exploded into global consciousness in late 2017, beginning with revelations about Harvey Weinstein and igniting a broader reckoning with gendered misconduct across industries. Nike's internal unrest now found itself aligned with a global narrative – one that demanded that institutions no longer protect silence over justice.

### Executive Shake-Up and Corporate Contrition

In March 2018, the findings of the survey made their way to Parker. The result was a dramatic reshuffling at the top. Eleven high-level executives left the company in quick succession, some under the guise of early retirement. Among them was Trevor Edwards, then president of the Nike brand and widely regarded as Parker's heir apparent. Edwards left under a severance arrangement that reportedly included a US$525,000 payout and up to US$9 million in unvested stock awards – a departure that stirred debate about accountability and reward.

In May, Parker addressed employees at the Beaverton, Oregon campus. He praised the courage of those who had spoken up, expressed regret that some employees felt marginalised, and acknowledged that Nike had not lived up to its ideals. He admitted that leadership had been slow to grasp the depth of internal discontent. He acknowledged that certain voices had been marginalised and pledged a new approach – one that would emphasise listening, accountability, and systemic reform. He also promised action. Compensation systems would be reviewed. Diversity metrics would be made more transparent. Internal reporting channels and managerial training programmes would be overhauled. He pledged the introduction of mentorship schemes, leadership training for under-represented groups, and initiatives to tackle unconscious bias.

The speech was received with cautious scepticism. Aside from a brief round of applause for acknowledging those who spoke up, the room remained largely silent. Some welcomed his acknowledgement; others found the tone evasive and the timing too convenient. Amanda Shebiel, a former Nike employee, openly questioned why it took an anonymous survey – rather than years of formal reports – to prompt change.

### Beyond Damage Control: Towards Structural Redesign

The aftermath did bring some material changes, though. In July 2018, Nike announced that it would adjust compensation for over 7,000 employees following a review of pay equity. Around 10 per cent of the global workforce would see raises. The following month, two former employees filed a lawsuit alleging sex-based discrimination – with the potential to expand into a class-action suit involving hundreds of women.

Nike's case stood out. While many companies swept problems under the rug or scapegoated individuals, Nike's internal revolt triggered visible structural action. As *The New York Times* noted, this went beyond disciplining perpetrators – it began to address the organisational culture that had allowed the behaviour to flourish.

Ultimately, the pressure did not come from shareholders, regulators, or journalists. It came from within – from employees who dared to hold their employer accountable, and from a cultural moment that forced even the most powerful brands to take a hard look in the mirror.

### Reflect

1. Track Nike's change process: which specific events sparked changes at Nike? Do you believe that similar changes could have been achieved without these events?
2. What ultimately changed at Nike? Did these changes alter Nike's balance of power?
3. How should Nike move forward? Who is to make such a call?

### Case Study Sources


Cowley, S. (2018, 23 July). Nike will raise wages for thousands after outcry over inequality. *New York Times*, www.nytimes.com/2018/07/23/business/nike-wages-raises.html.

Creswell, J., Draper, K., & Abrams, R. (2018, 28 April). At Nike, revolt led by women leads to exodus of male executives. *New York Times*, www.nytimes.com/2018/04/28/business/nike-women.html.

Draper, K., & Creswell, J. (2018, 5 May). Nike's C.E.O. vows changes after claims of workplace harassment and bias. *New York Times*, www.nytimes.com/2018/05/05/business/mark-parker-nike.html.

Germano, S. (2018, 3 May). Nike CEO apologizes for corporate culture that excluded some staff. *Wall Street Journal*, https://shorturl.at/mlGfN.

Germano, S., & Lublin, J. S. (2018, March 16). Second Nike executive leaves in wake of workplace complaints. *Wall Street Journal*, https://shorturl.at/4HK43.

Hsu, T. (2018, 10 August). *Ex-employees sue Nike, alleging gender discrimination. New York Times*, www.nytimes.com/2018/08/10/business/nike-discrimination-class-action-lawsuit.html.

Winkler, E. (2018, 23 March). Nike rides out #MeToo moment. *Wall Street Journal*, https://shorturl.at/P4UDZ.


## REFERENCES


[1] Bakhtin, M. M. (2010). *The dialogic imagination*. Austin: University of Texas Press.

[2] Baxter, L. A., & Montgomery, B. M. (1996). *Relating: Dialogues and dialectics*. New York: Guilford Press.

[3] Benson, J. K. (1977). Organizations: A dialectical view. *Administrative Science Quarterly*, *22*(1), 1–21.

[4] Bohm, D., & Weinberg, R. A. (2004). *On dialogue*. London: Routledge.

[5] Bryson, J. M. (2004). What to do when stakeholders matter: Stakeholder identification and analysis techniques. *Public Management Review*, *6*(1), 21–53.

[6] Carlsen, A. (2006). Organizational becoming as dialogic imagination of practice: The case of the indomitable Gauls. *Organization Science*, *17*(1), 132–149.

[7] Chanin, M. N., & Shapiro, H. J. (1985). Dialectical inquiry in strategic planning: Extending the boundaries. *Academy of Management Review*, *10*(4), 663–675.

[8] Costanzo, L. A., & Di Domenico, M. (2015). A multi-level dialectical-paradox lens for top management team strategic decision-making in a corporate venture. *British Journal of Management*, *26*(3), 484–506.

[9] Cule, P. E., & Robey, D. (2004). A dual-motor, constructive process model of organizational transition. *Organization Studies*, *25*(2), 229–260.

[10] De Keyser, B., Guiette, A., & Vandenbempt, K. (2019). On the dynamics of failure in organizational change: A dialectical perspective. *Human Relations*, *74*(2), 234–257.

[11] Eden, C., & Ackermann, F. (1998). *Making strategy: The journey of strategic management*. Thousand Oaks, CA: Sage.

[12] Eisenhardt, K. M. (2000). Paradox, spirals, ambivalence: The new language of change and pluralism. *Academy of Management Review*, *25*(4), 703–705.

[13] Farjoun, M. (2002). The dialectics of institutional development in emerging and turbulent fields: The history of pricing conventions in the on-line database industry. *Academy of Management Journal*, *45*(5), 848–874.

[14] Fligstein, N. (1991). The structural transformation of American industry: An institutional account of the causes of diversification in the largest firms, 1919–1979. In W. W. Powell & P. DiMaggio (eds.), *The new institutionalism in organizational analysis* (pp. 311–336). Chicago, IL: University of Chicago Press.

[15] Ford, J. D., & Ford, L. W. (1994). Logics of identity, contradiction, and attraction in change. *Academy of Management Review*, *19*(4), 756–785.

[16] Ford, J. D., & Ford, L. W. (1995). The role of conversations in producing intentional change in organizations. *Academy of Management Review*, *20*(3), 541–570.

[17] Greenwood, R., & Hinings, C. R. (1996). Understanding radical organizational change: Bringing together the old and the new institutionalism. *Academy of Management Review*, *21*(4), 1022–1054.

[18] Hargrave, T. J., & Van de Ven, A. H. (2017). Integrating dialectical and paradox perspectives on managing contradictions in organizations. *Organization Studies*, *38*(3–4), 319–339.

[19] Hoelscher, C. S. (2019). Collaboration for strategic change: Examining dialectical tensions in an interorganizational change effort. *Management Communication Quarterly*, *33*(3), 329–362.

[20] Jay, J. (2013). Navigating paradox as a mechanism of change and innovation in hybrid organizations. *Academy of Management Journal*, *56*(1), 137–159.

[21] Langley, A., & Sloan, P. (2011). Organizational change and dialectic processes. In D. Boje, B. Burnes, & H. Bernard (eds.), *The Routledge companion to organizational change* (pp. 261–275). London: Routledge.

[22] Lewis, M. W. (2000). Exploring paradox: Toward a more comprehensive guide. *Academy of Management Review*, *25*(4), 760–776.

[23] Lüscher, L. S., & Lewis, M. W. (2008). Organizational change and managerial sensemaking: Working through paradox. *Academy of Management Journal*, *51*(2), 221–240.

[24] Mason, R. O. (1969). A dialectical approach to strategic planning. *Management Science*, *15*(8), B403–B414.

[25] Mason, R. O. (1996). Commentary on varieties of dialectic change processes. *Journal of Management Inquiry*, *5*(3), 293–299.

[26] Mengis, J., & Eppler, M. J. (2008). Understanding and managing conversations from a knowledge perspective: An analysis of the roles and rules of face-to-face conversations in organizations. *Organization Studies*, *29*(10), 1287–1313.

[27] Mitchell, R., Boyle, B., Parker, V., Giles, M., Joyce, P., & Chiang, V. (2014). Transformation through tension: The moderating impact of negative affect on transformational leadership in teams. *Human Relations*, *67*(9), 1095–1121.

[28] Mitchell, R. K., Agle, B. R., & Wood, D. J. (1997). Toward a theory of stakeholder identification and salience: Defining the principle of who and what really counts. *Academy of Management Review*, *22*(4), 853–886.

[29] Mitroff, I. I., & Emshoff, J. R. (1979). On strategic assumption-making: A dialectical approach to policy and planning. *Academy of Management Review*, *4*(1), 1–12.

[30] Nielsen, R. P. (1996). Varieties of dialectic change processes. *Journal of Management Inquiry*, *5*(3), 276–292.

[31] Panayiotou, A., Putnam, L. L., & Kassinis, G. (2019). Generating tensions: A multilevel, process analysis of organizational change. *Strategic Organization*, *17*(1), 8–37.

[32] Piderit, S. K. (2000). Rethinking resistance and recognizing ambivalence: A multidimensional view of attitudes toward an organizational change. *Academy of Management Review*, *25*(4), 783–794.

[33] Powley, E. H., Fry, R. E., Barrett, F. J., & Bright, D. S. (2004). Dialogic democracy meets command and control: Transformation through the appreciative inquiry summit. *Academy of Management Perspectives*, *18*(3), 67–80.

[34] Putnam, L. L., Fairhurst, G. T., & Banghart, S. (2016). Contradictions, dialectics, and paradoxes in organizations. *Academy of Management Annals*, *10*(1), 65–171.

[35] Quinn, R. E., & Cameron, K. S. (1988). *Paradox and transformation: Toward a theory of change in organization and management*. New York: Ballinger/Harper and Row.

[36] Reed, M. I. (1997). In praise of duality and dualism: Rethinking agency and structure in organizational analysis. *Organization Studies*, *18*(1), 21–42.

[37] Rowley, T. J. (1997). Moving beyond dyadic ties: A network theory of stakeholder influences. *Academy of Management Review*, *22*(4), 887–910.

[38] Schweiger, D. M., Sandberg, W. R., & Ragan, J. W. (1986). Group approaches for improving strategic decision making: A comparative analysis of dialectical inquiry, devil's advocacy, and consensus. *Academy of Management Journal*, *29*(1), 51–71.

[39] Seo, M., & Creed, W. (2002). Institutional contradictions, praxis, and institutional change: A dialectical perspective. *Academy of Management Review*, *27*(2), 222–247.

[40] Thomas, K. W. (1992). Conflict and negotiation processes in organizations. In M. D. Dunnette & L. M. Hough (eds.), *Handbook of industrial and organizational psychology* (2nd ed., pp. 651–717). Palo Alto, CA: Consulting Psychologists Press.

[41] Thomas, R., & Hardy, C. (2011). Reframing resistance to organizational change. *Scandinavian Journal of Management*, *27*(3), 322–331.

[42] Thomas, R., Sargent, L. D., & Hardy, C. (2011). Managing organizational change: Negotiating meaning and power-resistance relations. *Organization Science*, *22*(1), 22–41.

[43] Tilly, C. (1978). *From mobilization to revolution*. Reading, MA: Addison-Wesley.

[44] Tsoukas, H. (2009). A dialogical approach to the creation of new knowledge in organizations. *Organization Science*, *20*(6), 941–957.

[45] Van de Ven, A. H., & Poole, M. S. (1995). Explaining development and change in organizations. *Academy of Management Review*, *20*(3), 510–540.

[46] Van de Ven, A. H., & Sun, K. (2011). Breakdowns in implementing models of organization change. *Academy of Management Perspectives*, *25*(3), 58–74.

# 5 A Reactive Perspective on Change

## PERSPECTIVE IN BRIEF

- **Concepts related to the perspective** – adaptation, revolutionary change, punctuated equilibrium, turnaround/recovery, and resilience
- **Keep reading to learn more about** – the role of crisis, technology, and disruption in change
- **Prime contributors** – D. Coutu, G. Hamel, A. Meyer, D. Miller, K. Romanelli, W. Starbuck, M. Tushman, and L. Välikangas
- **Guiding metaphor** – change as a spring

## Introduction

As much as most of us would like to navigate through life without encountering major crises, it's highly unlikely that anyone might do so. Unexpected events occur – and when they do, they challenge both individuals and the organisations they belong to. In Chapter 4, we explored how change can emerge from gradually building tensions and power struggles within organisations. However, not all transformation stems from socio-political friction – sometimes, change is forced upon organisations by sudden shocks that demand an immediate response.

Just imagine you were working at of one of the following companies during these pivotal moments:

- American Airlines, after the 9/11 terrorist attacks
- Goldman Sachs, during the global financial crisis of 2008
- Alibaba, during the 2003 SARS outbreak
- Toyota, after the 2011 Japanese earthquake and tsunami
- Your own restaurant, during the COVID-19 pandemic.

In each of these situations, your firm would have been compelled to transform operations almost overnight. Change, in these instances, would not unfold as a deliberate, step-by-step process towards a predetermined goal, nor would it be the result of political groups slowly working towards a better positioning for themselves; instead, it would be a reactive force, largely driven by events that are beyond any of our control. To understand transformation in such contexts, we must recognise that it often manifests as a response to external circumstances.

While not all situations may be as dramatic as the ones listed here, organisational life is filled with sudden events that may trigger change or transformation. Perhaps rapidly evolving customer preferences require a redesign of the product you've been offering. Maybe the bankruptcy of a key supplier forces you to rethink your value chain. Or a competitor's new, highly attractive service leaves you scrambling to pivot your business model. In many cases, the impetus for transformation is reactionary, and acknowledging this reactive nature can provide clarity in understanding the dynamics of change.

This chapter delves into **the reactive perspective on change**, which sees transformation as a response to sudden disruptions, crises, and unforeseen challenges. We will explore key ideas such as punctuated equilibrium, resilience, and robustness, which help us understand how organisations navigate instability and recover from setbacks. Unlike perspectives that view change as a structured process or a gradual adaptation, this approach highlights how uncertainty and adversity can act as catalysts for rapid, sometimes radical, shifts.

By the end of this chapter, you will have a comprehensive understanding of how change can operate reactively within organisations and how you, as a leader, can effectively manage and harness this type of transformation. Whether you're dealing with a global crisis or a localised disruption, the insights gained here will equip you with the tools to navigate change in a world where the unexpected is often the norm.

## 5.1 The Genesis of Thought

At its core, the reactive perspective on change stems from a fresh understanding of one of an organisation's harshest realities: sometimes, businesses don't thrive but simply face significant challenges. Yet when these challenges arise, they can create prime conditions for transformation. In this section, we will explore how the reactive perspective developed from ideas of crisis and disaster.

### 5.1.1 The Catastrophe Wake-Up Call

For much of the twentieth century, both executives and researchers concentrated on how to enhance organisational performance. The dominant focus was on making firms bigger, stronger, and more competitive.[40] In contrast, struggling or declining businesses received far less attention – partly because studying failure presented practical and reputational challenges. Managers were (and often still are) reluctant to have their setbacks exposed to academic scrutiny. This hesitation was reinforced by the broader orientation of the field: research on high-performing firms – especially in areas like mergers, acquisitions, vertical integration, and strategic alliances – was far more celebrated than studies of failure or decline.[3] Why study deterioration when practitioners were seeking blueprints for excellence? As a result, the body of knowledge available for navigating adversity remained limited for decades, leaving a significant blind spot in how organisations understood and responded to risk.[40]

By the 1980s, however, this focus shifted dramatically when the world came to face several high-profile disasters – such as the Tylenol poisoning, the Chernobyl meltdown, the Challenger explosion, and the Exxon Valdez oil spill. These events underscored a sobering reality: human-induced crises could be just as catastrophic as natural disasters.[42] As a result, the concepts of risk and uncertainty began to command serious attention in organisational thinking.

This shift prompted a deeper reckoning. If the world could be so suddenly and violently upended, why had managers and researchers invested so much energy in refining the routine – engaging in what now seemed, by comparison, like petty small talk?[12] Why had so little attention been paid to the prevention and management of failure? Consequently, fields such as crisis management[33, 34, 39, 41, 53] and high-reliability organising[45, 46, 61, 63] emerged, focusing on keeping organisations afloat. For many, success had never seemed so precarious.[17]

### 5.1.2 Turning Risk into Opportunity

Building on this new-found interest in what could go wrong, some scholars and practitioners began to reframe environmental jolts not just as threats but as potential opportunities.[31] Rather than viewing crises as periods of damage and recovery, they proposed that such events could serve as catalysts for innovation and renewal. Taking a hit – or even anticipating one – was increasingly seen not only as a test of resilience but also as a window through which to seize possibilities that would otherwise remain hidden. While crises certainly posed serious risks, they also had the potential to open doors that routine circumstances could not. The key was whether organisations could recognise these openings and summon the courage and creativity to walk through them.[55]

Among the most significant opportunities offered by crisis, many pointed to the rare chance to initiate deep, structural change. Under normal conditions, organisations often remain locked into established patterns – their so-called deep structure,[15] which preserves stability but resists transformation. However, in the face of profound disruptions, several authors noted that these structural rigidities could suddenly loosen.[7, 19, 31, 32, 58] By thrusting organisations into unfamiliar situations, crises could create space for unconventional experiments that revitalised the organisation, provided valuable lessons, and inspired renewed commitment to its core values.[31] It is from these observational seeds that the reactive perspective on change sprouted, and eventually bloomed.

## 5.2 Unpacking the Heart

If you've ever watched your car's suspension in action, you'll know that speeding over any kind of terrain is not in itself a smooth experience – it is *made* smooth by the way in which your vehicle is equipped to handle bumps and potholes. A reactive perspective on change, for its part, can be understood as precisely that: a way of equipping businesses with the means to withstand the bumps and potholes of organisational life. Figure 5.1 offers an overview of how to understand the essence of the reactive perspective on change.

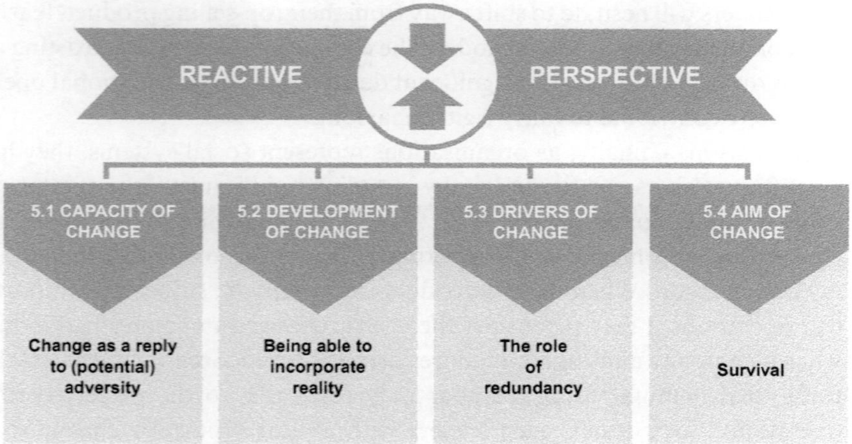


**Figure 5.1** Unpacking the heart of the reactive perspective.

### 5.2.1 Capacity of Change: Change as a Reply to (Potential) Adversity

The first core idea of the reactive perspective is that change is essentially a **reply** – either to prolonged poor performance of the company or to significant shifts in the competitive, technological, social, and legal aspects of its environment (with both often being interrelated).[58] From a reactive angle, change is fundamentally responsive, with the organisation developing by responding to problems that are critical now, or that may become critical in the (nearby) future.[20, 32, 37, 57]

As organisations confront crises and adversity, they will often see many of their standing choices raised to questions. Are we still organised in the 'right' way? Is our activity pattern still appropriate, given the hardship we're currently facing? While such questions can arise in periods of success, they often don't, due to the cognitive, motivational, and social dynamics inherent in any human system:[58]

- Cognitive reasons – if all is going well, organisational actors often lack awareness of potential alternatives or interpret such alternatives in unfair ways,[43, 58] with phenomena that do not fit their beliefs often not being seen at all.[24] To illustrate this, let's go back to pre-Covid times. Before the COVID-19 pandemic, few companies ever considered going fully remote in their way of working. In most cases, this lack of consideration was not due to a conscious choice or to malicious intent: it simply resulted from a lack of awareness that alternative ways of working could be considered at all.
- Motivational reasons – when an organisation is experiencing success, it is tough to motivate members to wilfully make a change as fears of failure, uncertainty, or loss of power impose quite formidable barriers.[14, 22] When there is no dire need to jump ship, most of us prefer the squeaky but well-known planks of the hull to the unknown dangers of the deep. For instance, imagine a company that is making truckloads of cash by selling a popular product. While new technologies may emerge, it is unclear whether these will really catch on. As a result,

most leaders will hesitate to shift away from their top-selling product, fearing the uncertainty of a completely new business model. The company's success with existing approaches makes it thus difficult to motivate a significant departure from its traditional operations, which can ultimately contribute to fairly rigid behaviour.

- Social reasons – finally, as organisations represent social systems, they have ample obligations for members to honour, hereby installing rigid frameworks of interdependent relationships and value commitments.[15, 24, 58] If I'm pushing for a change, there is a very reasonable chance that, at some point, I'll undermine the interests of another individual or group within my organisation. When these individuals or groups are sufficiently important to my day-to-day operations, I may reconsider the drastic change campaign I had in mind. For instance, when a company aims to adopt more sustainable practices, departments that rely heavily on traditional manufacturing methods may resist due to the perceived threat to their own operations. As a result, even leaders with a clear vision for change may delay or dilute their initiatives to avoid disrupting internal power dynamics.

**Box 5.1 The Point?**

A reactive view argues that organisations seldom make far-reaching changes unless they are forced to do so by (dire) circumstances. While crises can be disruptive, they also allow organisations to bootleg changes by camouflaging them as responses:[31] by leveraging significant, discontinuous events, organisations may have a better chance of making change stick. Crises, when labelled as such, provide organisations with energy, justify unconventional actions, and disrupt established power dynamics. In this way, despite their potentially disastrous impact, crisis and adversity come with a distinct silver lining: they offer a clean slate, allowing organisations more leeway in how to move forward.[47, 58, 64]

## 5.2.2 Development of Change: Changing as Incorporating Reality

But while crises may open the door to change, walking through it is another matter entirely: for many organisations, severe shocks simply prove fatal, not transformational. Merely reacting is not enough – what matters is how an organisation responds. To navigate disruption effectively and turn crisis into an opportunity for change, organisations must develop certain ways of **incorporating reality** into their structures, strategies, and ways of working.

### 5.2.2.1 Anticipation: Being Able to (Re)Imagine Reality

First, if an organisation wishes to translate adversity into change, it should work to continuously question the very basis of the reality it faces: what do we currently believe is true – and will such assumptions likely remain valid in the future?[17, 21] Those organisations that are able to transpose crises into meaningful change recognise the need to regularly update their risk assessments. They acknowledge their countermeasures' limitations and understand their operations' fragility. More 'brittle' organisations, on the other hand, are often found to equate success with an absence of hazards and a belief that countermeasures are sufficient to deal with all possible anomalies. They uphold the idea that deviations require evidence before being considered a problem: in other words, they retain a mentality of 'convince me it's an issue'.[60]

For example: if a food delivery company is currently experiencing big success due to explosive demand, it may want to question whether such preference for takeaway food is bound to last. In most cases, there is a very real possibility that the core assumptions fuelling success today will be toppled tomorrow – including consumer preferences, supplier availability, governmental support and regulations, or general economic conditions.

While the future can never be fully visualised, it is surprising how often seemingly 'unexpected' shocks can be anticipated by working to gather indicators, identify patterns of change, and envision possible outcomes.[44] An essential element of such efforts is becoming aware of the ideology or culture that organisational members draw on to explain their worlds in cause-and-effect relationships.[2, 31, 42, 50] Do the beliefs that tie our people together allow for the idea of crises happening to our organisation? Do they label our company as able to prepare for and manage such crises? In this sense, much of the required 'anticipation' involves how the organisation will interpret or see an uncertain and ambiguous environment that is not objectively knowable.[13]

#### 5.2.2.2 Acknowledgement: Being Able to Face Reality

Next, while being able to imagine a potential crisis can still be fun and games, an organisation must eventually face some hard truths: that is, it must be able to candidly acknowledge difficult events as they occur – and be harshly honest with itself. It will need to eliminate efforts that deliberately block early warning signals,[42] and dramatically reduce the time it takes to go from 'that cannot be true' to 'we must face the world as it is'.[17]

While such acknowledgement might seem relatively straightforward, it very much depends on the ways in which organisational members interpret or make sense of the 'barrage of noise'[42] that is their daily business.[9, 50, 54, 62] Do drops in competitor prices mark a new long-term strategy, or do they represent a short-term attempt to sell inventory? Is a decrease in revenue the outcome of poor marketing, improved competition, or an economy that is generally slowing down? While providing answers to these types of question may be easy in hindsight, it rarely proves so in the thick of things. Threats and opportunities do not come with a label: they are just material and symbolic actions, reconstructed afterwards by the people who try to give them meaning. It is people who are the architects of their realities, and it is to their interpretations that organisations ultimately react.[13]

#### 5.2.2.3 Leeway to Act: Being Able to Respond to Reality

Furthermore, while organisations may be open to the idea of adversity and may have successfully labelled a situation as requiring action, such action can only occur if there is sufficient leeway to respond. To what extent are members allowed to act on reality as it is, rather than on what the firm hopes it to be?[4, 21]

For instance, if hiring additional staff requires a multitude of approvals, chances are slim that a crisis will trigger expeditious redesign, with a very real possibility that the situation will still pull an organisation under – irrespective of how aware that firm was of the crisis in the first place. Similarly, if an organisation has little to no cash reserves to tap into in case of need, it may find that many of its induced intentions run dry for lack of resources. In this sense, a reactive perspective notes that change is largely dependent on the organisation's real options – with organisations being much more likely to transform through hardship when enabling conditions are in place.[29]

#### 5.2.2.4 Learning from Hardship: Being Able to Develop from Reality

Finally, to fully capitalise on adversity, organisations should develop the capacity to learn from challenging times.[6] What past actions led to the situation we eventually changed away from, and how can we avoid facing such situations in the future?[21, 60] In this sense, a reactive perspective advances change as going beyond simply reducing risk; rather, it should allow a company to gain an edge by learning to handle disruptions more effectively than its competitors.[12] By experiencing hardship – either directly or vicariously – the organisation can process new information, update mental models, and integrate new knowledge into organisational habits.[65]

Consider a manufacturing firm that suffers a major supply chain disruption due to geopolitical tensions. If the firm merely reacts by finding an alternative short-term supplier, it may mitigate immediate risks but fail to learn from the experience. However, if it systematically analyses what led to the vulnerability – such as over-reliance on a single region, lack of supplier diversification, or inadequate inventory buffers – it can extract deeper lessons. This might lead to strategic shifts, such as reshaping procurement strategies, investing in local suppliers, or adopting more resilient production models. By doing so, the firm not only recovers but also strengthens its ability to navigate future disruptions, turning adversity into a source of long-term competitive advantage. In this way, learning from hardship transforms reactive responses into proactive resilience, ensuring that setbacks become stepping stones for sustainable growth rather than mere survival.

**Box 5.2 The Point?**

While a reactive approach repositions change as capitalising on adversity, there are a few things to get sorted in order for that to really happen – specifically, it demands anticipation, acknowledgement, leeway to act, and the ability to learn from hardship. Organisations that continuously question their assumptions, face reality with honesty, empower action, and extract meaningful insights from challenges are better equipped to transform crises into opportunities. By embracing these characteristics, firms can move beyond merely surviving disruptions to using them as catalysts for long-term adaptability and competitive advantage.

### 5.2.3 Drivers of Change: The Role of Redundancy

Remember your car and its suspension? If you've ever broken that, you'll probably have some bumpy memories underscoring the following harsh truth: if buffers are lacking, your car is not going to purr along much farther.

From a reactive angle, organisations and their drivers for moving forward are not all that different: in fact, what are particularly supporting organisational change are **'slack' or 'redundant' means**[17, 25, 29, 44, 51, 60] – resources that do not find themselves tied up within yearly budget claims but are parked as auxiliary buffers.

While such non-committed resources might seem inefficient or ill-used in times of plenty, they may very well come to be the organisation's lifeline in times of need. By stacking uncommitted or unabsorbed resources during peaceful periods, the organisation might be able to cushion the impact of more turbulent periods – and thus change successfully. This cushioning may include mitigating the effects of capital constraints, seizing potential growth opportunities that present themselves due to decreased asset prices, or reducing the time that the organisation requires to transform, reorganise, and adapt to the shifted environment.[4, 31]

Think about a manufacturing firm that has been consistently setting aside a portion of its annual profits as a reserve fund, even while the company was operating smoothly. To some, this may have appeared overly conservative – those funds could have been reinvested into new projects or used to expand operations. However, when an unexpected economic downturn hits and supply chains are disrupted, this reserve allows the company to transform production while competitors struggle: it is able to quickly adapt its operations to source materials from new suppliers and even acquire smaller, distressed competitors at reduced prices. Here, slack resources not only cushion the impact of the crisis but allow the firm to emerge from it in a stronger competitive position.

#### Box 5.3 Be Aware!

While the availability of slack resources is a necessary condition for enabling change through adversity, it is by no means sufficient. An organisation may have a substantial reserve of funds sitting deep in a vault, but if access to those resources is tightly guarded by fire-breathing executives, they may have little practical effect. For slack to truly matter, managers must first acknowledge the limits of their own foresight. They need to distinguish between what they can reasonably predict and control, and what lies beyond their grasp.[44]

To adapt effectively, organisations must tap into a broad base of insight. Those closest to emerging problems – often at the front lines – are typically the first to spot weak signals that something is going wrong. If these signals are ignored or suppressed, critical opportunities for timely response may be missed. For slack resources to be used meaningfully, they must be liberated,[17] that is, made accessible in ways that respond to real-time input rather than internal politics or rigid routines. This requires creating a culture in which people from across the organisation feel safe and empowered to speak up. When this happens, the organisation can construct a more accurate and adaptive interpretation of reality as it is unfolding.[13, 42, 50]

At the same time, broad participation in sense-making does not necessarily mean broad participation in decision-making. While input should be widely sourced, decisions – especially in times of crisis – often need to be made quickly and firmly. This typically calls for a small, empowered coalition at the top that can integrate diverse insights and translate them into concrete action.[35] In other words, while the organisation must listen widely, it must act selectively. Without a clear decision-making centre, competing inputs can lead to gridlock, delay, or watered-down compromises that fail to address the core problem.[50]

Thus, effective responsiveness requires a careful balance: distributed sensing combined with centralised, accountable decision-making. In this model, those closest to the issue inform the agenda, while those entrusted with strategic authority steer the course.[13]

### Box 5.4 The Point?

Just like a car needs suspension to absorb shocks, organisations need slack resources to enable crisis-driven transformation. While keeping extra funds or capacity might seem inefficient in good times, these buffers can be the key to longevity and competitive advantage during downturns. However, having resources alone isn't enough – they must be accessible, free from bureaucratic constraints, and guided by a leadership team that can make bold, timely decisions. By balancing broad input with decisive action, organisations can turn adversity into opportunity and transformation.

## 5.2.4 Aim of Change: Survival

So, what's the aim here? Why is change a thing at all for organisations from a reactive point of view? From a reactive angle, change should be conducted for a clear purpose: to safeguard the organisation's very **survival**.[4, 6, 12, 41, 65] Organisations, in this view, don't change because they want to improve themselves; they do it because change allows them to endure the conditions of an onrushing environment.[5] In this sense, organisations change not because they wish to outperform their competitors; they change to keep standing upright. This emphasis on survival is underpinned by an emphasis on organisational improvisation or 'bricolage' – the ability to devise a solution to a problem without proper tools or materials. Resilient organisations consider improvisation to be a crucial competence: they are filled with individuals who are resourceful.[65]

For example, during the COVID-19 pandemic, some organisations proved incredibly resourceful with the limited means they had at their disposal. Some local breweries transformed their business-to-business (B2B) business models to business-to-consumer (B2C) ones, and this almost overnight. The way they did it often did not involve much conscious planning but drew almost exclusively on the craftiness of a few shrewd individuals. Somebody suggested repurposing a few old vans for door-to-door deliveries; another drew on the skills of a husband who was able to build a rudimentary e-commerce platform; and an employee's daughter redeveloped the brewery's parking lot into a public barbecue area. By making do with what was available and drawing on imagination to reconceptualise their extant activities, these local brewers eventually emerged from the pandemic unscathed – with some even pulling in more revenue than they did before the world was 'locked down'.

Ultimately, such a survivalist aim is meant to culminate in a state of 'zero-trauma' – where the firm can change through adversity while not finding itself strained by the effort. The goal is to create a company that undergoes transformational change in rapid, incremental steps, yet without any unexpected upheavals, major reorganisations, huge write-offs, or sweeping lay-offs. In a truly resilient organisation, there is plenty of dynamic energy, but no traumatic events.[17] Hence, while a reactive perspective stresses the organisation's bare survival as the actual aim of change, it also advances a more ambitious ideal towards which organisations should ultimately strive.

**Box 5.5 Be Aware!**

Firms always face a balance between what is possible and what is ideal. Given the extensive losses that usually accompany major crises, it's often unrealistic to consider effective only those efforts that get an organisation through unscathed. On the other hand, simply surviving a crisis may not be a strict enough standard for success. As such, the following may strike a reasonable middle ground: change efforts are effective when operations are continued or resumed (i.e., the organisation is able to maintain or restore the momentum of its core activities, which are necessary for transforming inputs to outputs that meet the requirements of crucial customers); losses for organisational and external stakeholders are minimised; and learning occurs so that insights can be transmitted to future situations.[41]

## 5.3 Extending Your Toolkit

If survival is the aim and improvisation the mindset, then organisations need the right tools to navigate disruption when it hits: just like a mechanic equips a car to handle bumps and potholes, the reactive perspective provides a set of frameworks to help organisations absorb shocks and adapt under pressure. In this section, I'll cover two of the most important in detail: (i) punctuated equilibrium theory; and (ii) resilience and robustness.

### 5.3.1 Punctuated Equilibrium Theory

Originally introduced as a reconceptualisation of biological evolution,[10] **punctuated equilibrium theory** has since spilled over into many other fields of research,[24, 28, 43] including organisational theory.[15, 47, 49] The core idea is that organisational change does not unfold gradually and continuously, but rather in sharp, discontinuous bursts. Because the social context of organisations often fosters inertia and resistance to change (as discussed in Section 5.2.1), meaningful transformation typically occurs only in response to significant internal or external pressures. In other words, organisations tend to experience extended periods of relative stability – equilibria – which are occasionally disrupted or punctuated by brief episodes of intense change:[15]

- Equilibrium periods – during equilibrium periods, the organisation's basic activity pattern remains the same: the organisation maintains and carries out the elementary strategic choices it has made.[15] These choices are buttressed by (i) core values and beliefs; (ii) the products, markets, and technology the organisation is in; (iii) the current distribution of power; (iv) the organisation's structure; and (v) the presence of control systems.[58] While alterations to the organisation can be made during equilibrium periods, changes will typically not affect the organisation's fundamental way of operating: as strong forces of inertia will prevent the system from generating alternatives beyond its boundaries, any significant deviations will often be rapidly extinguished. Although an organisation might thus appear to develop during equilibrium, few impactful changes will really be made.
- Revolutionary periods – in contrast, impactful changes can occur during revolutionary periods: here, the organisation will find itself momentarily unshackled from its set of systemic choices, allowing it to alter its fundamentals quite drastically. While such disruptions of the organisation's systemic choices may be deliberately planned for, they typically remain limited to: (i) occasions in which the organisation is experiencing significant amounts of internal strain due to the system having 'outgrown' the deep structure governing its perspectives and activities; or (ii) occasions in which the organisation faces environmental changes that threaten the system's ability to obtain resources. These disruptions will briefly dismantle the organisation's standing logic, leaving the system temporarily open for change. In this sense, oncoming adversity and failure work as a source of energy for organisations to develop: they set the stage for change in what is otherwise a very stable configuration.[15, 47, 49]

An illustrative, society-wide example of punctuated equilibrium theory can be found in the reuniting of Germany shortly after the 'revolution year' 1989. As long as the social system's deep structure remained intact, any predictions of West and East Germany reuniting long seemed hogwash, with experts estimating that it would take a very long time for these regions to merge again.[15] However, as repeated shocks temporarily dismantled the social system's deep structure in 1989 – such as the opening up of the Iron Curtain in May or the fall of the Berlin Wall in November – changes formerly thought unfeasible suddenly came within reach. As standing values, power distributions, structures, and so on were put into question by major shocks, landslide changes at once became abruptly doable. As a result, Germany was reunited only eleven months after the Berlin Wall had come crashing down.

Another example of change being brought about by the disruption of a system's deep structure can be seen in the lockdown measures implemented by many countries during the COVID-19 pandemic. Despite Western societies having long viewed freedom of movement, society, and speech as fundamental values that could never be compromised, their approach changed rapidly in response to a significant shock (the surge in COVID-19 cases). As this shock dismantled society's deep structure, it paved the way for changes that would formerly be considered totalitarian – with entire villages, cities, or even countries being 'locked down' or limited in their actions.

### Box 5.6 Be Aware!

Occasions for disruption often disappear as suddenly as they appear. As an organisation's deep structure usually consists of highly interdependent choices, the toppling of any basic premise quickly affects other premises contingent on it. Similarly, once a new set of choices is decided, the revolutionary period will rapidly close again. Hence, to draw sufficiently on them, organisations need to be swift in making changes during system disruptions.

Punctuated equilibrium theory suggests that change management efforts may be more effective if they focus on anticipating sudden, discontinuous shifts rather than trying to drive gradual, incremental improvements. It highlights the importance of being prepared for sudden change and having the capabilities to respond quickly and effectively.

## 5.3.2 Resilience and Robustness

If punctuated equilibrium theory highlights the need to recognise and leverage certain windows of disruptive opportunity, the concepts of **resilience and robustness** offer a lens for understanding how organisations can work to act on such disruptions as if on instinct: rather than focusing on predicting or avoiding shocks, these ideas emphasise how organisations may be designed to almost automatically respond to them. While the terms have been conceptualised in a variety of ways,[6, 16, 23] the following section outlines six general principles that may help organisations build the capacity to weather adversity – and emerge stronger from it.[44]

First, leaders must make sure that their organisation **maintains heterogeneity** – that is, diversity – along three dimensions: people, ideas, and activities. Such heterogeneity may be initialised by hiring people with different backgrounds and personalities, but it can also be maintained by active cultural and managerial support. Does our organisation allow people to risk failure and create new ideas?[44]

### Box 5.7 Practical Advice?

- Establish cross-functional teams that encourage collaboration between departments with different expertise and perspectives.
- Implement mentorship programmes where junior employees are paired with senior staff from different backgrounds.
- Regularly rotate employees across various projects or departments to expose them to new ideas and approaches.

Next, the organisation needs to **sustain modularity**. A modular system is one that consists of loosely connected components. Highly modular systems prevent shocks from escalating from one component to the next, thus rendering the system more resilient and robust. However, modularity in business also involves trade-offs: protecting against shocks requires sacrificing the advantages of increased interconnectivity.[44]

### Box 5.8 Practical Advice?

- Break large projects into smaller, self-contained modules that can be developed, tested, and deployed independently.
- Set up independent, autonomous teams that are responsible for specific aspects of the business to limit the risk of disruptions affecting the whole organisation.
- Use modular supply chains that allow the firm to shift between suppliers or logistics providers without significant disruption.

Third, the organisation needs to **preserve redundancy** among components. Redundancy in systems refers to having multiple components that perform the same function. This is important in environments with frequent adverse events as it allows for seamless continuation of operations: even when one component fails, another can take over. Too often, businesses shy away from redundancy, considering it the opposite of efficiency.[44]

### Box 5.9 Practical Advice?

- Maintain a back-up vendor or supplier network to ensure continuity in case of supply chain disruptions.
- Create overlap in job roles where employees are cross-trained so that teams can remain productive even if a person is absent.
- Invest in duplicate or back-up IT systems to ensure business continuity during outages or cyberattacks.

Fourth, the organisation must work to **expect surprise, but reduce uncertainty**. In the complexity of organisational life, the future state is uncertain and cannot be precisely predicted. What businesses can do, however, is collect data, look for patterns, and take action to try to prevent events from occurring.[44]

**Box 5.10 Practical Advice?**

- Invest in predictive analytics and data visualisation tools that help identify emerging patterns and potential risks.
- Run regular scenario planning sessions where leadership teams simulate possible future disruptions and test the organisation's readiness.
- Develop a crisis management plan that outlines clear actions for responding to unforeseen challenges.

Fifth, the firm needs to **create feedback loops and adaptive mechanisms**. Heterogeneity provides the diversity for selection to occur, and feedback loops make sure that selection happens and the system's fitness improves. Feedback mechanisms detect changes in the environment and amplify beneficial traits, making the system more adaptive. In nature, mutation and natural selection occur automatically, but in business it is a primarily managed process. The development, choice, and spread of innovations occur only when leaders actively establish and support systems that drive these processes.[44]

**Box 5.11 Practical Advice?**

- Set up continuous feedback channels from customers, partners, and employees to gauge performance and areas for improvement.
- Implement a culture of rapid prototyping and iteration, where new products or services are launched quickly, and learnings from initial feedback are applied to improve them.
- Develop a knowledge-sharing platform where teams can post lessons learnt from projects, allowing the whole organisation to benefit from individual feedback loops.

Finally, the organisation needs to **foster trust and reciprocity in business ecosystems**. As direct control over participants is usually not feasible, trust is needed to thrive, ultimately enabling users to establish norms of mutual benefit. To harness the power of trust, leaders should reflect on their company's impact on other stakeholders in their ecosystem and balance profit maximisation with adding value to the system.[44]

### Box 5.12 Practical Advice?

- Regularly engage with ecosystem stakeholders through forums or roundtables to discuss common challenges and opportunities for collaboration.
- Create transparency in relationships with suppliers and partners by sharing key information that fosters mutual trust.

Resilience and robustness aren't just about surviving disruption; they're about thriving in uncertainty and being able to transform because of it. Organisations can strengthen their adaptability by embracing diversity, designing modular systems, maintaining redundancy, anticipating surprises, leveraging feedback loops, and fostering trust within their ecosystems. These principles help businesses absorb shocks, seize opportunities, and evolve in the face of adversity. By balancing efficiency with flexibility and control with collaboration, companies can build structures that are not only resistant to failure but also capable of continuous growth and innovation.

## 5.4 Impact on the Ground

Equipped with these tools, the reactive perspective doesn't just help organisations brace for impact; it reshapes how they respond when the pressure is on. Its value becomes especially clear when we look at how it plays out in practice. Three key benefits stand out.

### 5.4.1 A Reactive Perspective Makes Change Pertinent to All

First, one of the biggest benefits of a reactive perspective is that it reframes change as universal and inevitable – something that no organisation can afford to ignore. Change isn't just an abstract concept or a strategic choice; it is often the difference between survival and obsolescence. All organisations, no matter how stable their conditions at any given time, might eventually confront situations that require significant adapting to.

For example, while publishing books has long been a stable occupation, the sudden onset of digital environments necessitated publishing organisations to radically reconsider their way of doing business. While the market of mobile phones was quite stable for a long time, the sudden shift by competitors towards increased software and hardware integration almost pushed dominant incumbents to bankruptcy. While banks and other financial institutions were long considered the pinnacle of stability, extreme market conditions can make them surprisingly prone to failure – an observation all of us learnt the hard way during the banking crisis of 2008. No organisation, however secure its current operations, escapes that logic. In this sense, the reactive perspective reminds organisations that no matter how strong their position seems today, change is always around the corner – and preparation for it should never be optional.[26, 38, 59, 66]

### 5.4.2 A Reactive Perspective Gives Adversity a Silver Lining

Hardship and crises can feel like overwhelming setbacks, but a reactive perspective highlights the silver lining: disruption is often a gateway to reinvention. When an organisation faces turmoil, it is presented with an opportunity to rethink outdated models, shed inefficiencies, and emerge stronger. Consider it like being caught in a downpour – yes, you're soaked, but it also presents you with the perfect moment to swap out drenched clothes for something better suited to the journey. Rather than viewing adversity as an insurmountable obstacle, a reactive mindset sees it as fuel for transformation. In this sense, while a reactive perspective on change originates from a notion of risk and uncertainty, it does not bring such an ominous outlook to the organisation: it claims that the organisation will ultimately benefit from – rather than be obstructed by – the hardship it faces.[11, 23, 30, 52]

### 5.4.3 A Reactive Perspective Emphasises the Importance of Ownership

Finally, a reactive perspective recognises that change isn't something that just happens to an organisation – it's something the people within it must actively drive. In this sense, the reactive perspective underscores the importance of ownership at every level. Those closest to a crisis must be empowered to both identify the problem and take action, while leadership must acknowledge its role in past decisions and take full responsibility for shaping the path forward. Without this sense of ownership, change becomes sluggish, weighed down by hesitation and bureaucracy. As such, organisations that embrace the reactive perspective develop a culture of brutal honesty – one where past missteps are acknowledged, lessons are learnt, and decisive action is taken to forge a more resilient future.[8, 9, 48]

**Box 5.13 The Point?**

A reactive approach to change doesn't just prepare organisations for uncertainty – it makes them more adaptable, more accountable, and ultimately more capable of turning adversity into useful transformations. By acknowledging that change is universal, seeing crises as opportunities, and fostering a culture of responsibility, organisations can ensure that they don't just survive disruptions but thrive because of them.

## 5.5 Drawbacks and Pitfalls

However, even adaptability has its limits: while embracing a reactive perspective on change has its merits, it's not entirely without risk. Two major pitfalls stand out, both of which can determine whether an organisation thrives in the face of adversity or gets caught in a spiral of miscalculated responses.

### 5.5.1 Is It Really Change That Results from Threat?

A key assumption of the reactive perspective is that organisations respond to adversity with adaptation. But is that always the case? Some researchers argue the opposite – that, when faced with a crisis, organisations often become more rigid rather than more flexible. Instead of using adversity as a springboard for transformation, they tighten their grip, centralise control, and narrow their field of vision. The result? They double down on existing processes, even when those very processes are what's dragging them down. As such, many high-profile corporate failures can be seen as failures to adjust in response to environmental changes, highlighting a broader tendency for individuals, groups, and organisations to act rigidly when faced with threats.[56]

History is littered with examples of companies that froze in the face of existential threats. Take the COVID-19 pandemic. Many bars and restaurants collapsed, unable to adapt to lockdowns and shifting consumer behaviours. Others, however, saw an opportunity. Some shifted to direct-to-consumer sales, launching online platforms and home delivery services. Some set strict spending limits to help them get through the worst of the crisis, while others started spending more to make drastic revisions to their practices. Some saw their traditions and history threatened, while others saw a new future opening up.

What made the difference? It wasn't their organisational structure; it was their interpretation of the crisis. Some businesses saw it as an insurmountable catastrophe, while others saw it as a catalyst for reinvention. This suggests that an organisation's response to threats isn't hard-wired; it's shaped by perception.[50] How leaders and employees interpret a crisis dictates whether they resist change, cautiously adapt, or seize the moment for bold transformation. In this sense, being able to distil change from hardship may be not just about what happens to an organisation but about how the organisation is wired to make sense of what's happening – and how such sense-making is allowed to further develop.[36, 50]

### 5.5.2 Is It Really Beneficial to Change in Response to Shocks?

Furthermore, even if an organisation recognises a crisis as an opportunity for change, that doesn't mean that change is always the right move. In fact, in some cases, reacting too quickly can do more harm than good.[1, 18, 27] As rearranging assets can often cause turmoil within organisations, it's not that difficult to think of companies that only sped up their demise by making frantic changes, rather than just staying put.

For example, when global supply chains get congested – due to the Suez Canal being blocked or container ships being insufficiently available – it is typical for many companies to frantically start buying any supplies they can get their hands on. For most, this means a severe pivoting away from more just-in-time ways of working. As the crisis resolves itself and global supplies start flowing again, many find the financial impact of their drastic changes to be more profound than if they had stayed immobile. In this sense, the reactive changes made in the heat of the moment end up being more damaging than if they had simply held their ground.

This highlights a crucial reality: just because change is possible in response to a crisis doesn't mean that it's necessary – or beneficial.[4] Sometimes, stability is the wiser course of action.

Change, when purely done reactively and without strategic foresight, can create chaos rather than progress. Organisations that overcorrect in response to disruption may find themselves worse off than if they had exercised restraint. Use your best judgement when navigating the challenge at hand.

> **Box 5.14 The Point?**
>
> A reactive approach to change is powerful – it can push organisations out of complacency and into much-needed transformation. But it's not a universal solution. Not every crisis demands an overhaul, and not every organisation will instinctively pivot in the face of adversity. The key is not just to react but to react wisely. Leaders must discern whether a crisis requires change, assess the risks of inaction versus action, and – most importantly – shape the way their people interpret and respond to uncertainty. In the end, survival isn't just about adapting; it's about knowing when and how to do it.

## SUMMARY

In Chapter 5, we examined the **reactive perspective** on change, which sees transformation as a response to external shocks, adversity, and uncertainty. Unlike approaches that emphasise long-term planning or gradual adaptation, this perspective focuses on how organisations transform by reacting to crises (see Table 5.1 for an overview).

◊ The **emergence of this perspective** was shaped by large-scale disasters that exposed the fragility of business operations and the hidden risks within organisational systems. These events prompted a shift in thinking, where risk was viewed no longer solely as a danger but also as a potential opportunity for renewal and strategic repositioning.

◊ At its **foundation**, this perspective defines change as a reaction to threats, emphasising the importance of acknowledging and incorporating reality rather than resisting it. Change unfolds not in a steady or linear manner but in response to disruptions that force organisations to adapt. Redundancy – having flexible systems, back-up plans, and excess capacity – plays a crucial role in enabling organisations to weather crises. From this standpoint, the primary objective of change is not necessarily growth or efficiency but survival in an unpredictable environment.

◊ To further explore this idea, we examined two influential **tools**. Punctuated equilibrium theory suggests that long periods of stability are periodically disrupted by sudden and transformative shifts. Meanwhile, the concepts of resilience and robustness highlight the capacity of organisations to endure shocks, recover from setbacks, and emerge stronger in the face of adversity.

◊ One of the major **contributions** of this perspective is that it broadens the relevance of change, making it a universal concern for organisations across different contexts. It also encourages a reframing of adversity, positioning crises as opportunities to rethink strategies and

**Table 5.1 A reactive perspective on change: overview**

| | |
|---|---|
| **Guiding metaphor** | Change as a spring |
| **The genesis of thought** | |
| Development 1 | The catastrophe wake-up call |
| Development 2 | Turning risk into opportunity |
| **Unpacking the heart** | |
| Capacity of change | Change as a reply to (potential) adversity |
| Development of change | Being able to incorporate reality |
| Drivers of change | The role of redundancy |
| Aim of change | Survival |
| **Extending your toolkit** | |
| Tool #1 | Punctuated equilibrium theory |
| Tool #2 | Resilience and robustness |
| **Impact on the ground** | |
| (+) | A reactive perspective makes the question of change pertinent to all. |
| (+) | A reactive perspective adorns adversity with a silver lining. |
| (+) | A reactive perspective emphasises the importance of ownership. |
| **Drawbacks and pitfalls** | |
| (−) | Is it change that results from threat? |
| (−) | Is it always beneficial to change in response to shocks? |
| **Related concepts** | |
| ► | Adaptation |
| ► | Revolutionary change |
| ► | Punctuated equilibrium |
| ► | Turnaround/recovery |
| ► | Resilience |

strengthen operations. Additionally, it underscores the importance of ownership in change, recognising that those who actively take responsibility for adaptation are often better equipped to navigate uncertainty.

◊ Despite these strengths, the reactive perspective raises some important **concerns**. It questions whether change should always be driven by external threats, potentially downplaying the value of proactive transformation. Furthermore, while responding to shocks can lead to positive shifts, not all crises necessitate change – sometimes stability and continuity may be the wiser path.

# CASE: BOUNCING BACK WITH MICKEY

## The Reactive Perspective in Practice

A source of comfort and positivity, the Walt Disney Company holds a special place in the hearts of many. Numerous generations have grown up with Disney's films – and, often, snuggling up on the sofa with a Disney film is still the perfect antidote when life is throwing curveballs.

Yet even for the Walt Disney Company itself, life hasn't always been smooth sailing. From humble beginnings to one of the most successful media conglomerates on the planet, the firm has had its fair share of rough patches and dramatic turnarounds. During its century-long existence, Disney has faced numerous challenges that have forced it to transform itself to survive.

In this case, we will look into what those challenges were and how Disney has developed accordingly. So, sit back, relax, grab a bag of popcorn – and immerse yourself in the world of Disney entertainment.

### The Birth of Mickey and the Walt Disney Company

In 1923, brothers Walt and Roy Disney launched the Disney Brothers Cartoon Studio in Los Angeles. Walt, a creative mind with a background in illustration, focused on storytelling and animation, while Roy took charge of the business side. From the outset, they sought to build a company that encouraged collaboration and informal interaction, promoting a relatively egalitarian ethos. While Walt could be a demanding figure, his insistence on high standards was balanced by his emphasis on creative teamwork and shared vision.

The studio's early breakthrough came with Oswald the Lucky Rabbit in 1927, a character that gained popularity but was ultimately lost when Universal Pictures claimed ownership. With little time to spare, Walt and Roy created a new character – a cheerful mouse named Mickey. The gamble initially met a lukewarm response, but Walt doubled down by introducing synchronised sound, a novelty in cartoons at the time. The 1928 release of *Steamboat Willie* with sound proved transformative, turning Mickey Mouse into a global icon and securing Disney's place in the entertainment industry.

By the early 1930s, the studio had rebranded as Walt Disney Productions, releasing a string of successful shorts and introducing characters like Goofy and Donald Duck. However, Walt envisioned a bolder path: full-length animated features. Despite scepticism and high production costs, *Snow White and the Seven Dwarfs* premiered in 1937 and became a commercial and critical triumph.

As Disney Productions went public in 1940, the company's financial future seemed secure – had it not been for World War II. During these years, Disney pivoted by producing training and propaganda films for the government, which helped the company survive. After the war, Walt expanded into television with the Disneyland TV programme, while also making strides in live-action filmmaking with hits like *Mary Poppins*.

In the mid 1950s, Walt capitalised on the popularity of his Disneyland TV show by building a theme park. Opened in 1955, Disneyland reimagined the amusement park experience with clean design, immersive storytelling, and careful theming. It was a financial risk, but one that paid off. Encouraged by its success, Walt began planning a second park in Florida along with an ambitious experimental city concept known as EPCOT.

### Holding On to Legacy

In 1966, Walt Disney passed away. In the years that followed, Disney adopted a cautious stance, intent on preserving his legacy. Yet this reverence for the past quickly came at a cost. In the film division, the creative energy that had once propelled the company began to fade. Unwilling to venture beyond Walt's playbook, executives leaned heavily on familiar formulas, resulting in a series of uninspired releases that failed to connect with evolving audience tastes.

At the theme parks, a rigid commitment to Walt's founding ideals – such as avoiding advertising and keeping ticket prices low – began to stifle growth. Leadership resisted substantial innovation, relying instead on the reliable revenue generated by the parks' enduring popularity. This financial stability, while reassuring on the surface, masked a deeper creative and operational stagnation, fostering complacency and delaying necessary change.

### The Oil Crisis Spilling into Disney

Then came the 1973 oil crisis. The economic downturn caused by the surge in oil prices had a direct and significant impact on the company's theme parks, which had become its main revenue generator. With rising fuel costs, many families found themselves tightening their belts, and travel – especially to distant vacation destinations like Disneyland – became less affordable. Attendance at Disney's parks, which had been steadily growing, began to drop. This decline in visitor numbers was compounded by higher costs for maintaining the parks and operating attractions, which were increasingly reliant on energy.

The crisis also highlighted a much deeper vulnerability at Disney: despite owning valuable assets like film libraries and the iconic theme parks, Disney's content and overall brand began to show signs of age. The family-friendly, wholesome films and shows that had once dominated the industry now seemed increasingly out of step with shifting audience preferences. In the 1970s, the entertainment market was rapidly evolving, with audiences seeking out edgier, more sophisticated fare like space epics, action-packed thrillers, and dramas that pushed the boundaries of storytelling. As the cultural zeitgeist shifted, Disney's traditional, family-centric content began to feel stale.

By the early 1980s, Disney found itself under attack from corporate raiders, culminating in a high-profile hostile takeover threat. The company managed to fend it off, but it became evident that significant changes were necessary. Many recognised that Disney's management had lost strategic direction, leaving the company vulnerable and at risk of deeper strategic decline.

### Turning Around the Steamboat and Setting Course for New Directions

In 1984, Michael Eisner was appointed CEO of Disney, bringing with him a firm belief that the company's greatest strength lay in its ability to manage creativity. He set out to revitalise this core capability by fostering bold, imaginative ideas – while also imposing clear expectations around strategic focus and financial discipline. Creative spending was welcomed, but only when aligned with well-defined objectives and sustainable growth.

Eisner respected Walt Disney's legacy but also made significant changes to the company's strategic direction, such as rebuilding Disney's declining TV and film business. Disney resumed the development of network shows in TV, which it had stopped pursuing after launching the Disney Channel. In addition, Eisner repositioned Disney's film studios by slightly broadening its target audience, occasionally producing R-rated movies.

In the following years, more than 80 per cent of Disney's live-action films made a profit. By the end of the 1980s, Disney Studios' film division held a share of almost 20 per cent of the total US box office, making it the market leader. Eisner even noted that Disney transformed from a nerdy outcast to the leader of the popular crowd almost overnight.

Although the animated division took longer to rebound, it made significant strides by reducing production time from four years to one year and transitioning from hand-drawn to blending with computer animation. These changes led to a string of highly profitable and critically acclaimed animated features in the late 1980s and early 1990s, including films like *Beauty and the Beast*, *Aladdin*, and *The Lion King*.

The Disney Stores, introduced in 1987, represented a novel approach to merchandising by turning shopping into a themed experience. Far from conventional outlets, each store was conceived as a miniature extension of the Disney universe – complete with immersive design elements that aimed to capture the magic of its films and characters. This experiential format proved commercially successful, with the stores generating sales per square foot well above the industry average.

In the Disney parks, major investments were accompanied by strategies to boost attendance, such as national TV ads, special events, and retail partnerships. Disney also removed restrictions on park capacity, opened Disneyland on previously closed Mondays, and raised ticket prices. Despite the price increases, market research indicated that guests believed they were getting their money's worth.

## A Changing World

Then, during the mid to late 1990s, Disney again began to lose some of its shine, with some of its operations becoming bloated due to its prolonged period of success. Changes in the executive team caused the cost of making films, both live-action and animated, to skyrocket. With the emergence of new competitors in the entertainment industry as well as new technologies like video games, Disney found itself struggling to keep up.

By the early 2000s, the Walt Disney Company found itself again grappling with a perfect storm of challenges that exposed significant vulnerabilities in its business model. The theme park division, once a pillar of the company's success, faced a sharp decline in attendance due to a confluence of global crises. The 2001 terrorist attacks on September 11 sent shockwaves through the travel and tourism industries, and Disney was no exception. Adding to the turbulence, the SARS epidemic of 2003 further compounded Disney's struggles. The outbreak, which primarily affected Asia, disrupted travel and negatively affected attendance at Disney-related parks and destinations, particularly in Japan.

Meanwhile, Disney's film division faced increasing pressure from rapidly advancing competition. Once a leader in animated filmmaking, Disney was now struggling to keep pace with Pixar, which had revolutionised the industry with its groundbreaking use of computer animation and innovative storytelling. Pixar's films, such as *Toy Story*, *Finding Nemo*, and *The Incredibles*, captured the imagination of audiences and critics alike, while Disney's own animated films were losing their lustre.

### Teaming Up, Digital Transformation, and Streaming

In 2005, Robert Iger became CEO of Disney and quickly recognised the need for bold transformation. Rather than relying solely on in-house innovation, he pursued strategic acquisitions to revitalise Disney's creative engine. This included the purchase of Pixar in 2006, Marvel in 2009, and Lucasfilm in 2012. Although initially questioned, these deals proved enormously successful, enabling Disney to monetise beloved franchises across film, merchandise, and theme parks. This cross-platform integration became central to Disney's renewed growth strategy.

By the mid 2010s, a new challenge emerged: the rise of digital streaming. While Disney had long profited from its traditional pay-TV model, shifting viewer habits threatened its dominance. Iger recognised the risk of losing ground to tech-savvy competitors and announced in 2017 that Disney would end its distribution deal with Netflix. Instead, the company would launch its own direct-to-consumer platforms.

To support this pivot, Disney acquired 21st Century Fox's entertainment assets – including Fox Film and TV Studios, FX Networks, National Geographic, and a controlling stake in Hulu – while Fox retained its news and sports divisions. Disney then launched ESPN+ in 2018, followed by Disney+ in November 2019, offering a vast catalogue of classic and new content. Together with Hulu, Disney could now target diverse audiences.

The streaming launch was a massive success: Disney+ gained 10 million subscribers on its first day. By 2022, Disney's combined streaming services rivalled Netflix in subscriber numbers, marking a powerful reinvention of its business model for the digital era.

### The Future of Disney

Moving forward, Disney's biggest challenge concerns profitability. While its streaming platforms have been a big success in attracting subscribers, rendering these assets profitable proves daunting. In November 2022, less than one year after his official retirement, Robert Iger was brought back as company CEO. Earlier that month, the company's earnings vastly underperformed Wall Street's expectations. During Iger's absence, Disney's stock had fallen more than 28 per cent, while the S&P 500 had posted notable gains over the same period. Even its theme park business, which reported a surge in revenue, delivered less than analysts had projected. The future, again, seemed challenging – but so far the House of the Mouse had always bounced back.

### Reflect

1. What events incited change at Disney?
2. Do you believe that Disney is an example of a resilient company? Why?
3. Going forward, how do you think Disney could improve its way of managing change?

### Case Study Sources

Barnes, B. (2012, 21 October). Disney, struggling to find its digital footing, overhauls Disney.com. *New York Times*, www.nytimes.com/2012/10/22/business/media/disney-struggling-to-find-its-digital-footing-overhauls-disneycom.html.

CNBC. (2023, 13 July). Disney's CEO Bob Iger speaks with CNBC's David Faber on 'Squawk Box' Today. www.cnbc.com/2023/07/13/cnbc-exclusive-cnbc-transcript-disney-ceo-bob-iger-speaks-with-cnbcs-david-faber-on-squawk-box-today.html.

Gabler, N. (2015, 12 September). Walt Disney: A visionary who was crazy like a mouse. *New York Times*, www.nytimes.com/2015/09/13/business/media/walt-disney-a-visionary-who-was-crazy-like-a-mouse.html.

Govindarajan, V. (2016, 3 June). How Disney found its way back to creative success. *Harvard Business Review*, https://hbr.org/2016/06/how-disney-found-its-way-back-to-creative-success.

Holson, L. M. (2002, 18 August). As Disney loses steam, insider loses patience. *New York Times*, https://web.archive.org/web/20160906013749/http://www.nytimes.com/2002/08/18/business/as-disney-loses-steam-insider-loses-patience.html?pagewanted=all.

Kunze, P. C. (2023, 16 October). How the Walt Disney Company made it to 100. *Time Magazine*, https://time.com/6323556/disney-100-history/.

Littleton, C. (2018, 8 November). Bob Iger talks Disney+, Hulu plans and his vision for enlarged TV studio. *Variety*, https://variety.com/2018/digital/news/disney-disney-streaming-service-launch-2019-1203023789/.

Luebering, J. E. (March 4, 2025). Disney Company. *Encyclopedia Britannica*, www.britannica.com/money/Disney-Company.

Reid, A., & Holmes, J. (n.d.). How Disney took over the world. *BBC News*, www.bbc.co.uk/news/extra/NUgROc189X/disney-100-years.

Smith, D., & Clark, S. (1999). *Disney: The first 100 years*. New York: Hyperion.

## REFERENCES

[1] Abrahamson, E. (2004). Avoiding repetitive change syndrome. *MIT Sloan Management Review*, *45*(2), 93.

[2] Beyer, J. M. (1981). Ideologies, values, and decision making in organizations. In P. C. Nystrom & W. H. Starbuck (eds.), *Handbook of organizational design: Volume 2 Remodeling organizations and their environments* (pp. 166–202). New York: Oxford University Press.

[3] Bibeault, D. B. (1982). *How managers turn losers into winners*. Boston, MA: McGraw-Hill.

[4] Chakrabarti, A. (2015). Organizational adaptation in an economic shock: The role of growth reconfiguration. *Strategic Management Journal*, *36*(11), 1717–1738.

[5] Chakravarthy, B. S. (1982). Adaptation: A promising metaphor for strategic management. *Academy of Management Review*, *7*(1), 35–44.
[6] Coutu, D. L. (2002). How resilience works. *Harvard Business Review*, *80*(5), 46–54.
[7] D'Aveni, R. A. (1989). The aftermath of organizational decline: A longitudinal study of the strategic and managerial characteristics of declining firms. *Academy of Management Journal*, *32*(3), 577–605.
[8] DesJardine, M., Bansal, P., & Yang, Y. (2019). Bouncing back: Building resilience through social and environmental practices in the context of the 2008 global financial crisis. *Journal of Management*, *45*(4), 1434–1460.
[9] Dutton, J. E., & Duncan, R. B. (1987). The creation of momentum for change through the process of strategic issue diagnosis. *Strategic Management Journal*, *8*(3), 279–295.
[10] Eldredge, N., & Gould, S. (1972). Punctuated equilibria: An alternative to phyletic gradualism. In T. J. Schopf (ed.), *Models in paleobiology* (pp. 82–115). San Francisco, CA: Freeman, Cooper and Company.
[11] Farjoun, M., & Starbuck, W. H. (2007). Organizing at and beyond the limits. *Organization Studies*, *28*(4), 541–566.
[12] Fiksel, J., Polyviou, M., Croxton, K. L., & Pettit, T. J. (2015). From risk to resilience: Learning to deal with disruptions. *MIT Sloan Management Review*, *56*(2).
[13] Ford, J. D., & Baucus, D. A. (1987). Organizational adaptation to performance downturns: An interpretation-based perspective. *Academy of Management Review*, *12*(2), 366–380.
[14] Gersick, C. J. (1989). Marking time: Predictable transitions in task groups. *Academy of Management Journal*, *32*(2), 274–309.
[15] Gersick, C. J. (1991). Revolutionary change theories: A multilevel exploration of the punctuated equilibrium paradigm. *Academy of Management Review*, *16*(1), 10–36.
[16] Gilbert, C., Eyring, M., & Foster, R. N. (2012). Two routes to resilience. *Harvard Business Review*, *90*(12), 65–73.
[17] Hamel, G., & Välikangas, L. (2003). The quest for resilience. *Harvard Business Review*, *81*(9), 52–65.
[18] Hannan, M. T., & Freeman, J. (1984). Structural inertia and organizational change. *American Sociological Review*, *49*(2), 149–164.
[19] Harrigan, K. R. (1980). Strategy formulation in declining industries. *Academy of Management Review*, *5*(4), 599–604.
[20] Keats, B. W., & Hitt, M. A. (1988). A causal model of linkages among environmental dimensions, macro organizational characteristics, and performance. *Academy of Management Journal*, *31*(3), 570–598.
[21] Kiesler, S., & Sproull, L. (1982). Managerial response to changing environments: Perspectives on problem sensing from social cognition. *Administrative Science Quarterly*, *27*(4), 548–570.
[22] Koberg, C. S. (1987). Resource scarcity, environmental uncertainty, and adaptive organizational behavior. *Academy of Management Journal*, *30*(4), 798–807.
[23] Kossek, E. E., & Perrigino, M. B. (2016). Resilience: A review using a grounded integrated occupational approach. *Academy of Management Annals*, *10*(1), 729–797.
[24] Kuhn, T. (1970). *The structure of scientific evolution* (2nd ed.). Chicago, IL: University of Chicago Press.
[25] Lawson, M. B. (2001). In praise of slack: Time is of the essence. *Academy of Management Perspectives*, *15*(3), 125–135.
[26] Lengnick-Hall, C. A., & Beck, T. E. (2005). Adaptive fit versus robust transformation: How organizations respond to environmental change. *Journal of Management*, *31*(5), 738–757.

[27] Leonard-Barton, D. (1992). Core capabilities and core rigidities: A paradox in managing new product development. *Strategic Management Journal*, *13*(Special Issue), 111–125.

[28] Levinson, D. J. (1978). *The seasons of a man's life*. New York: Random House.

[29] Linnenluecke, M. K. (2017). Resilience in business and management research: A review of influential publications and a research agenda. *International Journal of Management Reviews*, *19*(1), 4–30.

[30] McKinley, W. (1993). Organizational decline and adaptation: Theoretical controversies. *Organization Science*, *4*(1), 1–9.

[31] Meyer, A. D. (1982). Adapting to environmental jolts. *Administrative Science Quarterly*, *27*(4), 515–537.

[32] Meyer, A. D., Brooks, G. R., & Goes, J. B. (1990). Environmental jolts and industry revolutions: Organizational responses to discontinuous change. *Strategic Management Journal*, *11*(4), 93–110.

[33] Meyers, G. C., & Holusha, J. (1987). *When it hits the fan: Managing the nine crises of business*. New York: Berkley.

[34] Mitroff, I. I., & Pearson, C. M. (1993). *Crisis management: A diagnostic guide for improving your organization's crisis-preparedness*. San Francisco, CA: Jossey-Bass.

[35] Mone, M. A., McKinley, W., & Barker III, V. L. (1998). Organizational decline and innovation: A contingency framework. *Academy of Management Review*, *23*(1), 115–132.

[36] Ocasio, W. C. (1995). The enactment of economic adversity: A reconciliation of theories of failure-induced change and threat-rigidity. *Research in Organizational Behavior*, *17*, 287–331.

[37] Oliver, C. (1991). Strategic responses to institutional processes. *Academy of Management Review*, *16*(1), 145–179.

[38] Ortiz-de-Mandojana, N., & Bansal, P. (2016). The long-term benefits of organizational resilience through sustainable business practices. *Strategic Management Journal*, *37*(8), 1615–1631.

[39] Pauchant, T. C., Mitroff, I. I., & Lagadec, P. (1991). Toward a systemic crisis management strategy: Learning from the best examples in the US, Canada and France. *Industrial Crisis Quarterly*, *5*(3), 209–232.

[40] Pearce, J. A., & Robbins, K. (1993). Toward improved theory and research on business turnaround. *Journal of Management*, *19*(3), 613–636.

[41] Pearson, C. M., & Clair, J. A. (1998). Reframing crisis management. *Academy of Management Review*, *23*(1), 59–76.

[42] Pearson, C. M., & Mitroff, I. I. (1993). From crisis prone to crisis prepared: A framework for crisis management. *Academy of Management Perspectives*, *7*(1), 48–59.

[43] Prigogine, I., & Stengers, I. (1997). *The end of certainty*. New York: Simon and Schuster.

[44] Reeves, M., Levin, S., & Ueda, D. (2016). The biology of corporate survival. *Harvard Business Review*, *94*(Jan–Feb), 46–56.

[45] Roberts, K. H. (1990). Managing high reliability organizations. *California Management Review*, *32* (4), 101–113.

[46] Roberts, K. H. (1990). Some characteristics of one type of high reliability organization. *Organization Science*, *1*(2), 160–176.

[47] Romanelli, E., & Tushman, M. L. (1994). Organizational transformation as punctuated equilibrium: An empirical test. *Academy of Management Journal*, *37*(5), 1141–1166.

[48] Ronchi, L. (1980). The decision-making process for strategic adaptation. *Long Range Planning*, *13* (1), 48–54.

[49] Sabherwal, R., Hirschheim, R., & Goles, T. (2001). The dynamics of alignment: Insights from a punctuated equilibrium model. *Organization Science*, *12*(2), 179–197.

[50] Sarkar, S., & Osiyevskyy, O. (2018). Organizational change and rigidity during crisis: A review of the paradox. *European Management Journal*, *36*(1), 47–58.

[51] Schulman, P. R. (1993). The negotiated order of organizational reliability. *Administration and Society*, *25*(3), 353–372.
[52] Sheffi, Y. (2007). *The resilient enterprise: Overcoming vulnerability for competitive advantage*. Cambridge, MA: MIT Press.
[53] Shrivastava, P. (1995). Ecocentric management for a risk society. *Academy of Management Review*, *20*(1), 118–137.
[54] Smircich, L., & Stubbart, C. (1985). Strategic management in an enacted world. *Academy of Management Review*, *10*(4), 724–736.
[55] Starbuck, W. H., Greve, A., & Hedberg, B. (1978). Responding to crises. *Journal of Business Administration*, *1*(9), 111–137.
[56] Staw, B. M., Sandelands, L. E., & Dutton, J. E. (1981). Threat rigidity effects in organizational behavior: A multilevel analysis. *Administrative Science Quarterly*, *26*(4), 501–524.
[57] Tolbert, P. S., & Zucker, L. G. (1983). Institutional sources of change in the formal structure of organizations: The diffusion of civil service reform, 1880–1935. *Administrative Science Quarterly*, *28*, 22–39.
[58] Tushman, M. L., & Romanelli, E. (1985). Organizational evolution: A metamorphosis model of convergence and reorientation. *Research in Organizational Behavior*, *7*, 171–222.
[59] Van Der Vegt, G. S., Essens, P., Wahlström, M., & George, G. (2015). Managing risk and resilience. *Academy of Management Journal*, *58*(4), 971–980.
[60] Vogus, T. J., & Sutcliffe, K. M. (2007). Organizational resilience: Towards a theory and research agenda. In *2007 IEEE International Conference on Systems, Man and Cybernetics*, 3418–3422.
[61] Weick, K. E. (1987). Organizational culture as a source of high reliability. *California Management Review*, *29*(2), 112–127.
[62] Weick, K. E. (1993). The collapse of sensemaking in organizations: The Mann Gulch disaster. *Administrative Science Quarterly*, *38*(4), 628–652.
[63] Weick, K. E., Sutcliffe, K. M., & Obstfeld, D. (2008). Organizing for high reliability: Processes of collective mindfulness. *Crisis Management*, *3*(1), 81–123.
[64] Weitzel, W., & Jonsson, E. (1989). Decline in organizations: A literature integration and extension. *Administrative Science Quarterly*, *34*(1), 91–109.
[65] Williams, T. A., Gruber, D. A., Sutcliffe, K. M., Shepherd, D. A., & Zhao, E. Y. (2017). Organizational response to adversity: Fusing crisis management and resilience research streams. *Academy of Management Annals*, *11*(2), 733–769.
[66] Yasai-Ardekani, M. (1986). Structural adaptations to environments. *Academy of Management Review*, *11*(1), 9–21.

# 6 A Capability Perspective on Change

**PERSPECTIVE IN BRIEF**

- **Concepts related to the perspective** – organisational flexibility, organisational adaptability, dynamic capabilities, and organisational agility
- **Keep reading to learn more about** – change culture and organisational learning
- **Prime contributors** – Y. Doz, K. Eisenhardt, C. Helfat, M. Kosonen, M. Peteraf, G. Pisano, D. Teece, and S. Winter
- **Guiding metaphor** – change as a craft

## Introduction

While Chapters 2–5 varied significantly in their focus, they shared a common thread: each examined change as an action, something unfolding in the present. This chapter, however, marks a notable shift in emphasis – moving from action to potential. Rather than viewing change as a discrete event, this chapter explores the underlying capabilities and resources that enable organisations to evolve continuously. It reframes change not as something that simply happens to an organisation but as a capacity that organisations can develop to shape and sustain transformation over time.

Consider, for example, two artists, each with a major hit song. While both are equally popular, the first artist has a long discography of hit singles, whereas the second has only just achieved their first success. Imagine you had to predict which artist would enjoy greater long-term success. Most people would likely bet on the first artist. While personal preferences – such as a liking for their voice or style – might play a role, the more compelling reason is that this artist has consistently demonstrated their capability as a hit-maker, releasing multiple successful songs over time. In contrast, while the second artist's hit song may be equally massive, it could be a one-time phenomenon. There is little indication yet whether they have the skills to sustain their success.

This comparison illustrates the importance of capabilities in determining future success. The first artist's proven track record suggests a stronger ability to adapt and thrive in a changing musical landscape. The focus, therefore, is not merely on the success of a single hit but on the broader, more reliable skill set that underpins sustained achievement. Similarly, in an organisational context, success is not just about managing a single change effectively but about cultivating the internal capabilities that make adaptation and transformation a continuous, embedded process.

In this chapter, I'll discuss this way of thinking as representing a **capability perspective** on change. Together, we'll examine how organisations can develop and refine the skills necessary to implement change whenever it is needed, how stability and continuity can serve as foundations for adaptability, and how resources – both tangible and intangible – shape a firm's ability to navigate change. Finally, we'll consider how organisations can move beyond seeing change as a response to challenges and instead integrate it into their long-term strategy.

So, with that being said, let's start honing our skills and move into a capability perspective on change. No singing required (but feel free to).

## 6.1 The Genesis of Thought

As we embark on our exploration of the capability perspective, let's begin by again considering the first of our fundamental questions: why did this perspective on change emerge at all? Two key developments played a pivotal role in shaping the capability line of thought.

### 6.1.1 The Idea of the Ceaselessly Dynamic Environment

Between the 1980s and the 1990s, managers and organisational researchers had become increasingly baffled by the relentless pace by which organisational environments seemed to be developing.[2] Globalisation pushed firms to increasingly leave the safety of home;[31] technological developments greased the wheels of production ever more intensely; and individual choices were increasingly liberalised.[12] In these hyper-turbulent[33] or high-velocity[19] environments, it was believed that firms needed to fend off 'hyper-competition'[13] – that is, rivalry from actors who continually develop new competitive advantages that disrupt or invalidate those of the industry leader and render them obsolete or ineffective.[14]

Change, in this landscape, was no longer seen as an occasional hiccup; it seemed to have become the norm. The challenge for organisations was no longer just about navigating change periodically; it became necessary to embed adaptability at the very core of operations. Consequently, new forms of organisation were called for, which were to install change as both a deliberate and an ongoing feature in the firm's core set-up. Firms seemed to increasingly need structures that could institutionalise adaptability, ensuring that change was not just a mere fluke but a continuous and deliberate feature of the organisation itself: put differently, they needed flexible and agile designs that could thrive in environments characterised by constant, unpredictable change, rather than just periodic or major shifts.[5]

### 6.1.2 Turning to Resource-Based Theory and Practice

While the 1980s saw the initial outlines of what the capability perspective would be, it was not until the 1990s that these outlines gained tangible form.[21, 30, 32] Key in this blossoming was tapping into related fields of interest.

From a theoretical angle, the resource-based theory of the firm was instrumental.[6, 7, 35] Initially set out as a static understanding of how firms achieve competitive advantage based on what they have, resource-based theory offered a helpful platform from which to consider what organisations could potentially achieve with those means: in other words, firms can sustainably outcompete others because they have more or better resources. These resources can be both tangible (such as the money you have in your pocket) and intangible (such as the knowledge you have in your head). If resources belong only to you and other companies have no way of easily acquiring similar ones, your firm is believed to hold a competitive advantage over its adversaries. In this sense, your money-filled pockets or your knowledge-filled head may help develop your organisation in ways that others simply cannot achieve.[20, 41]

From a more practical angle, there were also several operational developments that offered sound empirical ground for a new change perspective to take root. Most notable are advances in so-called agile manufacturing, that is, production systems that became geared to reducing lead-times and working more adaptively to the wants and needs of the customer;[25] the introduction of 'agile development' in IT, that is, a more responsive way of coding software that was aimed at avoiding catastrophic misfires associated with the traditional waterfall system;[24] and experiments with the 'flexible' organisational designs of emerging tech firms, who considered the ability to keep up with external developments to be at the core of their business model.[5] These practices all emphasised the importance of being dynamic and responsive to external developments, and provided a wide range of examples of how (different parts of) organisations could deal with incessant environmental dynamism.

#### Box 6.1 The Point?

The developments discussed here laid bare the necessity for organisations to move beyond sporadic efforts for change, and design their features so that the overall group would become consistently responsive at its core. If the context in which organisations operated was turning more and more into a maelstrom, why not leverage the way in which some were experimenting with managing it in return? In this sense, the capability perspective emerged from the recognition that organisations needed to be more consistently responsive to an environment that was increasingly picking up its pace, and the presence of related knowledge that allowed organisations to pick up theirs as well.

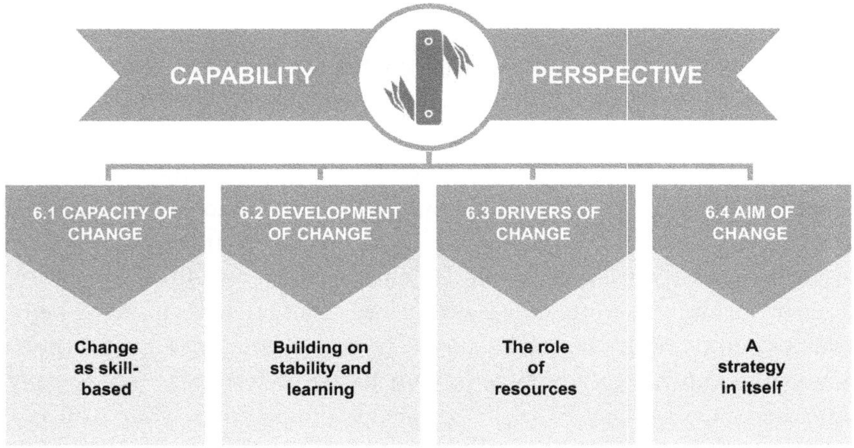


**Figure 6.1** Unpacking the heart of the capability perspective.

## 6.2 Unpacking the Heart

So, what does a capability perspective truly entail? What defining features have been carved from the vast block of organisational knowledge, shaping the way firms adapt, compete, and innovate? In the following subsections, we'll delve deeper into the perspective's core tenets. For an overview, see Figure 6.1.

### 6.2.1 Capacity of Change: Change as Skill-Based

When talking about change from a capability perspective, the focus is on the **organisational skills** that drive change. While there has been quite some debate on what skills should be emphasised, all recommendations essentially relate to the same principle: namely, that change should not be approached as a one-time effort but should concern a development of core proficiencies that can be applied whenever they are needed.[9, 41, 44] In this sense, approaching change from a capability angle is not about helping the fisher make that one catch; it is about making the fisher fit for fishing.

To render this a bit more tangible, it's helpful to look at some examples: what concrete skills are we talking about when beefing up our organisation for change? Over time, authors have marked a wide variety of relevant skills to consider.[20] Think of **product development routines**, by which the organisation is capable of successfully creating and recreating new products to follow up on changing customer wants and needs. Think of **transfer skills**, by which the organisation is able to quickly replicate crucial resources within the firm. Think of **strategic decision-making skills**, or the capacity of managers to smoothly reach visionary decisions by pooling their expertise together. Think of **alliance and acquisition routines**, which can allow the organisation to easily access resources available beyond organisational boundaries. As can be observed, there are many options when considering skills that make your organisation fit for change, and all may be of importance somewhere down the line.

For example, let's imagine a company that has long been a leader in consumer electronics, known for its ability to consistently innovate and release new products that capture the market's attention. Over time, this company has developed a set of core capabilities that allow it to adapt to rapidly changing technological landscapes. For one, it has established strong product development routines, enabling it to quickly prototype, test, and launch new devices in response to emerging trends. Additionally, the company has honed its ability to transfer knowledge across different teams, ensuring that breakthroughs in one area, such as software development, can be swiftly integrated into other areas, like hardware design. Moreover, the company excels in strategic decision-making, with a leadership team that regularly collaborates to anticipate market shifts and align the company's resources with future opportunities. Finally, the organisation has developed robust alliance and acquisition routines, allowing it to form strategic partnerships and acquire start-ups that bring in new technologies or expertise. These capabilities have allowed the company not only to maintain its market leadership but also to navigate the uncertainties of a fast-paced industry, continuously adapting to change and staying ahead of competitors.

**Box 6.2 The Point?**

A capability perspective emphasises the importance of building and nurturing a diverse set of organisational skills that make change continuously possibly. By focusing on the development of core proficiencies, organisations can move beyond viewing change as a one-time event and instead embrace it as an integral part of their ongoing strategy. This approach ensures that they are not just reacting to change but proactively shaping their futures, ready to seize new opportunities and overcome challenges as they arise.

### 6.2.2 Development of Change: Building on Stability and Learning

So far, we've seen that a capability perspective places primary emphasis on the skills that underlie change. But where do those skills or capabilities come from and how do they develop over time? The answer may be counter-intuitive: rather than treating **routine and stability** as obstacles to transformation, the capability perspective views them as its essential building blocks.[43, 44, 47] According to this perspective, stability is not in opposition to transformation; instead, it provides the foundation that allows organisations to evolve. When leveraged effectively, routines – or the firm's repositories of regular patterned behaviours and the firm's stored knowledge[3] – can act as stepping stones for facilitating change. Stability and change are believed to be deeply interconnected, with routines supplying the platform from which the capacity to transform can emerge.

For example, if I repeatedly engage with customers, I might discover that a more effective way to understand their evolving preferences is to let them lead the conversation rather than guiding it with specific questions. Over time, this routine practice would lead to a change in my behaviour that might otherwise have been overlooked. Similarly, a company might regularly conduct customer trials to pilot new products. Some products may succeed, while others may fail, but because the failures are small and manageable they provide insights that drive future success. By working through both repetition and minor failures, organisations can leverage their stable foundations to cultivate a more adaptable and resilient state.[28]

In this sense, developing a capability for change may hinge on how organisations manage learning and knowledge, involving the establishment of robust systems for accumulating, integrating, applying, and reconfiguring such knowledge across the firm.[22, 28, 36, 47] Organisations that recognise the value of repeated practice and embrace small failures as learning opportunities are believed to make more meaningful improvements. Repetition deepens individuals' understanding of processes, refining routines over time, while small failures provide critical insights without triggering the defensiveness that stifles growth.[20]

### Box 6.3 Be Aware!

Not all failures are created equal; nor are they equally instructive. Organisations must be cautious not to celebrate every misstep: basic failures, often caused by inattention or lack of skill in well-understood contexts, and complex failures, which result from unpredictable interactions in interdependent systems, rarely offer the clarity needed for effective learning. In contrast, intelligent failures – those that (i) explore an opportunity, (ii) in novel territory, (iii) whose assumptions are explicitly articulated, and (iv) keep cost and scope as small as possible – are the true goldmine for adaptive learning. Developing a culture that encourages prudent risk-taking and reflective experimentation can help distinguish useful failures from costly distractions.[11]

Think about a technology firm that has built its success on a consistent process of product iteration. This company has established a routine of releasing software updates every quarter, each time incorporating customer feedback and addressing known issues. Initially, these updates are straightforward, focusing on fixing bugs and improving performance. However, over time, the firm begins to notice patterns in customer feedback that suggest broader shifts in user expectations. Instead of simply responding to immediate needs, the company starts experimenting with more significant changes during its routine updates, such as introducing new features or redesigning the user interface. Some of these changes are met with resistance, but the firm views these small setbacks as opportunities to learn and refine its approach. Through this iterative process, the company not only maintains its product's relevance but also gradually transforms it to better meet the evolving demands of the market. Here, the routine of regular updates becomes a platform for ongoing innovation, allowing the company to adapt in an increasingly dynamic environment.

**Box 6.4 The Point?**

The key takeaway here is that the capability perspective does not require you to abandon stability; it requires you to leverage it. By carefully crafting routines and responses to failure, organisations can foster ongoing change without destabilising their core operations. Ultimately, the ability to evolve is not about rejecting predictability but about using it as a foundation for reinvention.

### 6.2.3 Drivers of Change: The Role of Resources

Having explored how routines and learning processes underpin an organisation's capacity to change, the next logical question is: what enables those routines to be enacted, with learning taking root? From a capability perspective, the answer lies in the strategic use of **resources**. Just as routines provide the 'how' behind organisational change, resources represent the 'what' fuelling it – the tangible and intangible assets that can be deployed, recombined, or redirected in response to evolving demands.[1]

According to the capability perspective, change is strongly related to the organisation's understanding of how best to make use of the resources it holds. If an organisation is to change successfully, it needs to be able to gather the necessary means; to integrate and allocate them wherever they are required; and to recombine them for the generation of new value-creating strategies.[7, 20, 26] In this sense, change becomes a matter of managing resources at the organisation's disposal: handling firms as bundles of assets[28] and aligning their resources in a way that supports the desired direction and maximises the creation of new value.

Now, before you go withdrawing all your cash from your local bank, be aware that this idea of resources can be interpreted quite broadly:

- financial resources – such as cash or capital investments;
- human resources – such as managerial talent or labour;
- physical resources – such as specialised equipment, office and production facilities, or materials; and
- information resources – such as usable data and information.

In this way, although your company may be starved of cash, it may still be sitting on a pile of resources that can help it outmanoeuvre competitors that lack them. For example, as a mining corporation, you may have access to a patented high-tech drill that other companies cannot duplicate; as a consulting firm, you may have snatched up all recently graduated top performers; or as a company of caretakers and nurses, you may have developed unique understanding of your local patient base. These are all 'resources' and they can help you develop your company in ways that others may not.

### Box 6.5 Be Aware!

A side effect of such a resource-driven understanding is that resources can also impose quite the constraint on firms' capacity for change. If the organisation doesn't have the right resources or doesn't manage them correctly, aiming for change may seem futile. In this way, the capability perspective considers the firm's management of resources as having the potential to prompt but also impede genuine organisational change. Resources can be a useful and very helpful tool to wield for changing – if one only knows how to.

### 6.2.4 Aim of Change: Change as a Strategy in Itself

Finally, by framing change through the lens of competitive advantage, the capability perspective brings it to the very heart of strategic thinking. In this view, change is no longer simply a means to achieve a predefined goal; **it becomes the strategy itself**.[11] Change is elevated from a supporting role to a central one, representing the primary way through which organisations create and sustain advantage in dynamic environments.[41, 46]

Whether this capacity for change translates into a lasting competitive advantage depends on how easily it can be replicated. Some argue that an organisation's ability to change is deeply embedded in its history, routines, and culture – making it path-dependent, firm-specific, and thus difficult for rivals to imitate.[7] From this angle, a capability for change becomes a source of sustained competitive advantage.

Others, however, contend that, as the capability perspective gains traction, best practices and frameworks for managing change will emerge, making adaptability a more accessible and imitable resource.[20] If change management becomes standardised, the notion of 'change as a strategy' may thus lose its potency as a differentiator. Ultimately, whether a dynamic capability for change can serve as a long-term advantage remains an open question.

### Box 6.6 The Point?

The capability perspective repositions change from a mere 'means to an end' into a strategic imperative. Whether this shift grants firms a sustainable edge, however, hinges on whether the ability to change remains unique or becomes widely replicable. The debate is far from settled, but one thing is clear: in an era of turbulence, organisations can no longer afford to treat change as an afterthought.

## 6.3 Extending Your Toolkit

If change becomes a strategic necessity, then organisations need more than intent – they need tools that help them stay ahead in unpredictable environments. The capability perspective has given rise to several such frameworks, two of which continue to shape how firms think about and act on change. Use both to your advantage.

## 6.3.1 Dynamic Capabilities

One of the most influential tools to emerge from a capability way of thinking is the concept of **dynamic capabilities**. Dynamic capabilities refer to a firm's ability to flexibly integrate, build, and reconfigure internal and external competencies to address rapidly changing environments.[41] They are the processes, skills, and strategies that organisations use to manage and adapt their resources and competencies to meet new challenges and opportunities. Dynamic capabilities are considered a crucial aspect of a firm's competitiveness as they enable organisations to quickly respond to changes in the market and capitalise on new opportunities.[38]

Dynamic capabilities are defined as being distinct from static capabilities, which are resources and competencies that may provide a firm with a competitive advantage at any given time but don't necessarily allow it to evolve. For example, a company may be excellent at producing goods in a highly efficient fashion, or it may have the skill to optimise its tax position. While very useful, these capabilities are static in that they allow the company to be more competitive at a given time. Dynamic capabilities, on the other hand, are those features that enable organisations to transform their static capabilities into new sources of competitive advantage. Overall, three categories of dynamic capabilities – sensing, seizing, and reconfiguring – are key.

### 6.3.1.1 The Capacity of Sensing

To be able to change, companies first need to be capable of picking up what opportunities and threats are developing in the marketplace. In this respect, the notions of both scanning information and interpreting what such information means are deemed vital.[38, 41]

Think, for example, of a global consumer electronics company that has a dedicated team for market intelligence. This team continuously monitors trends in consumer behaviour, technological advancements, and competitor strategies. Through sophisticated data analytics and direct engagement with customers, the team identifies an emerging demand for wearable technology that seamlessly integrates health monitoring with everyday activities. By interpreting this data, the company realises that the market is shifting towards more personalised, health-focused devices. As such, its sensing capacity has allowed the company to spot the opportunity early, giving it a head start in the development of new products tailored to these emerging consumer preferences.

### 6.3.1.2 The Capacity of Seizing

Next, once an opportunity or a threat is sensed, the organisation needs to have the capacity for acting decidedly on the momentum identified. Concretely, this means that the firm must be able to quickly step in with relevant new products, processes, or services, as well as being capable of framing such produce with an appropriate commercialisation strategy and set of investment priorities.[38, 41]

For instance, a fast-fashion retailer may sense a growing trend in eco-conscious consumerism. The company swiftly decides to launch a new line of sustainable clothing made from recycled materials. To seize this opportunity, it not only develops the new product line but also aligns its marketing strategy to emphasise sustainability, launching a campaign that highlights the environmental benefits of its products. The company reallocates resources to prioritise this initiative, ensuring that the new line reaches stores in record time. By being able to act decisively and strategically, the retailer can capitalise on the trend before competitors, enhancing its brand image and market share.

#### 6.3.1.3 The Capacity of Reconfiguration

Finally, the organisation needs to be able to recombine and reconfigure its assets and structure as growth ensues. By doing so, it avoids becoming locked up in the very successes the firm's capacities for sensing and seizing should have, by then, reeled in. In this category, think of concrete abilities such as redesigning business models, revamping routines, or realigning assets.[38, 41]

Consider a tech start-up that has successfully launched a groundbreaking software platform. As the company grows, it realises that its initial organisational structure, designed for rapid development and iteration, is no longer suitable for managing a larger, more diverse portfolio of products and services. To address this, the start-up reconfigures its internal processes, moving from a flat organisational structure to one that includes specialised teams focused on different aspects of the business, such as customer service, product development, and strategic partnerships. Additionally, it revamps its business model to include subscription services and partnerships with other tech firms, ensuring a steady stream of revenue while continuing to innovate. This reconfiguration allows the company to scale effectively, avoiding the pitfalls of rigid success and maintaining its competitive edge.

**Box 6.7 The Point?**

The dynamic capabilities framework was one of the first to emphasise an organisation's competence for change as being an essential aspect of its competitiveness. The concept emphasises that companies need to continuously adapt and evolve their strategies, capabilities, and competencies if they mean to remain competitive and succeed in the long term.

### 6.3.2 Strategic Agility

Whereas dynamic capabilities centre on the skills and processes needed to adapt, **strategic agility** ties this adaptability more directly to long-term direction – emphasising not just movement but movement with coherent purpose. Specifically, strategic agility refers to an organisation's ability to quickly adapt to changes in its internal and external environment while still maintaining its strategic objectives and direction.[42] It involves having the flexibility to pivot and adjust plans as needed, while remaining focused on the long-term vision.[16] Three sets of capabilities are highlighted: strategic sensitivity (Section 6.3.2.1), leadership unity / collective commitment (Section 6.3.2.2), and resource fluidity (Section 6.3.2.3).

#### 6.3.2.1 Strategic Sensitivity

Almost identical to the 'capacity of sensing' as put forward by the dynamic capabilities framework, strategic sensitivity involves becoming rapidly aware of emerging trends and making proper sense of what such trends might implicate for the organisation at large. The following skills matter here particularly:[17]

- anticipating – sharpening foresight;
- experimenting – trying out new stuff;
- distancing – mentally moving away from the internal company towards the environment and its periphery;
- abstracting – capturing particular trends in conceptual terms; and
- reframing – highlighting the need for business model renewal.

Imagine a global technology firm that seeks to enhance its strategic sensitivity in response to the fast-paced evolution of artificial intelligence. To improve its skill of anticipation, the company sets up a dedicated AI foresight team tasked with continuously monitoring technological advancements and market shifts. To experiment, the firm launches pilot projects that explore the integration of AI into different product lines, allowing it to test new ideas with minimal risk. Recognising the importance of understanding the broader environment, the firm encourages its leaders to practise distancing by engaging with external experts and attending industry conferences, thereby gaining fresh perspectives on AI trends. Abstracting these insights, the company's strategists distil complex technological developments into actionable concepts that can be communicated across the organisation. Finally, the leadership team regularly revisits or reframes the company's value propositions and explores how AI can transform its existing business models. By cultivating these skills, the firm positions itself to swiftly sense what's going on in the AI revolution and thus maintain its competitive edge.

#### 6.3.2.2 Leadership Unity / Collective Commitment

After becoming aware of what is actually going on, the organisation's top team should be capable of quickly committing to a decision without being hampered by internal politics and power conflicts. To do this, you might want to consider working on the following skills:[17]

- dialoguing – surfacing and sharing assumptions;
- revealing – laying bare personal motives;
- integrating – defining a valuable common agenda;

- aligning – building common meaning; and
- caring – providing empathy and compassion in discussion.

Let's visualise a multinational corporation working on its leadership unity. The company begins by fostering dialogue among its leaders, creating open forums where assumptions and perspectives are shared transparently. To ensure that personal motives do not cloud judgement, the company emphasises revealing, encouraging leaders to openly discuss their individual goals and concerns. Integrating these diverse viewpoints, the team works on defining a common agenda that aligns with the company's long-term vision, ensuring that everyone is on the same page. Aligning follows, as the leadership team collectively builds a shared understanding of the strategic direction, fostering a unified sense of purpose. Finally, caring becomes a cornerstone of their discussions, with leaders demonstrating empathy and compassion, particularly in navigating the tough decisions that the regulatory changes demand. By nurturing these skills, the company ensures that its leadership can make swift, unified decisions, maintaining organisational coherence in the face of external challenges.

#### 6.3.2.3 Resource Fluidity

Finally, to make decisions materialise, the organisation will need to be able to quickly reconfigure its business systems and redeploy resources. To manage such capability, executives must nurture the following organisational skills:[17]

- decoupling – organising the firm according to customer segmentations;
- modularising – developing 'plug-and-play' functionalities for organisational processes and business systems;
- dissociating – separating resource use and ownership;
- switching – using multiple business models; and
- grafting – acquiring others to transform oneself.

For example, aware of ongoing developments in sustainable and eco-friendly product lines, a leading consumer goods company decides to work on enhancing its resource fluidity. It kicks off by first organising teams according to customer segments that prioritise sustainability, thus allowing the company to target and serve eco-conscious consumers more effectively. Next, the company develops plug-and-play functionalities in its manufacturing processes, enabling it to quickly adapt production lines to new, sustainable materials without extensive re-tooling. Furthermore, the company starts separating resource ownership from use, opting to lease rather than own machinery, which provides greater flexibility to scale production up or down based on market demand. Switching between different business models, the company experiments with subscription services for eco-friendly products alongside its traditional retail approach, thereby diversifying its revenue streams. Finally, the company engages in grafting by acquiring a smaller, innovative firm specialising in biodegradable packaging, integrating this new capability into its existing operations to accelerate the transition to sustainability. Through these efforts, the company ensures that its resources remain flexible and aligned with its evolving strategic goals, allowing it to stay competitive in a rapidly changing market.

**Box 6.8 The Point?**

It's important to note that strategic agility should not be confused with impulsiveness or a lack of planning. Strategic agility is about having a clear vision and direction while being flexible enough to adjust the plan as needed. Organisations must balance the need for agility with the need for stability and consistent execution of their strategy. It requires a combination of strong leadership, a supportive culture, and having the right systems and processes in place to facilitate quick and effective decision-making.

## 6.4 Impact on the Ground

Having seen how routines, resources, and frameworks shape the capability perspective, you might be asking yourself: what difference does mastering this perspective really make in practice? Thinking about change from a capability angle offers several distinct advantages, the most noted of which I've outlined in this section.

### 6.4.1 A Capability Perspective Affirms Collective Responsibility

The first major benefit of adopting a capability perspective is that it redistributes the responsibility for change. Instead of portraying transformation as the achievement of heroic leaders or isolated employee initiatives, this view anchors change in the organisation's collective skills and systems. By shifting agency from individuals to the organisation as a whole, change comes to be seen less as the result of exceptional personal effort and more as the innate outcome of coordinated systems – creating conditions in which adaptation can occur almost naturally.

This doesn't mean that individuals have no place in the perspective whatsoever: managers are still expected to ensure that a proper organisational configuration is installed, and employees are to signal where such configurations can still be improved.[8] Yet, from such tinkering onwards, it is the organisation as a whole – its entire membership base – that is assumed to deal with change, as if on instinct.[4, 23, 27, 28, 37] In this sense, just like you don't have to think about catching a ball that you see flying towards you, the organisation should be prepped to pick up on change as if by reflex, with each individual working near automatically for the group to realign.

### 6.4.2 A Capability Perspective Spotlights Repeatability

A second major benefit of the capability perspective is that it reframes change as repeatable rather than exceptional. Instead of treating transformation as a sporadic or extraordinary event, this view emphasises change as a continuous process of adjustment to shifting circumstances.[7, 26, 30, 40]

By embedding adaptability into their core capabilities, organisations make change a structured, habitual process rather than a one-time happening. This means that instead of scrambling to react to sudden plans or shifts, they are always in motion, continuously fine-tuning their strategies, structures, and resources. The truly adaptable firm is not necessarily the one making the most changes today; it's the one best prepared to change whenever necessary.

### 6.4.3 A Capability Perspective Introduces Pre-emptive Action

Finally, perhaps the most profound transformation brought by the capability perspective is its shift from reaction to anticipation. If change is deeply embedded within an organisation's DNA, it no longer needs to wait for external forces to dictate its next move. Instead, it can act on opportunities and threats before they fully materialise, gaining a strategic advantage over less prepared competitors.

In this sense, viewing change from a capability angle shifts the focus from what has already been achieved to what could be realised: it puts emphasis on what the organisation has the potential to achieve, rather than solely on its current output.[40] By prioritising the development of organisational skills, organisations can ensure that they are better equipped to handle future changes and better able to meet their goals and objectives. Organisational change thus becomes a topic that is no longer strictly confined to the here and now but extends into a more broadly formulated future.

By framing change as a preparation, the capability perspective encourages organisations to invest in change even when there is no immediate need. This proactive approach pries loose what might otherwise remain static, motivating the organisation to cultivate its capacity for change in order to capture a more promising future.

**Box 6.9 The Point?**

Ultimately, the capability perspective transforms change from a burden to a strategic asset. The most successful organisations are not necessarily those outperforming others today but those best positioned to embrace change whenever it becomes crucial.

## 6.5 Drawbacks and Pitfalls

Yet even as the capability perspective reframes change as a strategic asset, it is not without its blind spots: alongside its advantages come pitfalls that, if overlooked, can undermine its promise. The most notable ones are outlined here.

### 6.5.1 A Capability Perspective Is Buzz-Driven

Of all the different perspectives related to organisational change, few have been as littered with conceptual fads and fuzzy lingo as the capability perspective. Flexibility, adaptability, agility, dynamic capabilities . . . The list goes on. Many of the concepts used within the perspective lack clear and concise definitions, leading to confusion and misinterpretation.[10, 15, 42] Additionally, many of the concepts within the capability perspective have diffuse origins, making it difficult to determine what is essential and what is not. This has caused many to struggle with some sense of common ground, for if concepts are everything and more, how can we make sense of what is shared and what is not?

What makes the state of confusion even worse is that the relations between concepts have often been redefined according to the whims of the author in question.[29] For instance, when reading articles on organisational flexibility, one will soon learn that the concept supposedly overarches the more subordinate notions of dynamic capabilities and agility.[10] Yet when reading articles that focus on the idea of dynamic capabilities, this relationship seems frequently overturned – with flexibility being portrayed as subsidiary to the notion of dynamic capabilities.[22] As the conversation lacks clear definitions, the relationships between constructs often seem informed by the preferences of the authors in question. It often turns conceptual clarity into a nasty pickle.

### 6.5.2 A Capability Perspective May Be Geared Towards the Consulting Industry

A cynical way of looking at the capability perspective – with its rather vague conceptual outlines and measurement difficulties – is to interpret it as a cash cow for the management consulting industry. As the perspective urges all organisations to develop capabilities for change, who else is to make money out of it other than the advising expert?[18] True enough, scanning through current-day consulting outlets, it is hard to find a firm that does not explicitly warn organisations of the consequences of not becoming flexible, agile, dynamic, or any combination of these terms – with the implicit solution, of course, being to solicit the consultant for aid. In this way, the capability perspective finds itself increasingly adorned with a shroud of scepticism and wariness: its outlines considered too vague to straightforwardly build upon, and its practical translation thought to be a potential money-making racket for self-acclaimed experts and consultants of all sorts.[10, 34]

#### Box 6.10 Practical Advice?

When working on capability-related projects, organisations should aim to reach clear outcomes. Rather than making vague promises of increasing agility or flexibility, set out for specific examples of how these capabilities will be developed and how their impact will be assessed. Work on pilot projects or trial periods where the effectiveness of proposed changes can be evaluated before committing to large-scale implementations. Additionally, consider building internal expertise to reduce dependency on external consultants. By training your own staff in the principles of capability development, you can retain more control over the process and outcomes.

### 6.5.3 A Capability Perspective May Over-Promote Change

A final critical remark is the tendency of the capability perspective to implicitly advance change as the more developed or advanced side of the organisational spectrum – put out against a more under-developed and banal counterpart of non-change. A good example of such connotation can be found in the literature's common tendency of marking dynamic capabilities as 'higher level', rising above 'ordinary' or 'zero-level' capabilities associated with present-day efficiency.[7, 20, 40, 45] In this way, while the idea of stability is certainly not lost from view, it is attributed a clear subservient role – a base platform that the sensible firm should develop further and further away from.

**Box 6.11 Practical Advice?**

To avoid the pitfall of over-promoting change, organisations must strike a balance between adaptability and operational control. Leaders should resist the urge to pursue transformation for its own sake and instead assess whether change aligns with strategic goals, market realities, and core competencies. One effective approach is to define clear criteria for when change is necessary – for instance, prioritising adaptability in turbulent markets while maintaining operational consistency in more predictable environments. Additionally, firms should value and nurture their 'ordinary' capabilities – the processes, routines, and efficiencies that keep the business running smoothly. A well-functioning organisation is not one that constantly reinvents itself but one that knows when to evolve and when to hold steady.[7, 28, 32, 39]

## SUMMARY

Chapter 6 explored the **capability perspective** on change, which emphasises skill, expertise, and the ability to navigate an ever-evolving environment. Rather than viewing change as a reaction to external pressures or a rigidly planned process, this perspective sees it as an ongoing craft – something that organisations develop, refine, and strategically leverage over time (see Table 6.1 for an overview).

- The **roots of this perspective** lie in the recognition that the business environment is ceaselessly dynamic, requiring organisations to continuously adapt and refine their capabilities. Over time, insights from resource-based theory and operational practices spilled over into change management, leading to a greater focus on how organisations can build and sustain competitive advantages through their internal skills and resources.
- At its **core**, this perspective defines change as skill-based, unfolding through continuous learning rather than abrupt shifts. Unlike approaches that emphasise disruption, it views change as something that builds on existing stability, allowing organisations to improve and evolve without losing their foundations. Resources – both tangible and intangible – are central to this process, shaping an organisation's ability to respond, innovate, and reposition itself in a competitive landscape. Within this view, change is not just a means to an end; it is a strategy in itself, embedded in the way an organisation operates.

**Table 6.1 A capability perspective on change: overview**

| | |
|---|---|
| **Guiding metaphor** | Change as a craft |
| **The genesis of thought** | |
| Development 1 | The idea of the ceaselessly dynamic environment |
| Development 2 | Turning to resource-based theory and practice |
| **Unpacking the heart** | |
| Capacity of change | Change as skill-based |
| Development of change | Building on stability and learning |
| Drivers of change | The role of resources |
| Aim of change | A strategy in itself |
| **Extending your toolkit** | |
| Tool #1 | Dynamic capabilities |
| Tool #2 | Strategic agility |
| **Impact on the ground** | |
| (+) | A capability perspective affirms collective responsibility. |
| (+) | A capability perspective spotlights repeatability. |
| (+) | A capability perspective introduces pre-emptive action. |
| **Drawbacks and pitfalls** | |
| (−) | A capability perspective is buzz-driven. |
| (−) | A capability perspective may be geared toward the consultancy industry. |
| (−) | A capability perspective may over-promote change. |
| **Related concepts** | |
| ► | Organisational flexibility |
| ► | Organisational adaptability |
| ► | Dynamic capabilities |
| ► | Organisational agility |

◊ To deepen our understanding of this approach, we examined two **key frameworks**. The concept of dynamic capabilities highlights how organisations can develop, integrate, and reconfigure their resources to stay ahead in changing environments. Strategic agility, on the other hand, focuses on the ability to anticipate change, to pivot when necessary, and to sustain long-term adaptability.

◊ A capability perspective offers several **advantages**. It reframes individuals as part of a larger system, emphasising their role in building and sustaining organisational capabilities. It also acknowledges the importance of repeatability, suggesting that organisations can develop routines and expertise that allow them to navigate change more effectively over time. Additionally, it highlights the value of pre-emptive action, recognising that organisations can shape their own futures rather than simply reacting to external forces.

◊ Despite its strengths, this perspective is not without its **criticisms**. It has been described as buzz-driven, relying on trendy terminology that may not always translate into practical application. Some argue that it is particularly beneficial for the consultancy industry, offering frameworks that may be more appealing in theory than in practice. There is also the risk of over-promoting change, encouraging continuous transformation even when stability or consolidation might be the wiser approach.

## CASE: TEACHING A FINANCIAL BEHEMOTH TO DANCE

### The Capability Perspective in Practice

When thinking about companies that can pivot swiftly, sleek tech firms like Spotify, Netflix, or Google often come to mind. However, even in industries as deeply rooted in tradition as banking, organisations can reinvent themselves to embrace change.

One striking example is ING, a Dutch financial services company that was an early adopter of agile methodologies. In 2015, as the financial sector faced sweeping transformations fuelled by digitalisation, ING recognised the urgency of staying competitive. With fintech start-ups and tech giants encroaching on the market, banking products were becoming commoditised. The key differentiator was no longer the product itself but the customer experience. ING aimed to set itself apart by delivering seamless, high-quality service across all channels – whether visiting a branch for investment advice or finalising transactions online or by phone. To execute this strategy, the company saw agility as the only viable path forward.

Unlike many companies that embrace change in response to a crisis, ING embarked on its transformation from a position of strength. The organisation was performing well, yet there was growing frustration with inefficiencies – an excess of meetings, endless handovers, and a lack of end-to-end ownership. It became clear that a fundamental shift in working methods was necessary.

What followed was a journey that positioned ING as a benchmark for agility in the financial world. This case demonstrates that the ability to drive change is not about having cutting-edge technology or the sheer size of a company; instead, it hinges on boldness, perseverance, and a relentless commitment to improvement.

#### Reimagining How to Organise a Financial Institution

ING first introduced agile practices in 2010 within its IT department, emphasising engineering talent and implementing scrum methodologies to enhance flexibility and collaboration. However, by 2014, the company realised that incremental tweaks were not enough:

customers' needs were evolving faster than ING could respond, and its executives saw the need to rethink processes from the ground up.

To chart a new course, ING's leadership sought inspiration outside the banking sector. They studied leading tech firms to understand how these companies thrived in fast-changing environments. The goal? To bring ING's leaders up to speed on innovative organisational models and translate those insights into a blueprint for transformation. Peter Jacobs, CIO of ING Netherlands, explained that when talented young people are asked to name their ideal employer, companies like Facebook, Google, Netflix, Spotify, and Uber are often mentioned. That got him wondering: with all these companies being in different industries, what is it that makes them so attractive? He realised that what these companies share is a unique way of working: they operate in small, purpose-driven teams, follow an agile approach, maintain close interactions with customers, and are always adapting and reshaping their work.

Drawing on the insights gained from these visits, ING launched its pilot transformation programme at its Dutch retail operations headquarters in November 2014. Starting at the core was a strategic move to establish a strong foundation before scaling across the organisation. The company outlined several key objectives: reducing time to market, improving operational efficiency, and enhancing customer experience. While the transformation aimed to future-proof the organisation, it also entailed some tough decisions, including reducing the workforce at its Dutch headquarters. Employees had to reapply for their positions, with selections based on both skill sets and alignment with the company's new way of working.

Despite widespread agreement on the need for change, few anticipated just how profound the transformation would be. Roles were redefined, responsibilities shifted, and traditional structures were dismantled. Many employees initially struggled to grasp the full scale of the shift, but as the new model took shape, the benefits became evident.

## Building an Agile Organisation

By spring 2015, the headquarters of ING Netherlands had transformed its traditional structure into a more agile organisation consisting of tribes, squads, and chapters. Thirteen **tribes** were established to focus on specific domains such as mortgages, securities, and private banking. Each tribe was led by a leader who set priorities, managed budgets, and facilitated knowledge-sharing both within and across tribes. The tribe leader was also responsible for creating cross-disciplinary self-steering **squads** of nine or fewer members (with input from tribe members), to address specific customer needs. These squads were composed of a mix of marketing specialists, data analysts, user-experience designers, IT engineers, and product specialists. One squad member was designated as the **product owner** and was responsible for coordinating activities and setting priorities. The squads remained together until the customer need was met, with task completion times ranging from two weeks to eighteen months. Some squads disbanded and the members joined new ones, while others that were working well stayed together and tackled additional customer needs. In this sense, ING's agile organisational model had no fixed structure – it constantly evolved. **Chapters**, finally, brought together members with similar disciplines, such as data analytics or systems processes, who were spread across different squads. The chapter leads were in charge of monitoring and sharing the best practices and taking care of professional development and performance evaluations. The chapters served as a way to maintain the beneficial aspects of conventional management while eliminating tedious hand-offs and bureaucracy.

The various business units at ING had the autonomy to manage their daily operations and determine their own objectives. Yet such autonomy did not necessarily imply a lack of order and common direction. At ING, clear rules and safeguards were implemented that were meant to maintain organisational stability. For example, each tribe was assigned agile coaches who assisted in fostering productive collaboration among the squads and individuals by encouraging problem-solving at the grassroots level, instead of relying on higher-ups to resolve issues. Another illustration of such safeguards can be found in the regular evaluations incorporated into the system. Every day, squads jointly looked at expectations, headway, and goals during stand-up meetings. Every fourteen days, squads reviewed their progress. Furthermore, during quarterly business reviews, each tribe was expected to showcase its achievements, key insights gained, and future goals, recognising both successes and challenges, and identifying any other tribe or squad with which it would need to collaborate. The reports from such quarterly reviews were openly accessible to all tribes, inviting them to provide input and feedback, which was transparently disseminated throughout the bank.

For ING, adopting agile practices represented a radical departure from the previous hierarchical mode of operation, where goals were set by managers. Now, leaders served as facilitators and sounding boards for the teams who were empowered to determine their own paths to success. By working in cross-functional, small teams, squad members could quickly resolve problems that might have otherwise been hindered by departmental silos. Additionally, the hands-on experience of bringing a project from start to finish seemed to give each squad a sense of pride and a connection to the customer. Bart Schlatmann, COO at ING Netherlands, commented on this: ‘the whole atmosphere of the organisation is much more that of a tech campus than an old-style traditional bank where people were locked away behind closed doors’.

### Challenges and Lessons Learnt

The shift to agile working brought undeniable benefits, but it also posed challenges. While the model excelled at driving incremental innovation, it proved more difficult to implement large-scale, disruptive changes. As teams were autonomous and nimble, they tended to focus on the tangible improvements they could achieve here and now. Hence, the challenge in this new way of working was ensuring that teams stayed aligned with the company’s overarching goals and objectives. Without regular alignment check-ins, there was a possibility that individuals would pursue their own initiatives that may not align with the company’s strategic priorities. To avoid this, leaders needed to offer sufficient direction and support to secure alignment, yet refrain from controlling too stringently how such directions would ultimately be pursued. Rather than explicitly telling employees to build a bridge – or hoping that someone would focus on crossing the river at all – leaders were expected to point their co-workers in the right direction, but let them figure out how to proceed from there.

Additionally, some employees found the transition difficult, particularly those accustomed to hierarchical structures. The emphasis on autonomy and self-direction required a shift in mindset, and not everyone adapted at the same pace. Training and support systems became essential to help employees navigate the new work environment. Furthermore, agility required ongoing commitment; without continuous reinforcement, old habits risked resurfacing. Leaders had to ensure that agile principles were not just implemented as a one-time initiative but became ingrained in the company's DNA.

### Results and Pride

ING's leadership took a bold leap, but the results validated the decision. The bank achieved significant efficiency gains, reducing handovers and improving productivity despite a reduction in workforce. Employees reported higher engagement, and customer satisfaction soared. Two years after implementation, ING staff overwhelmingly preferred the new way of working over the old hierarchical model. Encouraged by these results, the company scaled its agile approach to other countries and units across ING.

As ING's transformation gained attention, other organisations sought to learn from its experience. The bank became a global reference for agility, attracting visitors eager to understand its model. Recognising the widespread interest, ING even created dedicated teams to host study tours for other companies.

For ING, agility became more than a methodology – it became a mindset that reshaped the way the entire organisation functioned. The company recognised that adopting agile was not just about introducing new team structures; it was about fostering a collaborative, customer-centric culture that empowered employees to take ownership of their work.

### Reflect

1. What makes the agile different from traditional ways of working? Or is it essentially nothing new under the sun?
2. How did the agile way of working improve ING's ability to change?
3. ING utilised a 'big-bang' approach. What could be the benefits/drawbacks of this approach?

### Case Study Sources

Barton, D., Carey, D., & Charan, R. (2017, March–April). One bank's agile team experiment. *Harvard Business Review*, https://hbr.org/2018/03/one-banks-agile-team-experiment.

Economist Impact. (2022). Agile banking transformation. www.scribd.com/document/703451138/Economist-Agile-banking-transformation.

ING. (2017, 23 November). Squads, sprints, and standups – Working agile in a big multinational: What's it like? https://ing.com/news/2020/07/squads-sprints-and-stand-ups.html.

Mahadevan, D. (2017, 10 January). ING's agile transformation. *McKinsey Quarterly*, www.mckinsey.com/industries/financial-services/our-insights/ings-agile-transformation.

Schotkamp, T., & Danoesastro, M. (2018, 1 June). HR's pioneering role in agile at ING. *BCG*, www.bcg.com/publications/2018/human-resources-pioneering-role-agile-ing.
van Kemenade, R. (2016, 27 July). *The agile transformation at ING* [video]. www.youtube.com/watch?v=EKEaMeaiZOw.

## REFERENCES


[1] Amit, R., & Schoemaker, P. J. (1993). Strategic assets and organizational rent. *Strategic Management Journal, 14*(1), 33–46.
[2] Ansoff, H. I. (1965). *Corporate strategy: An analytic approach to business policy for growth and expansion*. New York: McGraw-Hill.
[3] Arndt, F., & Pierce, L. (2017). The behavioral and evolutionary roots of dynamic capabilities. *Industrial and Corporate Change, 27*(2), 413–424.
[4] Augier, M., & Teece, D. J. (2009). Dynamic capabilities and the role of managers in business strategy and economic performance. *Organization Science, 20*(2), 410–421.
[5] Bahrami, H. (1992). The emerging flexible organization: Perspectives from Silicon Valley. *California Management Review, 34*(4), 33–52.
[6] Barney, J. (1991). Firm resources and sustained competitive advantage. *Journal of Management, 17*(1), 99–120.
[7] Barreto, I. (2010). Dynamic capabilities: A review of past research and an agenda for the future. *Journal of Management, 36*(1), 256–280.
[8] Birkinshaw, J. (2017). What to expect from agile. *MIT Sloan Management Review, 59*(2), 39–42.
[9] Bowman, C., & Ambrosini, V. (2003). How the resource-based and the dynamic capability views of the firm inform corporate-level strategy. *British Journal of Management, 14*(4), 289–303.
[10] Brozovic, D. (2018). Strategic flexibility: A review of the literature. *International Journal of Management Reviews, 20*(1), 3–31.
[11] Cannon, M. D., & Edmondson, A. C. (2005). Failing to learn and learning to fail (intelligently): How great organizations put failure to work to innovate and improve. *Long Range Planning, 38*(3), 299–319.
[12] Crozier, M. (1993). Will a new logic of management emerge? In J. Child, M. Crozier, & R. Mayntz (eds.), *Societal change between market and organization* (pp. 19–29). Aldershot: Avebury.
[13] D'Aveni, R. A. (1994). *Hypercompetition: Managing the dynamics of strategic maneuvering*. New York: Free Press.
[14] D'Aveni, R. A. (1998). Waking up to the new era of hypercompetition. *Washington Quarterly, 21*(1), 183–195.
[15] Di Stefano, G., Peteraf, M., & Verona, G. (2010). Dynamic capabilities deconstructed: A bibliographic investigation into the origins, development, and future directions of the research domain. *Industrial and Corporate Change, 19*(4), 1187–1204.
[16] Doz, Y., & Kosonen, M. (2008). The dynamics of strategic agility: Nokia's rollercoaster experience. *California Management Review, 50*(3), 95–118.
[17] Doz, Y., & Kosonen, M. (2010). Embedding strategic agility: A leadership agenda for accelerating business model renewal. *Long Range Planning, 43*(2), 370–382.
[18] Easterby-Smith, M., Lyles, M. A., & Peteraf, M. A. (2009). Dynamic capabilities: Current debates and future directions. *British Journal of Management, 20*, S1–S8.
[19] Eisenhardt, K. M. (1989). Making fast strategic decisions in high-velocity environments. *Academy of Management Journal, 32*(3), 543–576.

[20] Eisenhardt, K. M., & Martin, J. A. (2000). Dynamic capabilities: What are they? *Strategic Management Journal*, *21*(10–11), 1105–1121.

[21] Eppink, D. J. (1978). Planning for strategic flexibility. *Long Range Planning*, *11*(4), 9–15.

[22] Eriksson, T. (2014). Processes, antecedents and outcomes of dynamic capabilities. *Scandinavian Journal of Management*, *30*(1), 65–82.

[23] Felin, T., & Powell, T. C. (2016). Designing organizations for dynamic capabilities. *California Management Review*, *58*(4), 78–96.

[24] Fowler, M., & Highsmith, J. (2001). The agile manifesto. *Software Development*, *9*(8), 28–35.

[25] Hayes, R., & Pisano, G. (1994). Beyond world class: The new manufacturing strategy. *Harvard Business Review*, *72*(1), 77–86.

[26] Helfat, C. E., Finkelstein, S., Mitchell, W., Peteraf, M., Singh, H., Teece, D. J., & Winter, S. G. (2007). *Dynamic capabilities: Understanding strategic change in organizations*. Malden: Blackwell.

[27] Helfat, C. E., & Peteraf, M. A. (2015). Managerial cognitive capabilities and the microfoundations of dynamic capabilities. *Strategic Management Journal*, *36*(6), 831–850.

[28] Hitt, M. A., Keats, B. W., & DeMarie, S. M. (1998). Navigating in the new competitive landscape: Building strategic flexibility and competitive advantage in the 21st century. *Academy of Management Perspectives*, *12*(4), 22–42.

[29] Kraatz, M. S., & Zajac, E. J. (2001). How organizational resources affect strategic change and performance in turbulent environments: Theory and evidence. *Organization Science*, *12*(5), 632–657.

[30] Krijnen, H. G. (1979). The flexible firm. *Long Range Planning*, *12*(2), 63–75.

[31] Levitt, T. (1983). The globalization of markets. *Harvard Business Review*, *61*(3), 92–102.

[32] Mascarenhas, M. B. (1981). Planning for flexibility. *Long Range Planning*, *14*(5), 78–82.

[33] McCann, J. E., & Selsky, J. (1984). Hyperturbulence and the emergence of type 5 environments. *Academy of Management Review*, *9*(3), 460–470.

[34] Pascale, R., Millemann, M., & Gioja, L. (1997). Changing the way we change. *Harvard Business Review*, *75*(6), 126–139.

[35] Penrose, E. (1959). *The theory of the growth of the firm*. New York: John Wiley and Sons.

[36] Pisano, G. P. (2000). In search of dynamic capabilities: The origins of R&D competence in biopharmaceuticals. In G. Dosi, R. R. Nelson, & S. G. Winter (eds.), *The nature and dynamics of organizational capabilities* (pp. 129–154). New York: Oxford University Press.

[37] Rindova, V. P., & Kotha, S. (2001). Continuous 'morphing': Competing through dynamic capabilities, form, and function. *Academy of Management Journal*, *44*(6), 1263–1280.

[38] Teece, D. J. (2007). Explicating dynamic capabilities: The nature and microfoundations of (sustainable) enterprise performance. *Strategic Management Journal*, *28*(13), 1319–1350.

[39] Teece, D. J. (2012). Dynamic capabilities: Routines versus entrepreneurial action. *Journal of Management Studies*, *49*(8), 1395–1401.

[40] Teece, D. J. (2014). The foundations of enterprise performance: Dynamic and ordinary capabilities in an (economic) theory of firms. *Academy of Management Perspectives*, *28*(4), 328–352.

[41] Teece, D. J., Pisano, G., & Shuen, A. (1997). Dynamic capabilities and strategic management. *Strategic Management Journal*, *18*(7), 509–533.

[42] Weber, Y., & Tarba, S. Y. (2014). Strategic agility: A state of the art. *California Management Review*, *56*(3), 5–12.

[43] Weick, K. E., & Quinn, R. E. (1999). Organizational change and development. *Annual Review of Psychology*, *50*(1), 361–386.

[44] Winby, S., & Worley, C. G. (2014). Management processes for agility, speed, and innovation. *Organizational Dynamics*, *43*(3), 225–234.

[45] Winter, S. G. (2003). Understanding dynamic capabilities. *Strategic Management Journal*, *24*(10), 991–995.

[46] Worley, C. G., Williams, T., & Lawler III, E. E. (2014). *The agility factor: Building adaptable organizations for superior performance*. Hoboken, NJ: John Wiley and Sons.

[47] Zollo, M., & Winter, S. G. (2002). Deliberate learning and the evolution of dynamic capabilities. *Organization Science*, *13*(3), 339–351.

# 7 A Paradox Perspective on Change

## PERSPECTIVE IN BRIEF

- **Concepts related to the perspective** – ambidexterity, exploration-exploitation, and paradoxes in change
- **Keep reading to learn more about** – strategy and sustaining organisational change
- **Prime contributors** – J. Birkinshaw, M. Lewis, J. March, C. O'Reilly, W. Smith, M. Tushman, and H. Volberda
- **Guiding metaphor** – change as yin and yang

## Introduction

When people first start working in an organisation, they often believe that clear-cut solutions exist for every problem. Employees are frustrated about not having a say in important decisions? Simply loosen control and involve them more. Customers going elsewhere because your goals are not sustainable enough? Just emphasise your social responsibility. Resources are available but don't fully meet market expectations? Double down and find a way to make the most of them. For most people starting out, organisational problems are often made sense of in an 'either A or B' way: that is, if we can only learn how to pick the right option, we believe that we will eventually do well.

Yet, with time, most people come to realise that organisational problems rarely allow for such simple answers. In reality, organisations need both control over employees *and* their cooperation. They must pursue a just cause while also ensuring financial viability. They have to leverage existing resources while adapting to changing market demands. Unlike a situation that is characterised by simple tension, these problems cannot – and should not – really be 'resolved': successfully navigating them does not mean discovering which side of the spectrum to opt for but figuring out how you can continuously keep closely attuned with both conflicting ends. In a word, these problems are paradoxical in nature – and organisations, it turns out, are full of them.

Change presents a similar challenge. Just as firms may experience simultaneous conflicting needs for control and cooperation or purpose and profit, changing organisations sustainably may require coping with two seemingly contradictory forces: between stability and innovation, or tradition and transformation. Like the Taoist seeking harmony between yin and yang, organisations must navigate these seemingly contradicting forces to achieve sustainable growth.

The **paradox perspective** on change encourages us to embrace this dynamic interplay rather than becoming gridlocked by it. It highlights how effective change management is not about picking a single path but about harmonising competing forces to ensure both immediate effectiveness and long-term adaptability. The perspective challenges conventional wisdom about change as a linear or clear-cut process, instead portraying it as an ongoing balance between seemingly contradictory demands.

In this chapter, we will explore what it means to approach organisational change from a paradox perspective. We will examine how organisations can benefit from adopting this mindset, investigate practical tools for managing competing demands, and consider how embracing paradoxes can lead to more durable organisational change.

## 7.1 The Genesis of Thought

As with every perspective discussed so far, thinking paradoxically about organisational change has some clear roots. The following two developments are the most noteworthy.

### 7.1.1 Connecting the Dots between Exploration and Exploitation

With all of the perspectives discussed so far, one striking feature stands out: they are all primarily concerned with the dynamics of change itself. While stability often appears in the background, it is typically cast as something to overcome or at least outgrow – an obstacle to tackle by effective change agents. In this framing, change is treated as a distinct and self-contained topic, largely divorced from the day-to-day work of running reliable operations. Managers, it seems, have to choose: either focus on driving transformation or concentrate on maintaining order – but not both at once.[3, 8, 17, 37]

Yet by the early 1990s, some thinkers began to recognise that an organisation's capacity for change and innovation – its activities of 'exploration' – could simply not be fully understood without also considering its pursuit of stability and efficiency – its 'exploitation' activities. Specifically, there was always a trade-off to be considered: resources allocated to explorative efforts such as research and development (R&D) were, by definition, unavailable for exploitative tasks like process optimisation – and vice versa.[27] Both were deemed essential for long-term success, yet they competed for the same limited attention, funding, and managerial bandwidth. As a result, organisations had to always make conscious (and unconscious) choices about where to focus, balancing the push for novelty with the pull of reliability.

This seemingly simple insight marked a sharp departure from earlier thinking. Previously, it was assumed that competing demands were best handled by committing consistently to either one or the other. Now, such demands were increasingly framed as paradoxes, with both opposing ends to be managed in tandem.[32, 36] The central challenge of organisational success, then, was reframed: it was not just about embracing change or mastering stability but about navigating the dynamic balance between exploration and exploitation.

### 7.1.2 When Change Theories Fall Short in Practice

Some years after these observations, both scholars and practitioners started to recognise that the impact of change initiatives on practice was disappointingly limited, despite decades of development in the field. Change initiatives continued to report low success rates, and companies faced increasingly shortened lifespans.[29] As more incumbent firms struggled to adapt to disruptive innovation,[10] confidence in traditional change theories began to erode. After all, what was the value of change frameworks if they couldn't deliver better outcomes? And was change alone sufficient or did it need to be reconciled with the more stable, enduring aspects of organising?

Influenced by the exploration-exploitation logic outlined earlier,[27] many began to question the prevailing tendency to treat change and organising as separate, even opposing, concerns. Rather than prioritising change over stability, a more integrated view began to take shape.[4] While change remained important – especially in the face of technological shifts, political upheaval, and economic volatility – it was increasingly seen as insufficient on its own. Enduring success also required alignment: the ability to coordinate value creation, leverage internal capabilities, and optimise operations.[24, 25, 30, 40, 41]

This reconceptualisation shifted the lens: organisations were cast no longer solely as agents of change but as entities navigating the balance between adaptation and coherence. To make change meaningful and sustainable, it had to be reconciled with continuity – bringing together traditions of thought that had long seemed at odds.

> **Box 7.1 The Point?**
>
> As managers and researchers came to see that a firm's ability to explore was often inseparable from its capacity to exploit, a new way of thinking took hold. Theories advocating unrestrained change had proven less effective than hoped, and gradually a paradoxical perspective on change began to crystallise. In Section 7.2, we take a closer look at what this paradoxical view entails.

## 7.2 Unpacking the Heart

It used to be that those interested in uncovering the mysteries of yin and yang were to go meditating on a lonely mountain somewhere in the Chinese highlands. You will be pleased to learn that such an act of reclusion is no longer necessary: today, reading the next few pages will get you started. When tapping into the essence of what the paradox perspective entails for organisations dealing with change, four core tenets should be highlighted (see Figure 7.1).

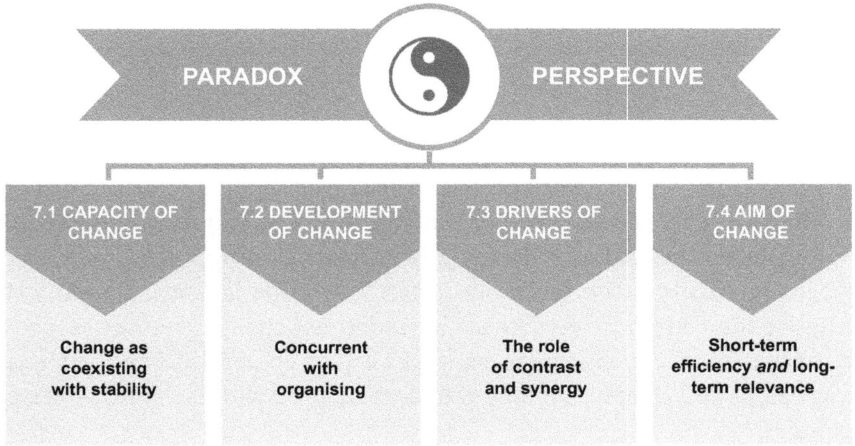


**Figure 7.1** Unpacking the heart of the paradox perspective.

## 7.2.1 Capacity of Change: Change as Coexisting with Stability

At its core, the paradox perspective calls for a **reconciliation of change and stability**. Rather than viewing change in isolation, it emphasises that meaningful transformation must be balanced with considerations of efficiency, routine, and continuity. Put differently, if change represents the dynamic, white half of the yin-yang symbol, it must be counterbalanced by the grounded, black half of stability. In this view, change and stability are treated no longer as opposing or sequential states but as interdependent forces that coexist and enable one another.[29]

For example, if you, as a manager, decide to move forward with a drastic new change programme, you need to be aware of the repercussions that said programme may have on your organisation's capacity to steadily meet its clients' needs. As the organisation will be in turmoil, it is possible that its ongoing operations may suffer – for instance, when some of your employees forget to respond to an important customer enquiry due to ongoing change stress. The right amount of change thus becomes a question of balance. If your organisation is only able to change on the dime, its customers will likely forsake it for a more trustworthy or cheaper competitor; yet, if your company is only able to offer steady services, it will probably see its relevance in the marketplace diminish over time. In this sense, according to the paradox perspective, the real organisational challenge lies in continuously living through both change and stability. Such contradiction is not to be resolved but to be accepted, embraced, and made the most of.[31, 40]

### Box 7.2 Be Aware!

Before you squat down in lotus position and consider yourself the Zen master, know that successfully maintaining balance between change and stability is not easy. In fact, keeping in touch with both requires continuous tending to.[13, 39] While managers can always take measures that can restore harmony – for example, by revising structure or by altering incentive mechanisms – such balancing acts tend not to last forever: shifts in political behaviour, customer demands, or competitor strength (to name but a few) may lead organisations to again emphasise either too much exploration or too much exploitation over time.[21] In this way, the harmony called for between the two counterparts is not to be understood as static and fixed, but should instead be looked at as dynamic and ongoing – as an act of balancing more than as balance in itself.[19, 23, 33] Think of it not in terms of a set of scales but rather as an artist walking a tightrope. For a ropewalker, retaining balance is not a one-time effort: they are able to keep standing upright only by continuously making small adjustments to their distribution of weight. For the organisation balancing between stability and change, the effort is not all that different.

By emphasising change as a question of sensible inclusion, the paradox perspective represents a clear shift away from the either/or focus that long dominated the conversation.[23, 29] Now, building a competitive advantage is deemed to require a sustained bond between two starkly contrasting forces, with the benefits of either only being realised through sensible integration.[2]

### 7.2.2 Development of Change: Concurrent with Organising

Having established that advantage stems from integrating opposites, the next step is to consider how this plays out in practice. From a paradox perspective, managing change is inseparable from **managing the broader organisation** – its structures, cultures, strategies, and systems – all of which must be configured to sustain both stability and transformation.[13, 19, 40] In this sense, a paradox perspective places the act of changing in parallel to the act of organising – with the firm's entire way of doing things becoming pertinent.

Imagine a multinational technology company. To achieve a balance between change and stability, the company might adopt a dual structure: one division is dedicated to R&D, focusing on exploring new technologies and products, while another division is tasked with refining and optimising the production and delivery of established offerings. The company's culture is deliberately crafted to support this duality, encouraging creativity and risk-taking in the R&D division while promoting efficiency and precision in the operations division. Managerial roles are designed to bridge these divisions, with leaders tasked not only with overseeing their respective areas but also with fostering collaboration and knowledge-sharing between them. Incentive plans are tailored to reward both innovation and operational excellence, ensuring that employees are motivated to contribute to both the company's growth and its stability. In this way, the organisation's entire configuration – from its structure and culture to its strategy and incentives – is aligned to manage the paradox of change and stability, allowing the company to thrive in a competitive and dynamic environment.

This attention to organising does not limit itself to any particular level:[5] from a paradox view, all levels can contribute to balancing change and stability. From individuals to teams, subunits, broader units, and even the entire firm ... All levels can – and should – be looked at when dealing with the question of how to harmonise change with non-change. In most cases, lower levels can help higher levels to live through contradictory tensions noted.[33] For instance, a business unit may achieve both exploration and exploitation by setting up two subdivisions with complementary targets,[4] or a team may reconcile these contradictory notions by assigning participating individuals to different roles.[22] In this sense, not only does the paradox perspective link the act of changing with organising in a horizontal way (meaning, across units or functions), it also calls for dealing with such interactions vertically, through hierarchy.

**Box 7.3 The Point?**

A paradox perspective emphasises that effective management of an organisation involves harmonising change and stability across all aspects of its configuration. By aligning structure, culture, strategy, technology, and incentives, organisations can create an environment where innovation and efficiency coexist, enabling them to adapt to change while maintaining the reliability necessary for ongoing success.

### 7.2.3 Drivers of Change: The Role of Contrast and Synergy

At first glance, the yin-yang symbol is all about **contrast** – black against white, each the opposite of the other. But look closer and you'll notice something else: balance and **synergy**. Despite their differences, the two halves fit together seamlessly, forming a perfect whole.

Thinking about change and stability through a paradoxical lens reveals a similar dynamic. While they may seem like opposing forces, they are deeply interconnected, working together to drive an organisation's ongoing evolution. Rather than representing a zero-sum game – where one must weaken for the other to thrive – change and stability are believed to reinforce each other. Strengthening an organisation's ability to adapt can create greater stability, while reinforcing stability can provide a stronger foundation for innovation and transformation.[15, 38]

Diversity and experimentation, for example, can drive change and innovation while also ensuring more stable operations during disturbances. To illustrate this point, just imagine a car manufacturer that has always been experimenting prolifically with different engine types. In this firm, there is a good chance that operations are far less bothered by the trend of electrification than the operations of its more conservative peers. In this sense, the company's emphasis on change has, ironically enough, made it easier for it to keep steady in the long run.

Similarly, stable mechanisms such as routines and control may support stability while also fostering adaptability, innovation, and exploration. For instance, if your pharmaceutical company is able to rely on a rigorous set of R&D processes that run like clockwork, it will probably be more likely to ultimately churn out a new groundbreaking drug. Here, having routine processes makes it easier to ultimately push for change.

**Box 7.4 The Point?**

Achieving either change or stability may benefit from the presence of the other – it all depends on how we look at these phenomena. This means that while organisations may need to pay attention to both change and stability, they may not necessarily be mutually exclusive activities. When done well, each penny spent on either may ultimately generate returns on both.

### 7.2.4 Aim of Change: Short-Term Efficiency and Long-Term Relevance

If change and stability can reinforce one another, then the aim of managing their balance goes beyond theory – it becomes a question of organisational longevity. From a paradox perspective, the harmonic balance between change and stability is not to be looked after for fun: it is meant to take care of the very success that a company can hope to accomplish in **the short term and in the long term**.[15]

From a paradox view, being obsessed with fluidity is just as harmful as being knee-deep in rigid bureaucratic policy.[13] To understand why, imagine two companies. The first is holding true to the way things have been done for years; the second is transforming its processes, structures, and values according to every changing whim. Now, while the former would quickly fail to remain relevant in a world that is constantly developing, the latter would soon find itself outcompeted by those that are more operationally savvy. Generally, it takes time for people to adopt a new approach – and during that time, other, more experienced firms may offer a better service. In this sense, when a company changes incessantly without retaining a sense of stability, it opens itself up to competition from peers that are more operationally grounded. Retaining a proper balance between change and stability ultimately aims at securing both long-term relevance and short-term efficiency – however precarious such a balancing act may prove to be.[11, 33]

As a result, leadership should concern itself with aligning strategy, structure, culture, and processes, all while preparing for environmental change.[39] From a paradoxical angle, the ability to effectively balance both change and stability is what sets successful organisations, groups, and individuals apart. Rather than making a choice between either change or stability, entities should work to develop the capacity to handle both and create an environment of dynamic tension that provides a competitive edge. Embracing this duality, rather than avoiding it, enables organisations to outshine those who have opted for a more simplified approach. The contradiction and friction inherent in this balancing act can be challenging, but it is precisely in this zone of discomfort that organisations can find the strength and adaptability to thrive.[13]

## 7.3 Extending Your Toolkit

Now that we've unpacked the essence of a paradox perspective, let's bring it to life with practical frameworks. One of the most valuable tools to add to your strategic toolkit here is the concept of **ambidexterity**. Borrowed from its everyday meaning – the ability to use both hands equally well – the term was first introduced in an organisational context to describe firms that have dual structures to handle operations with different time frames or management needs.[12] Over time, this idea evolved, shifting its focus to an organisation's ability to balance both incremental and radical change.[39] Today, ambidexterity is widely understood as the capacity to excel in current business operations while remaining flexible and responsive to future challenges.[32] It's this final definition that has been largely retained.

Although the conversation on ambidexterity is one of many dealing with the idea of harmonising change and stability, it does stand out for having brought forth several concrete tracks for how to make the idea work in practice. In what follows, I will touch upon three distinct approaches: (i) temporal ambidexterity; (ii) structural ambidexterity; and (iii) contextual ambidexterity.

### 7.3.1 Temporal Ambidexterity

One of the most basic ways of balancing efficiency and flexibility is to do both at different times: **temporal ambidexterity** refers to the ability of organisations to switch back and forth between a focus on exploration (i.e., change) and exploitation (i.e., stability), depending on what the environment and internal workings require. At one instance, workers may focus on predictable tasks, only to switch to more novel tasks later on. In this way, the organisation succeeds to do both by shifting emphasis.[14, 35] Historic examples of this kind of harmonisation between change and stability include, among others, the Toyota Motor Corporation, where workers repeatedly shifted between their standard production tasks and more flexible roles focused on improvement initiatives, such as participating in quality circles, conducting trial runs, or taking on short-term projects with the Pilot Team.[1] This requires strong leadership and a flexible organisational structure that can adapt to changing needs and goals. By being able to sequence a focus on exploration and exploitation, an organisation can both create new opportunities and capitalise on existing ones, allowing it to remain competitive and relevant over time.

To see why this could be useful, just imagine a software company that alternates between product development and maintenance. During the development cycle, teams focus on exploration – designing new features, experimenting with innovative technologies, and pushing the boundaries of what their software can achieve. This phase is characterised by a more informal, creative environment where rapid prototyping and iterative testing are encouraged. Once the product is launched, the focus shifts to exploitation. The same teams now prioritise stability – addressing bugs, optimising performance, and ensuring that the software runs smoothly. This phase requires a more formalised approach, with established procedures and rigorous quality checks. By switching between these phases, the company can continuously innovate while maintaining the reliability and performance of its existing products.

> **Box 7.5 Be Aware!**
>
> A common criticism of temporal ambidexterity is that it is not really all that ambidextrous: as the organisation essentially oscillates between states of stability and change, temporal ambidexterity does not exactly allow an organisation to do both at the same time. The next approach, however, addresses that issue, proposing structural, rather than time-based, separation.

### 7.3.2 Structural Ambidexterity

A second track for acting out the tenets of a paradox perspective is what has been labelled **structural ambidexterity**. Rather than addressing the contradicting demands of change and stability at different moments in time, organisations can do both by sensibly leveraging their structure. Two options stand out.

First, one can choose to **spatially separate** business units with different emphases. This means that leaders set up a corporate structure in which some business units focus more on novel and dynamic tasks, and others take up the more routine and operationally focused activities. Both types of unit are physically separated, thus preserving the autonomy of their operations, culture, and ways of thinking.[14]

A good example of structural ambidexterity is multinationals that acquire promising start-ups: while the start-up will become part of the corporate portfolio from the acquisition onwards, it will typically remain a separate entity. By doing this, the multinational behemoth can ensure to keep focused on its steady course, while the start-up is able to remain operating in the same flexible way that allowed it to be creative and innovative.[16, 20, 23]

Second, one can also choose to **partition tasks**, assigning different types of job to different subgroups within a unit. Under such task-partitioning, one subgroup can come to fall under a more command-and-control type of regime, with another subgroup being managed more organically.[1, 19] While the business unit will still be addressed as one entity, reality will thus be somewhat more segregated, with the unit representing a mix of differentiated subgroups.

Think about what large financial services firms look like nowadays. In most, there will be a clear partitioning in distinct subgroups within the same firm. A traditional banking team, responsible for managing established products like loans, savings accounts, and mortgages, may operate under a command-and-control structure. This subgroup focuses on risk management, compliance, and efficiency, with clear hierarchies and standardised procedures ensuring that operations are stable and secure. Meanwhile, a fintech innovation team, tasked with developing new digital banking solutions, operates under a more organic management style. This subgroup encourages experimentation, rapid iteration, and cross-functional collaboration, with a flat structure that promotes creativity and agility. While both subgroups contribute to the firm's broader goals, they function differently to best suit the nature of their tasks. This partitioning allows the firm to maintain the reliability and compliance necessary in traditional banking while fostering the innovation required to stay competitive in the rapidly evolving fintech landscape.

### Box 7.6 Be Aware!

Given the significant amount of physical separation that this track suggests, it should not come as a surprise that structural ambidexterity has been criticised for overlooking problems of reintegration, that is, how to eventually bring back together what has been created separately.[19] In a final ambidexterity track, this pitfall is explicitly addressed[34] – leading to a paradoxical interweaving of stability and change not through separation but through context management.

## 7.3.3 Contextual Ambidexterity

A final track in the ambidexterity conversation is what has been noted as **contextual ambidexterity**. In this line of thinking, it is the individual who is responsible for balancing the contradictory demands of change and stability, seamlessly navigating between different paradigms in their daily actions.[34] To allow someone to perform such a difficult balancing act, the organisational context – or the systems, processes, and beliefs that shape individuals' behaviour in an organisation – is key.[7, 18] Specifically, the context must be organised so that four specific attributes – discipline, stretch, support, and trust – are promoted. When these are taken care of, both change and stability are believed to almost naturally occur.[19]

First, the organisation's context must induce members to work towards the fulfilment of all pledges made. To nurture such **discipline**, managers should focus on setting clear standards for performance and behaviour, this by installing a clear system of candid feedback, and advancing incentive mechanisms that both motivate proper behaviour and sanction improper conduct.[19]

### Box 7.7 Practical Advice?

How to promote discipline in practice:

- Performance standards – review whether clear and measurable performance standards are established and communicated to all employees.
- Feedback mechanisms – check if there is a consistent and transparent system for providing candid feedback on performance and behaviour.
- Incentive systems – evaluate whether the incentive mechanisms effectively reward proper behaviour and appropriately sanction improper conduct.
- Consistency in enforcement – ensure that rules and standards are applied consistently across all levels of the organisation, without exceptions.

Second, the context must push members to keep striving for more ambitious objectives. To nurture **stretch**, managers can work on a shared vision, on setting out a shared sense of identity, and on emphasising the contribution of the individual to the larger whole.[19]

### Box 7.8 Practical Advice?

How to promote stretch in practice:

- Shared vision – assess if the organisation's vision is well articulated and if employees understand how their roles contribute to this larger goal.
- Ambitious goal-setting – verify that goals are set at challenging levels, pushing individuals and teams to strive for continuous improvement.
- Recognition of efforts – review if individual contributions to the organisation's success are regularly acknowledged and celebrated.

Third, the context must nudge members towards helping each other out. Managers can allow **support** by providing organisational members the freedom to access resources available to others, by promoting initiative at lower hierarchical levels, and by giving guidance rather than strictly exercising authority.[19]

### Box 7.9 Practical Advice?

How to promote support in practice:

- Resource accessibility – confirm that employees have the freedom and tools to access resources across different departments or teams as needed.
- Empowerment – evaluate if employees at lower hierarchical levels are encouraged to take initiative and make decisions within their scope of work.
- Guidance versus authority – ensure that managers focus more on providing guidance and support rather than strictly exercising top-down authority.

Finally, the context must drive members to have confidence in the commitments of their fellow colleagues. Managers can develop **trust** by showcasing fairness and equity in decision-making, by involving individuals in decisions affecting them, and by staffing positions with people capable of what is expected.[19]

### Box 7.10 Practical Advice?

How to promote trust in practice:

- Fair decision-making – review decision-making processes to ensure that they are perceived as fair and equitable by employees at all levels.
- Inclusive decision-making – check if employees are meaningfully involved in decisions that impact their work or roles.

- Competency-based staffing – evaluate whether positions are filled with individuals who are competent and capable of meeting the organisation's expectations.
- Transparency – confirm that communication within the organisation is open and that information is shared transparently, to build trust among team members.

Contextual ambidexterity requires organisations to find the right combination of discipline, stretch, support, and trust that will allow them to achieve both short-term performance and long-term growth. If these attributes are imbued in the organisational context, it is argued that ambidexterity will come almost naturally, through individual behaviour.[19]

## 7.4 Impact on the Ground

If you've made it this far, you'll appreciate that upholding a paradoxical perspective is hard work. However, although inherently demanding, it should be noted that a paradoxical mindset offers distinct advantages for those working with change. The most notable benefits are as follows.

### 7.4.1 A Paradox Perspective Balances Out Change

In traditional views, successful change is often regarded with almost reverent awe – a holy grail that organisations are compelled to pursue if they intend to stay competitive. Change is often associated with positive attributes such as progress, development, and innovation, while non-change is often devalued as being uninspired or stagnant. According to the paradox perspective, this univocal hailing of change just doesn't cut it: although change and stability both have perks, they also have specific drawbacks – with one not topping the other. The result is a fundamental ambivalence about what is often called 'innovation' and even progress.[13]

For example, imagine a tech company that is constantly pushing for innovation. While this drive for change can lead to groundbreaking products, it can also result in burnout, a lack of focus, and a disconnect from core competencies. By adopting a paradox perspective, the company might recognise the value in periodically slowing down to consolidate gains, optimise existing products, and ensure that its innovations are aligned with its long-term strategy. This approach prevents the organisation from becoming overly obsessed with fluidity and perpetual transformation, allowing it to maintain a healthy balance between change and stability.

Consequently, one of the major benefits of thinking paradoxically is that it redirects the conversation away from a state of absolute change, which leaves little to no room for stability.[29] If anything, the perspective's emphasis on retaining a sense of harmony with stability counteracts the trend towards excessive change and helps to correct organisations from becoming overly focused on transformation[34] – hence cutting loose the stereotype of new organisational forms as being overly fixated on fluidity.[14]

### 7.4.2 A Paradox Perspective Puts Boundaries on Change

Furthermore, the paradox perspective reasserts the importance of maintaining boundaries in the face of change. Many other approaches to change implicitly encourage organisations to align as closely as possible with their external environment – mirroring the movements of suppliers, customers, competitors, and other outside forces. This often leads to a mindset of continuous adaptation, where responsiveness is prioritised above all else. When taken too far, such constant alignment can erode an organisation's core identity and operational coherence.

In contrast, the paradox perspective warns that blurring corporate boundaries in pursuit of flexibility can undermine the very foundations of organising. While adaptation is necessary, so too are elements like stability, structure, and a clear sense of purpose. Unrestrained improvisation in response to every environmental shift risks displacing these anchors, leaving the firm fragmented and directionless. Paradox thinking, therefore, calls for a more balanced approach – one that embraces responsiveness without sacrificing internal integrity.

> **Box 7.11 The Point?**
>
> By connecting change to core concepts such as identity, institutional logics, and culture, the paradox perspective not only sheds light on the topic of change but also provides a more comprehensive perspective on organising.[6] By interlacing these ideas, the paradox perspective implicitly steps up the game of change theory, moving it away from the niche in which it was originally constituted and pushing it more towards the realms of overarching organisational theory.[5, 15]

## 7.5 Drawbacks and Pitfalls

Still, every strength carries its shadow. Even as the paradox perspective puts change in perspective and extends it into the broader terrain of organising, it brings with it several pitfalls that cannot be ignored. Three stand out.

### 7.5.1 A Paradox Perspective May Kindle Unrealistic Ambitions

The first major drawback that a paradoxical perspective on change faces is that it can sometimes lead to unrealistic expectations due to its inherent complexity. Balancing change with continuity demands a level of sophistication and precision that goes beyond the typical challenges of managing change alone.[28] The need to juggle these two conflicting forces often creates uncertainty, as the solutions are rarely straightforward.[14] For instance, the idea that some parts of an organisation can remain completely stable while others are highly adaptable seems at odds with the demands faced by modern organisations. Can certain units truly remain unaffected by changes in their environment, while others must be agile and flexible?[34]

Additionally, while the tension between change and stability touches all parts of an organisation, it places a particularly heavy burden on leaders.[26] They are expected to uphold structured, disciplined resource commitments while also enabling swift, agile responses to emerging challenges. Striking this balance is far from easy. The push and pull between competing demands often generates ambiguity, tension, and internal conflict, conditions that can heighten defensiveness and resistance among both leaders and their teams. Mastering this balancing act is a central challenge of paradoxical leadership.

Therefore, while the paradox perspective offers a comprehensive framework for understanding organisational dynamics, it comes with significant challenges.[5, 23, 34] Successfully managing change involves not just adapting to new circumstances but also ensuring that the organisation remains stable enough to handle those changes – an intricate balancing act that is far from easy to achieve.

### Box 7.12 Practical Advice?

Start by developing clear boundaries for adaptability. Leaders may encourage experimentation within these boundaries, allowing teams to explore new ideas while also maintaining core organisational stability. For instance, creating 'safe zones' for innovation where certain teams or projects can operate with greater flexibility can help balance the need for stability in other areas. Additionally, regular check-ins and feedback loops can ensure that both stability and change are being managed effectively, allowing for adjustments as needed.

### 7.5.2 A Paradox Perspective May Get You Constricted in Ideals

Next, while the paradox perspective prescribes what an organisation needs to do, it offers relatively little guidance on how organisations are to do it. In other words, while the perspective may be clearly normative, it may not be very directive.[14, 29]

It's important to highlight here what the paradox perspective essentially is: a more fundamental perspective on change, rather than an applied one. Think of it as maths preluding the field of physics: just as maths feels less practical in its use than does the more applied field of physics, so does the paradox perspective feel less forthright in its application than, for example, the managerial perspective. This does not mean that either maths or the paradox perspective is useless as a stream of thought: it simply means that their tenets can rarely be extrapolated directly from theory to practice. Instead of being dismissed as academic jargon without practical value, the paradox perspective deserves recognition for its ability to challenge conventional thinking, which paves the way for more pragmatic approaches to be developed in turn.

### 7.5.3 A Paradox Perspective May Confuse

Finally, when thinking paradoxically about change, one needs to be careful not to get lost in translation. What do people really mean when talking about harmonising change and stability?

Do they mean for both objectives to be balanced, traded-off against one another, reconciled, or simply managed?[5, 9] Despite – or maybe due to – the incredible volume of texts revolving around a paradox perspective of change, these questions have been addressed in remarkably different ways, with some authors claiming one point of view and others claiming the other (and some, paradoxically, broadcasting several views at the same time).

Here, it should be noted that some level of divergence is part of every legitimate debate. That fields have not yet reached certitude regarding their topic of interest is not necessarily all that bad; it keeps open the dialogue where convergence would shut it down. In this sense, while advocates of the paradox perspective should certainly make up their minds on what to understand when talking change and stability, they should not be pushed to do so topsy-turvily. Many of the world's most interesting ideas have come from letting go of general conventions; so why numb to convergence what is still thriving in hectic conversation?

### Box 7.13 Practical Advice?

Begin by clearly defining what change and stability mean within the context of your organisation. This can involve developing a shared language around these concepts, ensuring that all team members are on the same page. Hold workshops or discussions to explore how these ideas can be applied in practice, encouraging input from various levels of the organisation. By fostering an environment where questions and divergent views are welcomed, you can help reduce confusion and ensure that the paradox perspective is applied in a consistent and meaningful way.

## SUMMARY

Chapter 7 examined the **paradox perspective on change**, which highlights the dynamic interplay between stability and transformation. Rather than treating change as a process of replacing the old with the new, this perspective emphasises the coexistence of opposing forces, where contrast and synergy drive progress (see Table 7.1 for an overview).

◊ The **origins of this perspective** emerged from the realisation that exploration and exploitation – two seemingly opposing forces – are deeply interdependent. Organisations striving for innovation must still maintain operational efficiency, while those focused on stability must also adapt to remain relevant. Additionally, many existing theories of change struggled to hold up in practice, failing to account for the reality that organisations must simultaneously manage continuity and transformation rather than choosing one over the other.

◊ At its **core**, the paradox perspective defines change as something that does not replace stability but rather coexists with it. Instead of unfolding in distinct phases, change develops concurrently with organising, meaning that organisations are constantly in flux even as they maintain structured operations. The key drivers of change in this view are contrast and synergy – opposing forces that, when balanced effectively, create sustainable momentum.

**Table 7.1 A paradox perspective on change: overview**

| | |
|---|---|
| **Guiding metaphor** | Change as yin and yang |
| **The genesis of thought** | |
| Development 1 | Connecting the dots between exploration and exploitation |
| Development 2 | When change theories fall short in practice |
| **Unpacking the heart** | |
| Capacity of change | Change as coexisting with stability |
| Development of change | Concurrent with organising |
| Drivers of change | The role of contrast and synergy |
| Aim of change | Short-term efficiency *and* long-term relevance |
| **Extending your toolkit** | |
| Tool #1 | Temporal ambidexterity |
| Tool #2 | Structural ambidexterity |
| Tool #3 | Contextual ambidexterity |
| **Impact on the ground** | |
| (+) | A paradox perspective balances out change. |
| (+) | A paradox perspective puts boundaries on change. |
| **Drawbacks and pitfalls** | |
| (−) | A paradox perspective may kindle unrealistic ambitions. |
| (−) | A paradox perspective may get you constricted in ideals. |
| (−) | A paradox perspective may confuse. |
| **Related concepts** | |
| ► | Ambidexterity |
| ► | Exploration-exploitation |
| ► | Paradoxes in change |

The ultimate goal is to achieve both immediate efficiency and long-term adaptability, ensuring that organisations do not become either too rigid or too chaotic.

◊ To better understand how organisations manage this balance, we explored three **tools** related to ambidexterity. Temporal ambidexterity refers to shifting between exploration and exploitation over time; structural ambidexterity involves designing separate units within an organisation to handle different priorities; and contextual ambidexterity focuses on embedding flexibility within individuals and teams so that they can navigate both demands simultaneously.

◊ A paradox perspective brings **valuable insights** by helping to reframe change as a continuous and multidimensional process rather than a simple shift from one state to another. It allows organisations to put change into perspective, recognising when and how stability should be preserved. It also reinstates boundaries around change, challenging the idea that organisations must always be in a state of reinvention.

◊ However, this perspective is not without its **complications**. It risks fostering unrealistic ambitions, as balancing paradoxes in practice can be far more difficult than in theory. Additionally, its conceptual complexity may lead to excessive academic theorising, making it difficult to translate into actionable strategies. Some may also find it inconsistent, as its emphasis on maintaining both stability and change can seem contradictory rather than complementary.

The paradox perspective challenges the notion that organisations must choose between change and stability, instead advocating for a more integrative approach where both coexist. While it offers a compelling way to navigate complexity, it also requires leaders to develop the capability to embrace tensions without defaulting to either extreme. By acknowledging the interplay of opposites, this perspective encourages a more holistic and sustainable approach to change – one that values both transformation and continuity as essential forces in organisational life.

## CASE: WALKING THE TIGHTROPE AT GOOGLE

### The Paradox Perspective in Practice

Many companies excel at one of two approaches: making sure that customers can rely on dependable operations or exciting clients with new and swanky stuff. Very few manage to combine both approaches – but the ones that do reap big rewards. One example of a company that has long successfully connected change with stability is Google. In 2024, Google – or, more precisely, its parent company, Alphabet – was the fourth most valuable company in the world, with a market capitalisation exceeding US$2 trillion. To put this into perspective, that's roughly equivalent to the annual economic output of countries such as Italy or Canada.

For decades, Google has been known as one of the most profitable companies on the planet, while also being consistently flagged as one of its most innovative. It developed products that most of us have been using daily for years – such as its search engine (Google Search), its web browser (Google Chrome), its mobile operating systems (Android), its email system (Gmail), or its mapping platform (Google Maps). Many of these products broke new ground, pushing the envelope of what technology was capable of.

Yet, even for a company as wildly successful as Google, retaining a balance between current operations and future developments proves tricky. In 2023, the aggressive launch of several artificially intelligent chatbots (e.g., ChatGPT) and search engines (e.g., Microsoft's revamped Bing) made it increasingly questionable whether Google would sustain as strongly as it had done for so many years. For many, Google had leant too heavily into exploiting its current ventures, with not enough attention being paid to leveraging its own AI explorations.

Whether that will be the case, only time can tell. For now, let's start by peeping under the hood of one of the most successful companies our planet has ever seen – let's see how Google was able to reconcile its role as a stable profit machine with that of a groundbreaking agent of change.

### The Rise and Set-Up of Google

Google saw the light of day in the late 1990s, at the dawn of the consumer internet. At the time, due to the proliferation of webpages, finding valuable information online had become increasingly challenging: while search engines such as Yahoo! alleviated such issues a bit, they depended on a model of human editors that proved largely unscalable. Google, however, rewrote the rules of the game. Its founders, Larry Page and Sergey Brin, developed an algorithm that ranked webpages based on the number of links directed to them – a measure that proved to be a good proxy for relevance. Impressed by the engine's accuracy when scouring the web, investors put up US$1 million to allow Page and Brin to establish a company. Not a year later, Google was working through over 500,000 search requests per day.

From the very beginning, Page and Brin fostered an informal work culture – using exercise balls as office chairs, wooden doors as desks, and allowing dogs in the workplace. The company strategically placed amenities like cafés and informal meeting spaces throughout its campuses to promote 'casual collisions', facilitating cross-departmental engagement and the free flow of ideas. Beyond spatial arrangements, Google even considered the social dynamics within its cafeterias – designing its dining areas to encourage employees to sit with colleagues they may not know, and thus fostering a culture of inclusivity and diverse idea exchange.

As the year 2000 came to a close, Google was already processing a whopping 100 million search requests daily. In 2004, the company went public, raising close to US$2 billion. In the company's initial public offering (IPO) prospectus, Page and Bring expressed their vision, stating that Google was not a typical company and did not intend to become one. They highlighted their commitment to creating a corporate structure focused on long-term stability. By investing in Google, they explained, investors were making a unique long-term investment in the team and in their innovative approach. Their goal was for Google to evolve into a significant institution, which they believed would require time, stability, and independence.

One of the most remarkable things investors noted in the IPO letter was Google's view on how employees should spend their time. Later informally referring to it as the '20 per cent rule', Page and Brin actively encouraged their employees to spend about a fifth of their time (or one day each week) working on anything they wanted. According to Page and Brin, allowing employees the opportunity to focus on their own ideas outside of ongoing projects resulted in their becoming more imaginative in their thinking. Later, this idea was refined into the '70–20–10' system, in which 70 per cent of an employee's time was to be dedicated to Google's core business, 20 per cent to projects related to that core business, and 10 per cent to projects unrelated to the core business.

To allow such a system to work, Google depended heavily on the quality of its staff. As a result, the company's hiring philosophy became centred on ensuring that every single person recruited was an 'A' player. For most vacancies, the company reviewed hundreds of résumés from various sources to identify candidates that matched specific success factors that Google had identified. These markers were tailored to each role, but the company always prioritised general cognitive ability as a key attribute for success. Self-governance, in this respect, was key to the company's hiring policy.

Additionally, it was the duty of managers to ensure that their subordinates received performance reviews at least once or twice a year. These evaluations were conducted with great importance and all employees were involved in 360-degree review programmes. Such programmes allowed individuals to receive feedback from their managers, peers, and subordinates to identify areas of strength and improvement. Setting stretch goals and achieving high standards for performance became the norm, with many of its employees perceiving it as challenging to achieve even the 'meeting expectations' rating. Employees that demonstrated outstanding forms of innovation were often rewarded handsomely, sometimes even with extensive stock grants.

While management thus had an important function at Google, it was also significantly less prominent than in many other firms. Although managers could be depended on as coaches or mentors, they were to steer clear of strictly controlling or micromanaging subordinates' behaviour: in fact, it was not rare for employees to believe that their managers worked for them instead of the other way around. Top-down management was to be avoided at all cost, and employees were stimulated to be self-managed and self-motivated at all levels of the organisation.

Furthermore, Google held various forums for employees to offer suggestions on how to improve the company, including regular 'bureaucracy buster' meetings. The overall philosophy was to encourage employees to find ways to solve problems and improve processes, especially if they were experiencing pain points from repetitive tasks. If employees noticed examples of red tape, they were encouraged to signal them so that they could be addressed and resolved. In this respect, ideas were given first place – not structure, procedures, or titles.

Such a form of trust also resonated throughout the company's attitude towards risk and failure. While good ideas were celebrated, initiators of failing ideas were not to be looked at crossly. Central to this ethos was the principle of 'Fail Fast, Learn Fast', which encouraged employees to quickly identify what didn't work, learn from these experiences, and iterate rapidly.

As a result of this tolerance for failure and experimentation, ideas were often developed quite quickly. Employees regularly collaborated during their 20 per cent time to create what looked like an internal start-up, and once the project gained momentum, they would recruit colleagues with time on their hands to participate in the project as well.

## From Google to Alphabet

Over time, these organising measures paid off and Google grew at a rapid pace, introducing a flurry of hit products such as Google Calendar, Google Docs, Gmail, and Google Maps – with quite a few of these products allegedly having been spawned during an employee's '20 per cent time'. Additionally, beside acquiring a truckload of small start-ups, the company also successfully acquired several major firms and platforms, including the mobile operating system Android (2005), the video platform YouTube (2006), the telecommunications firm Motorola Mobility (2011), the GPS navigation software Waze (2013), robotics company Boston Dynamics (2013), and artificial intelligence developers DeepMind (2014).

Yet, while mixing these unrelated investments, acquisitions, and businesses offered the company a great deal of opportunities, it also made investors slightly uneasy – worried as they were because of the limits this approach put on accountability, transparency, and discipline. Internally, Google's executives started to notice that a disproportionate part of its meetings were spent on discussing projects of radical innovation, and were thus drawing attention away from the core business. For instance, while Google Search was making more than 90 per cent of the company's revenues through its advertising services, discussions rarely revolved around it.

As a result, in 2015, Google was reorganised as a set of distinct companies, all of which were owned by the parent holding company called Alphabet. According to Larry Page, Alphabet represented two distinct concepts. Firstly, the name was a collection of letters representing language, which served as the foundation for Google's indexed search results – being the company's established business. In this type of industry, success was typically driven by scale, efficiency, and incremental improvements to remain competitive. Yet, secondly, Alphabet also represented 'alpha bets' – or investments in ventures that have the potential to generate returns beyond a benchmark. Concretely, this meant that Alphabet created a new corporate structure that separated Google's core and mature businesses like Google Search and YouTube from riskier ventures like Google X – which was largely geared to working on risky big breakthroughs or 'moonshot' projects.

According to analysts, the new structure allowed Google – or Alphabet – to tailor its approach more closely to the needs of its different units. For example, due to its position as the market leader in online advertising, Google AdWords required a more traditional strategy that focused on planning, economies of scale, and optimising its business model. On the other hand, Google's more innovative businesses needed a visionary approach that prioritised recognising and addressing unmet needs with novel products or business models at a fast pace. Applying a single approach to these distinct situations was considered detrimental to competitiveness and performance. Therefore, it was necessary to tailor strategies, capabilities, and resources to suit the specific needs and characteristics of each business, rather than relying on a one-size-fits-all approach.

### Retaining Balance and Moving Forward

For almost two decades, Google's search engine has been the primary entry point for internet worldwide, and the primary means for advertisers to access consumers. Since 2011, the company's revenue has grown at sustained double-digit rates, generating hundreds of billions of dollars in free cash flow, with the majority coming from search. In 2023, it processed approximately 100,000 web searches every second – a feat that has turned the company name into an actual verb for many ('to google something'). The accuracy of its search results has kept users loyal and has enabled Google to maintain its dominant market position, with other search engines accounting for just a fraction of daily search traffic.

However, with the rise of artificially intelligent chatbots and search engines, this business seems increasingly at risk. As chatbots have gained the capacity to engage in human-like conversations, they have started to outperform more traditional types of search engine. Chatbots driven by AI are not limited to answering queries in the way that Google does, but go beyond that and provide responses to a broader range of questions.

According to some, Google has only itself to blame. While the company was initially at the forefront of AI-driven technology – having developed the Transformer architecture that underpins today's AI chatbots – it was reluctant to proceed with this new tech because it was not suited to delivering digital ads – ads that, in 2022, still provided more than 80 per cent of the firm's total turnover. So even if Google nowadays catches up and perfects its own chatbots, it faces a daunting question: how to avoid this new technology from cannibalising its existing business? In this respect, while Alphabet has had a hard time maintaining pace (being closely monitored by regulators due to concerns regarding monopolistic practices), its main difficulty may lie in parting ways with a business model and technology that have consistently generated profits for over two decades. In this sense, Google faces a heavy business model challenge – for if the company provides the perfect answer to every query, users will no longer click on ads.

It is far too soon to claim that Google has run its course; in fact, by the time you are reading this, the company may already have recovered its throne. How the future turns out remains to be seen. It's an exciting new road, filled with opportunities and challenges. It will require the courage to explore, yet also the cunning to exploit.

### Reflect

1. How did Google incorporate temporal ambidexterity into its organisation?
2. How did Google incorporate structural ambidexterity into its organisation?
3. How did Google incorporate contextual ambidexterity into its organisation?
4. How did Google 'lose its balance' regarding artificially intelligent technology?

### Case Study Sources

The Economist. (2023, 8 February). *Is Google's 20-year dominance of search in peril?* www.economist.com/business/2023/02/08/is-googles-20-year-search-dominance-about-to-end?

Grant, N., & Metz, C. (2022, 21 December). *A new chat bot is a 'code red' for Google's search business*. *New York Times*, www.nytimes.com/2022/12/21/technology/ai-chatgpt-google-search.html.

Hof, R. (2015, 10 August). The real reasons Google will become Alphabet. *Forbes*, www.forbes.com/sites/roberthof/2015/08/10/the-real-reasons-google-will-become-alphabet/.

Kaufmann, M. (2022, 18 November). Reimagining physical spaces to foster connection. *Google Workspace*, https://workspace.google.com/blog/future-of-work/reimagining-physical-spaces-to-foster-connection.

Lebowitz, S. (2021, 23 November). Here's a step-by-step guide on how performance reviews work at Google. *Business Insider*, www.businessinsider.com/how-google-performance-reviews-work-2015-6.
Levy, S. (2011). *In the plex: How Google thinks, works, and shapes our lives*. New York: Simon and Schuster.
Page, L., & Brin, S. (2004). *Google founder's IPO letter*. https://abc.xyz/
Reeves, M. (2015).*Google couldn't survive with one strategy*. Boston, MA: Boston Consulting Group. https://bcghendersoninstitute.com/google-couldnt-survive-with-one-strategy/.
Schmidt, E., & Rosenberg, J. (2017). *How Google works*. New York: Grand Central.
Valinsky, J., & Sherman, I. (2018, 13 December). Google's incredible growth: A timeline. *CNN*, https://edition.cnn.com/interactive/2018/12/business/google-history-timeline/index.html.
Vise, D., & Malseed, M. (2005). *The Google story*. New York: Bantam Dell.

## REFERENCES

[1] Adler, P. S., Goldoftas, B., & Levine, D. I. (1999). Flexibility versus efficiency? A case study of model changeovers in the Toyota production system. *Organization Science*, *10*(1), 43–68.
[2] Ahmed, P. K., Hardaker, G., & Carpenter, M. (1996). Integrated flexibility: Key to competition in a turbulent environment. *Long Range Planning*, *29*(4), 562–571.
[3] Barnard, C. I. (1938). *The functions of the executive*. Cambridge, MA: Harvard University Press.
[4] Birkinshaw, J., & Gibson, C. B. (2004). Building ambidexterity into an organization. *MIT Sloan Management Review*, *45*(4), 47–55.
[5] Birkinshaw, J., & Gupta, K. (2013). Clarifying the distinctive contribution of ambidexterity to the field of organization studies. *Academy of Management Perspectives*, *27*(4), 287–298.
[6] Boynton, A. C., & Victor, B. (1991). Beyond flexibility: Building and managing the dynamically stable organization. *California Management Review*, *34*(1), 53–66.
[7] Burgelman, R. A. (1983). A model of the interaction of strategic behavior, corporate context, and the concept of strategy. *Academy of Management Review*, *8*(1), 61–70.
[8] Burns, T., & Stalker, G. (1961). *The management of innovation*. London: Tavistock.
[9] Cao, Q., Gedajlovic, E., & Zhang, H. (2009). Unpacking organizational ambidexterity: Dimensions, contingencies, and synergistic effects. *Organization Science*, *20*(4), 781–796.
[10] Christensen, C. M., Raynor, M. E., & McDonald, R. (2015). What is disruptive innovation? *Harvard Business Review*, *93*(12), 44–53.
[11] Collins, J., & Porras, J. (1994). *Built to last: Successful habits of visionary companies*. New York: Harper Collins.
[12] Duncan, R. B. (1972). Characteristics of organizational environments and perceived environmental uncertainty. *Administrative Science Quarterly*, *17*(3), 313–327.
[13] Eisenhardt, K. M. (2000). Paradox, spirals, ambivalence: The new language of change and pluralism. *Academy of Management Review*, *25*(4), 703–705.
[14] Eisenhardt, K. M., Furr, N. R., & Bingham, C. B. (2010). Microfoundations of performance: Balancing efficiency and flexibility in dynamic environments. *Organization Science*, *21*(6), 1263–1273.
[15] Farjoun, M. (2010). Beyond dualism: Stability and change as a duality. *Academy of Management Review*, *35*(2), 202–225.

[16] Galunic, D. C., & Eisenhardt, K. M. (2001). Architectural innovation and modular corporate forms. *Academy of Management Journal*, *44*(6), 1229–1249.

[17] Ghemawat, P., & Ricart i Costa, J. (1993). The organizational tension between static and dynamic efficiency. *Strategic Management Journal*, *14*(S2), 59–73.

[18] Ghoshal, S., & Bartlett, C. A. (1994). Linking organizational context and managerial action: The dimensions of quality of management. *Strategic Management Journal*, *15*(S2), 91–112.

[19] Gibson, C. B., & Birkinshaw, J. (2004). The antecedents, consequences, and mediating role of organizational ambidexterity. *Academy of Management Journal*, *47*(2), 209–226.

[20] Gilbert, C. G. (2006). Change in the presence of residual fit: Can competing frames coexist? *Organization Science*, *17*(1), 150–167.

[21] Graetz, F., & Smith, A. C. T. (2008). The role of dualities in arbitrating continuity and change in forms of organizing. *International Journal of Management Reviews*, *10*(3), 265–280.

[22] Jansen, J. J., George, G., Van den Bosch, F. A., & Volberda, H. W. (2008). Senior team attributes and organizational ambidexterity: The moderating role of transformational leadership. *Journal of Management Studies*, *45*(5), 982–1007.

[23] Lavie, D., Stettner, U., & Tushman, M. L. (2010). Exploration and exploitation within and across organizations. *Academy of Management Annals*, *4*(1), 109–155.

[24] Leana, C. R., & Barry, B. (2000). Stability and change as simultaneous experiences in organizational life. *Academy of Management Review*, *25*(4), 753–759.

[25] Lewis, M. W. (2000). Exploring paradox: Toward a more comprehensive guide. *Academy of Management Review*, *25*(4), 760–776.

[26] Lewis, M. W., Andriopoulos, C., & Smith, W. K. (2014). Paradoxical leadership to enable strategic agility. *California Management Review*, *56*(3), 58–77.

[27] March, J. G. (1991). Exploration and exploitation in organizational learning. *Organization Science*, *2*(1), 71–87.

[28] Martinez, A. C. (1997). Transforming the legacy of sears. *Strategy and Leadership*, *25*(4), 30–34.

[29] Nasim, S., & Sushil. (2011). Revisiting organizational change: Exploring the paradox of managing continuity and change. *Journal of Change Management*, *11*(2), 185–206.

[30] O'Reilly, C. A., & Tushman, M. L. (2013). Organizational ambidexterity: Past, present, and future. *Academy of Management Perspectives*, *27*(4), 324–338.

[31] Pettigrew, A. M., Woodman, R. W., & Cameron, K. S. (2001). Studying organizational change and development: Challenges for future research. *Academy of Management Journal*, *44*(4), 697–713.

[32] Raisch, S., & Birkinshaw, J. (2008). Organizational ambidexterity: Antecedents, outcomes, and moderators. *Journal of Management*, *34*(3), 375–409.

[33] Raisch, S., Birkinshaw, J., Probst, G., & Tushman, M. L. (2009). Organizational ambidexterity: Balancing exploitation and exploration for sustained performance. *Organization Science*, *20*(4), 685–695.

[34] Schreyogg, G., & Sydow, J. (2010). Organizing for fluidity? Dilemmas of new organizational forms. *Organization Science*, *21*(6), 1251–1262.

[35] Siggelkow, N., & Levinthal, D. (2003). Temporarily divide to conquer: Centralized, decentralized, and reintegrated organizational approaches to exploration and adaptation. *Organization Science*, *14*(6), 650–669.

[36] Smith, W. K. (2014). Dynamic decision making: A model of senior leaders managing strategic paradoxes. *Academy of Management Journal*, *57*(6), 1592–1623.

[37] Thompson, J. D. (1967). *Organizations in action: Social science bases of administrative theory*. London: Routledge.

[38] Turner, S. F., & Rindova, V. (2012). A balancing act: How organizations pursue consistency in routine functioning in the face of ongoing change. *Organization Science*, *23*(1), 24–46.

[39] Tushman, M. L., & O'Reilly, C. A. (1996). The ambidextrous organizations: Managing evolutionary and revolutionary change. *California Management Review*, *38*(4), 8–30.

[40] Volberda, H. W. (1996). Toward the flexible form: How to remain vital in hypercompetitive environments. *Organization Science*, *7*(4), 359–374.

[41] Volberda, H. W., Baden-Fuller, C., & Van Den Bosch, F. A. (2001). Mastering strategic renewal: Mobilising renewal journeys in multi-unit firms. *Long Range Planning*, *34*(2), 159–178.

# 8 A Persistence Perspective on Change

## PERSPECTIVE IN BRIEF

- **Concepts related to the perspective** – critical theories of change, population ecology theory, path dependence theory, structural inertia, escalating commitment, and imprinting
- **Keep reading to learn more about** – resistance to change and change ethics
- **Prime contributors** – J. Freeman, M. Hannan, D. Leonard-Barton, G. Schreyögg, J. Sydow, and B. Staw
- **Guiding metaphor** – change as an illusion

## Introduction

So far, we've explored six distinct perspectives on change. While each offered a different angle – whether focusing on leadership, power, skills, or something else – they all shared at least one key assumption: that change is, in some way, both possible and worthwhile. This belief may seem intuitive, even self-evident. After all, why else would so many organisations pour time, energy, and resources into transformation efforts?

But is it really so obvious? In fact, the idea that change is both good and possible may be more fragile than it first appears. To see why, consider the following questions:

- Have the changes you've so far witnessed in organisations always improved their operations?
- Have these changes consistently fostered a sense of unity among employees?
- Did the changes you observed or implemented always yield the desired outcomes?
- How many proposed changes were ultimately abandoned?
- And finally – have any of the changes you've witnessed hindered the organisation, causing it to lose its competitive edge?

For those who have even the slightest interest in organisational change, these questions might evoke images of rather nasty situations. Maybe you're thinking of a change that evoked widespread strikes and employee unrest. Perhaps you're seeing images of companies that went down the toilet because they tried pivoting into a direction that, afterwards, proved ill-advised. Maybe you've even reflected on firms that, despite grand claims, really didn't change that much at all.

Yet whatever your thoughts may be, let's try to delve a bit deeper into them: in instances where change failed, was incompetence the underlying cause? Or was it something more elusive – an underlying force within the organisation that resisted, disrupted, or simply prevented change from taking root?

While there are undoubtedly cases where gross negligence played a role, it's likely that most failures stemmed from the latter – instances where something just didn't click or didn't align with the organisation's goals. Perhaps it was the clash between what people valued and the new direction the organisation sought to pursue. Maybe it was the legacy customers' preferences that didn't support a fresh approach. Or it could have been the complex interplay between various organisational systems that ultimately undermined the change initiative. These scenarios underscore a fundamental – and often painful – truth about organisational transformation: that sometimes, despite our best efforts, change simply doesn't work out.

This chapter introduces the **persistence perspective** on change, which challenges the assumption that transformation is always possible – or even desirable. Rather than focusing on how organisations change, this perspective examines why they so often remain the same. It explores the forces that sustain stability, the limits of change initiatives, and the ways in which change can sometimes serve more as an illusion than a reality. By doing so, it offers a necessary counterbalance to the dominant narratives of transformation, encouraging a more critical and nuanced understanding of when, why, and how change occurs – or, just as importantly, why it sometimes does not.

## 8.1 The Genesis of Thought

Let's start by tracking roots: as we have consistently observed throughout this book, perspectives on change do not simply emerge out of thin air – they are born from a series of (uncomfortable) observations that eventually give rise to new ways of thinking. The persistence perspective is no exception, spawning from two core developments.

### 8.1.1 The Struggle to Make Change Stick

By the 1990s, organisational change had long been a central preoccupation for both scholars and executives. Yet, despite decades of attention, increasingly sophisticated models, and countless well-meaning initiatives, it was becoming clear that change remained one of the most difficult and unpredictable aspects of management. Success was elusive; failure, all too common.

This mounting pattern of disappointment began to unsettle even the most committed advocates of change. Although discomfort with the status quo had been simmering for years, it came into sharper focus with the publication of Hammer and Champy's influential *Reengineering the Corporation*. Their bold claim – that up to 70 per cent of re-engineering efforts ended in failure – cut through the optimism that had long surrounded change efforts and forced a more sobering reckoning with the limits of transformation.[16]

While the accuracy of this statistic was fiercely debated – and in some cases outright contested[40, 52] – it came to reflect a deeper realisation: implementing change is far more complex and difficult than often anticipated. Some took this as a challenge to improve change management frameworks, advocating for better planning, communication, and leadership to mitigate failure rates. Others, however, viewed it as a sign that organisational structures and cultures possess an intrinsic resistance to transformation. From this angle, change was no longer a matter of refining best practices – it became understood as a battle against fundamental forces that shape organisational life.

### 8.1.2 Confronting the Unintended Consequences of Change

Beyond the sheer difficulty of implementing change, people also began to notice the significant toll it could take on organisations and their members, with symptoms including an excess of initiatives, operational chaos, employee scepticism, and exhaustion.[1]

While change had long been championed as essential for staying competitive, a more sobering reality was beginning to take shape: change could be just as damaging as it was promising. This growing awareness marked a turning point. Rather than viewing change solely as a path to greater productivity, innovation, and engagement, scholars and practitioners alike began to confront its darker side – the disruptions to work life, declines in organisational health, and strains on personal well-being that often accompanied even the most well-intentioned initiatives.[42]

Sparked by these two observations, several organisational thinkers started to shift their beliefs about the role of change in organisational life. Maybe failures happened not solely because theoretical models were inadequate but also because of the inherent challenges of implementing change in an organisational context? This raised several critical questions: should scholars and practitioners continue to promote change as a pathway to organisational growth? Or would these efforts, despite their intentions, contribute to greater harm and hardship for organisations and society at large?[42]

From these seeds of scepticism, more critical approaches to change began to emerge. Drawing inspiration from diverse fields – including biological evolution theory,[17] sociological structuration theory,[36] and theories of social structures within organisations[26] – scholars began challenging the assumption that new is always better than old. This perspective questioned what some described as the 'pro-change bias'[42] or even the 'totalitarianism of change',[48] bringing a more nuanced and critical lens to the conversation. Rather than treating change as an unequivocal good, the emerging perspective urged a more thoughtful and measured approach – one that considers both the potential benefits and the (often very real) costs of organisational transformation.

## 8.2 Unpacking the Heart

As we continue to explore a persistence perspective on change, it will become clear that the path to successful organisational transformation is neither straightforward nor guaranteed; instead,

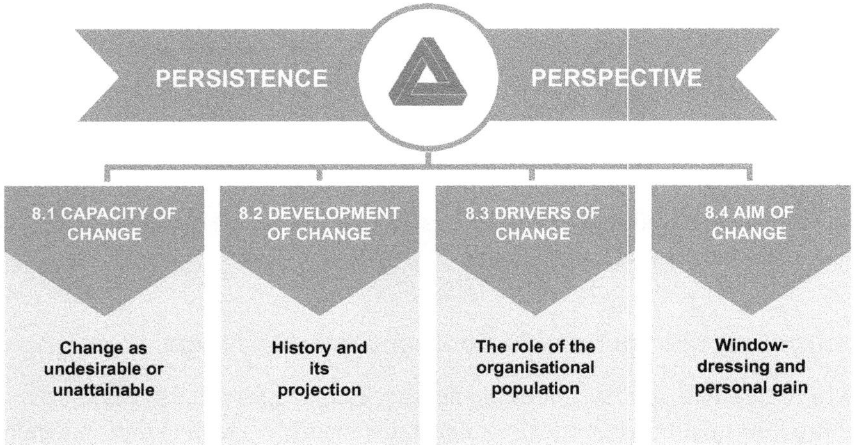


**Figure 8.1** Unpacking the heart of the persistence perspective.

it requires a deep understanding of the inherent difficulties and potential downsides of change, as well as a willingness to critically assess whether change is truly the best course of action in any given context. With that in mind, let's delve deeper into the perspective's four core tenets (see Figure 8.1).

### 8.2.1 Capacity of Change: Change as Undesirable or Unattainable

First, just as it would be challenging to transform this book into a cookbook, the persistence perspective raises fundamental questions about an organisation's ability to undergo deep and meaningful transformation. At its core, this perspective posits that organisational change is either (i) **undesirable** or (ii) **unattainable**.

First, from a persistence perspective, shifting an organisation can be highly undesirable, this by jeopardising its very survival through exposure to significant risks.[2, 26] Over time, several arguments have been developed to support this point of view:[7]

- Change may break a durable strategic commitment – to begin with, some have argued that steering organisations towards change is inherently at odds with offering a signal of durable strategic commitment.[40, 41] Stability is often viewed as a cornerstone of trust in business. When an organisation frequently shifts its strategies or core offerings, it risks undermining the confidence that customers, investors, and employees have in its long-term vision.[28] To illustrate this point, think about a bakery renowned for its exquisite cupcakes and frosty toppings. If the bakery, driven by the owner's new-found interest in rustic farmhouse bread, abruptly pivots away from its signature cupcakes, it risks confusing its loyal customer base. Customers who once relied on the bakery for their cupcake fix might feel alienated or uncertain about the bakery's future offerings, leading them to take their business elsewhere. In this sense, change, by rendering the organisation's strategy less steadfast, may inadvertently reduce its chances of survival.

- Change may erode people's morale – next, change often has profound implications for the workforce, affecting job roles, compensation, and interpersonal dynamics. When leaders push for significant, and often destabilising, changes, they may inadvertently sow seeds of discontent among employees. The fear of the unknown, coupled with the potential for job insecurity, can lead to apathy, resistance, or even outright opposition. Employees who once felt valued and secure in their roles may become disillusioned, reducing their engagement and productivity. Over time, this erosion of morale can lead to higher turnover rates, as skilled employees seek stability elsewhere, further compounding the challenges of implementing change. In extreme cases, an organisation that fails to maintain employee morale during periods of change may find itself struggling to maintain the talent and expertise necessary for long-term success.[1] Let's return to our bakery for a moment, switching from cupcakes to rustic farmhouse bread. While the baker may feel motivated by the prospect of doing something new and sexy, their staff may not feel the same way. Some may feel confused about why this move was necessary at all; others may perhaps feel that rustic bread isn't really their cup of tea. As a result, these staff members don't go the extra mile anymore, and customers may start sensing that something is off. If left unchecked, this erosion of staff morale may hurt the bakery more than the move ultimately ends up benefiting the business.
- Change may break the organisation's competitive advantage – finally, changing an organisation may break down the competencies, such as reliability and accountability, by which it often outcompetes others.[17, 18] When operating steadily, most organisations have an almost uncanny capacity to produce products of a given quality repeatedly. They document how resources have been used and reconstruct the sequences of organisational decisions, rules, and actions that produce certain outcomes. Yet when the organisational set-up is changed, these fundamental aspects are curtailed, resulting in a reduction of the organisation's attractiveness as a provider of solutions.[18] In our bakery example, as the baker shifts focus from cupcakes to farmhouse bread, the well-oiled processes for producing cupcakes become obsolete. New processes must be developed and perfected, which may lead to inconsistent quality in the new product line. During this transitional period, the bakery risks losing its reputation as a reliable producer of high-quality goods, making it vulnerable to competitors who can offer more consistency. Even if the switch to farmhouse bread eventually proves successful, the short-term impact on the bakery's reputation and customer loyalty might be severe enough to make the change a poor decision overall.

Second, in addition to change being undesirable, a persistence perspective also suggests that meaningful organisational change may simply not be possible. Why? The easy answer is because it's too hard. Numerous factors can contribute to inertia, reinforcing the status quo over efforts to change.[6, 10, 22, 26, 28, 43] For the sake of clarity, I here boil them down to two categories, internal and external:

- Internal resistance and power dynamics – first, within organisations, power dynamics often play a significant role in resisting change. Managers and employees who have built their careers and reputations on the existing system may be reluctant to embrace change that could diminish their influence or disrupt established hierarchies. This resistance can manifest as overt opposition or more subtle forms of sabotage, where change initiatives are deliberately slowed or undermined. Additionally, risk aversion is a common trait in many organisations, particularly those with a history of success. Leaders may fear that change could introduce uncertainties or failures, leading them to favour the safety of the status quo. To see this point in action, imagine you're a manager who's reporting directly to the CEO. Your position in the organisation gives you quite a lot of power and influence – since you have a direct line to the chief, you can easily bounce around ideas, express your thoughts on current happenings, or vie for additional resources. Now suppose that the organisation is looking to restructure according to geographical regions, where you'd be reporting to a regional manager instead. For you, the change would result in quite a big loss of informal power: while you would still be able to pass along your grievances through the regional manager, your direct line with the CEO would be severed. For this reason, you feel uncomfortable with the change and you start arguing against it, not because it would necessarily harm the company but because it would harm your position.

- External pressures and social embeddedness – furthermore, organisations do not exist in a vacuum; they are deeply embedded in broader social, economic, and cultural contexts. These external factors can also act as significant barriers to change. Long-standing relationships with suppliers, customers, and other stakeholders may create expectations that limit an organisation's ability to pivot. Similarly, regulatory environments, industry standards, and market conditions can impose constraints that make significant changes impractical. Even when an organisation recognises the need for change, these external pressures can make it difficult to implement new strategies without risking disruption or backlash. For example, think about a fast-food chain looking to connect with increasingly healthy eating habits. After reviewing the caloric intake of the company's menus, company leaders decide to rework many of the firm's offerings, by including an option to have carrots with your burger and by switching the standard sauce for one that is less fatty and includes fewer preservatives. However, after a few weeks, a social media thread has gone viral in which one of the company's long-standing customers burns this new direction to the ground. #HandsOffMySauce rapidly becomes of the most popular hashtags of all time, and leadership quickly reconsiders. With much ado, they soon announce the comeback of the original sauce, and the riddance of carrots. Customers cheer and let out a sigh of relief – nothing has changed after all.

### Box 8.1 Be Aware!

While these examples illustrate why change can be either ill-advised or tremendously hard for organisations, note that a persistence perspective does not suggest that it is therefore entirely absent; on the contrary, a quick glance at organisational reality reveals that firms are quite often in motion. However, what this perspective underscores is that change should be confined to peripheral areas of organisational activity, leaving the core largely intact.[18, 23] Adjustments to peripheral elements – whether in processes, structures, products, or policies – allow organisations to evolve without fundamentally disrupting their identity or operational continuity.[20] In this way, organisations can refine their ways of working while safeguarding the essence of who they are.

## 8.2.2 Development of (Non-)Change: History and Its Projection

So far, we've established that a persistence perspective is more about non-change than it is about change. Hence, from a persistence perspective, the question of how organisations develop might not be the most pressing one; in fact, coming to terms with how organisations don't develop may be at least equally, if not more, important.[14, 23, 39, 50] In general, three phases are highlighted – origin, reinforcement, and perpetuation.

### 8.2.2.1 Historical Origin

Every organisation begins somewhere – it is founded and comes into being (congratulations!). Yet while the founding stage may feel full of freedom and possibility, the choices made during this period are far from trivial. Like the early development of a child, the way an organisation is born – and the path it takes through its formative years – can leave a lasting imprint on everything that follows:[21] as organisational history is created, it will come to matter for all decisions made further down the line – with 'past becoming prologue',[39] and events and decisions taking place during the initial stages of organisational life having a profound influence on those that succeed them.[22, 37]

To better understand how this happens, imagine a start-up founded by a group of engineers who are passionate about open-source software. In the early days, the founders choose to adopt an open-source business model, believing that it aligns with their values and the tech community's ethos. This decision, while seemingly straightforward at the time, sets the stage for the company's future trajectory. As the company grows, this commitment to open source becomes a core part of its identity, influencing its hiring practices, partnerships, and even its approach to customer relations. Years later, when the company faces pressure to adopt a more traditional, proprietary software model to increase profitability, the founders and employees find themselves constrained by their initial decision. The very history that propelled the company to success now acts as a barrier to change, as abandoning the open-source model could alienate loyal customers, disrupt internal culture, and erode the company's foundational values.

### 8.2.2.2 Reinforcement of Initial Choices

In the second phase, initial decisions are gradually reaffirmed, with different organisational mechanisms naturally supporting the status quo.[37] Various such mechanisms have been highlighted over time,[14, 17, 23] with the most prominent being coordination effects, complementarity effects, learning effects, and adaptive expectation effects:[50]

- Coordination effects – first, as organisational actors come to abide by a particular routine, their cost of coordinating with each other reduces significantly: as behaviour can be anticipated on account of the routine, actors do not have to explicitly communicate about what they intend to do.[50] Such coordination effects make it very attractive for organisations to stick to what is already known, with the outlook becoming even better when a routine becomes more deeply embedded. An excellent example of coordination effects is the installation of working-time regimes. Such regimes allow us to depend on others without having to spend much thought on it. At 11 a.m., it's reasonable to pick up the phone and call a supplier for clarity on a missing part. You don't have to look up the supplier's opening hours because 11 a.m. falls within the range of typical working-time regimes. However, while such clear schedules guarantee an efficient operation, they also make it hard for the organisation to revise things drastically. If the supplier, for some reason, means to change its shifts to only start from noon, it will lose out on the coordination effects it previously enjoyed: any customers now calling at 11 a.m. would reach an empty office. As a result, the supplier will probably stick to what is already known because of coordination effects.

- Complementarity effects – for many activities, the organisation may experience a 'bonus' when carrying them out in combination with a complementary activity,[30, 46] that is, there is some form of combined benefit arising from the interaction of two or more distinct yet interconnected resources, rules, or practices.[50] For example, as an organisation aligns with the tenets of 'Fordism', it will have complementary management systems in place in operations (mass production), organisational structure (hierarchy of control), and human resources (hiring and firing of low-skilled labour). As a result, should the organisation aim to change its way of structuring, it will have a hard time prying loose such structure from the complementary features to which it is related. As a strict hierarchical structure is supported by the organisation's mode of operations and its approach to managing human resources, implementing a new (and potentially more modern) structure would make the whole system shaky. In this way, the organisation's current activity pattern becomes progressively dominant because of complementarity effects.
- Learning effects – next, as an organisation performs a particular activity more often, it will get more skilled in it, reducing the time needed to do it and the number of errors. Yet, while such learning effects make the activity gain in terms of efficiency, they also make it harder for the organisation to drop the activity altogether – this would mean the firm having to give up on its accumulated learning and decreased cost, starting from scratch again with something entirely new.[50] Think, for example, of your own learning. While it is possible to reorient yourself completely and become, let's say, a dentist, the learning effects you have by now accumulated in business and management – pursuing a degree or reading this book – could render such a choice rather painful: for some, it would involve tossing away years of study or expertise. As a result, you burrow your dentistry dream and continue capitalising on your learning in management.
- Adaptive expectation effects – finally, as people tend to conform their choices to those they expect others to make, dominant solutions come to be outlined.[8] For example, when choosing between web browsers or video calling software, people in organisations tend to select the solution they expect to be mainstream within their organisation or broader field. While such dominant solutions offer the advantage of conformity, they gradually rule out inconsistent practices: while some people might prefer Apple Pages over Microsoft Word, the prevalence of the latter over the former renders it challenging to use Pages. As such, the organisation will find its choices solidified by adaptive expectation effects – limited in its prospective movement by what is currently working out.[50]

#### 8.2.2.3 Perpetuation of Past to Present

Due to these effects, organisations will eventually continue their initial decisions and actions, extrapolating past to present. In this way, while organisations are initially consciously developed to align with the existing environment, they continue to display traces of their original context and decisions because of inertia and institutionalisation.[26]

Think about a large manufacturing company that has been in operation for over a century. It was initially established during the early twentieth century when industrial production was dominated by hierarchical structures and rigid processes. These early decisions, such as the implementation of a top-down management approach and a focus on mass production techniques, were well-suited to the environment of the time. Over the years, these practices became deeply ingrained in the organisation's culture and operations. Even as the external environment evolves with the rise of digital technologies and more flexible work practices, the company finds it difficult to adapt. The inertia of its institutionalised practices means that, despite attempts at modernisation, the company continues to operate with a strong hierarchical structure and a focus on efficiency over innovation. This persistence of past practices limits the company's ability to respond to new market demands and leaves it vulnerable to more agile competitors. In this stage, the company's history, once a source of strength, has become a constraint, perpetuating outdated practices that no longer align with the current environment.

**Box 8.2 The Point?**

As much as other perspectives have highlighted how change unfolds in organisations, a persistence perspective offers a better understanding of how it does not. As organisations become anchored in past decisions and reinforce them over time, they create a trajectory that resists deviation. In the end, they may find themselves left with little choice but to hold on and see where the waves take them.

### 8.2.3 Drivers of Change: The Role of the Organisational Population

So, if organisations are believed to be largely resistant to developments, what's important to visualise as drivers for change? Are there any? According to a persistence perspective, there sure are – it's just that they are not at the level of the single organisation. Instead, it's the larger **population** that is deemed to change. When societies evolve and new needs emerge, existing organisations are believed to be too rigid to act (for all the reasons discussed before). But just as you do things differently than your parents or grandparents did – with habits that they would struggle to master – new organisations tend to introduce ways of doing things that incumbents have a hard time pulling off. As such, according to the persistence perspective, change is not something that tends to happen at the organisational level: rather, if real change is to be observed, we must step up towards the level of the organisational population.

Why would that be the case? If you've been paying attention so far, you might suspect that 'history' – or age – has something to do with it. As young organisations have little in the way of routines yet in place – and, as such, experience few effects of coordination, complementarity, learning, and adaptive expectation – they tend to be able to introduce things that organisations long since established are no longer capable of picking up. As a result, existing organisations will wither, with new organisations gradually taking their place. In this way, the persistence perspective advances change as a process of perishing and restarting, with each organisational 'generation' introducing elements that might appear vastly foreign to those organisations already established.[17, 18, 31, 34, 56] Major change is not something that can – or should – be intentionally advanced; it happens because of the passing of organisational generations.[18]

Although there are many industries that illustrate this observation, one of the most drastic is photography. It was long dominated by a few key players, but then the rise of digital technology quickly pushed traditional photography to the near brink of extinction. While dominant companies had the means to push for a change towards digital photography, there were many reasons why they didn't – fear of cannibalising their traditional sales, power plays and vested interests, supplier relations, and so on – all of which were, essentially, remnants of past decisions or of these firms having considerable history. As a result, when digital technology improved, established players became increasingly irrelevant and ultimately filed for bankruptcy. New, less embedded players came to dominate the marketplace – and change, rather than having been enacted by an organisation, was thus installed at the level of the population.

**Box 8.3 The Point?**

A persistence perspective claims change to be driven primarily by the organisational population, where various configurations compete and the ones that are most suited to present conditions are selected. Organisations will thrive until the conditions they started in have changed sufficiently for new organisations to trump them. In this way, it is the population that is believed to be the primary source of change, not the single firm embedded within.[4, 11, 12, 59]

## 8.2.4 Aim of Change: Window-Dressing and Personal Gain

But if organisations cannot (or should not) change, why are there so many examples of change out there? Why is it that large multinationals often announce sweeping change programmes and restructuring efforts? Why is that employees are so often sitting in town-hall meetings, listening to another round of transformation being promoted? From a persistence perspective, the answer to these questions may be slightly crummy. When organisations do set out on major change initiatives, the persistence perspective often considers the intentions behind such initiatives to be somewhat reproachable: rather than aiming to advance the best interests of the organisation, organisational change is believed to be all too often run to advance the interests of its leading individuals.

For many managers, initiating change is a way of making their mark and showing how their leadership matters. It signals to shareholders and analysts how they have taken the reins and highlights how they are actively working towards a better future. In many cases, change increases the profile and media exposure of the manager who leads it: it is exciting, new, and worthy of talk. It puts the changing company in the spotlights, and the manager leading such change with it. It is a way of showing how you, as a leader, matter; and how the organisation that you are leading is a force to be reckoned with.

Hence, from a persistence perspective, the primary goal of change may be not necessarily to benefit the organisation but to create the appearance of progress and improvement. This dynamic highlights how change processes, along with the models and theories surrounding them, often serve to advance the interests of the managerial class. Rather than being value-neutral, these processes frequently reflect the priorities of those in the lead, particularly the financial elite who dominate many organisations.[42]

To better understand this point, try to imagine yourself as a newly brandished executive manager. Either you've been hired after an extensive hiring process or you've been promoted after toiling away at the company for many long years. Your arrival is announced with much aplomb, and you're not entirely sure that all these people really understand what you can and cannot do – after all, it's only you, right? In any case, expectations are high and markets are looking for a sign of strong leadership. What do you do? Do you sit tight in your corner office and let everything run its course? Do you go out and say, 'This firm seems to know how to handle itself pretty well – no need for me acting up here'. Or do you step out to meet the press, explaining how your vision will take the company in exciting new directions? All too often, it's the latter, for it gives your leadership meaning and supposed impact. Most of us want to leave a mark, in one way or another, and whether that mark is beneficial is surprisingly often of secondary importance.

**Box 8.4 The Point?**

Organisational change, when driven by the personal ambitions of managers, can sometimes lead to outcomes that are more harmful than beneficial to the organisation.[40] While organisations exist primarily to address specific societal needs – whether fulfilling consumer demands, treating the sick, or providing employment – change initiatives that prioritise individual or selfish goals over these broader purposes can undermine the very foundations of the organisations. From a persistence perspective, change is seen not as a strategy for organisational improvement but as a tool for advancing the careers and agendas of those in power – often to the detriment of the organisation's long-term health and societal contributions.

## 8.3 Extending Your Toolkit

Having established an elementary understanding of the persistence perspective's core, let's delve deeper into a few frameworks that will help you action these ideas in practice. In this section, I'll zoom into four essential ones: (i) path dependency and imprinting, (ii) escalating commitment, (iii) authenticity, and (iv) the law of diffusion. Some of these frameworks will resemble the general understanding we have established up to this point; however, since they all offer specific nuances and further refinements, I believe that they offer interesting extensions, nonetheless. With that in mind, let's jump right in.

### 8.3.1 Path Dependency and Imprinting

The first frameworks I'll set out are path dependency and imprinting – frameworks that capture the very essence of persistence by showing how either yesterday's choices or contextual features narrow today's options and shape tomorrow's trajectory.[50] In these frameworks, decisions are historically conditioned, with bygones rarely being bygones.[53]

In **path dependency theory**, the organisation gradually tapers to a well-defined path,[22] or a fixed and possibly inefficient pattern of actions developed through the unintended effects of past decisions and reinforcing feedback loops.[50] Three stages are generally noted: (i) the pre-formation phase; (ii) the formation phase; and (iii) the lock-in phase.

Initially, in the **pre-formation phase**, the organisation enjoys a largely unrestricted scope of action, with choices not being predefined by prior events or determinants. During this phase, options remain largely reversible, and many are discarded after being tested against reality. Although numerous choices will eventually be revised, some of these seemingly insignificant or even random decisions may become pivotal 'events' that shape the organisation's trajectory. This critical juncture, where choices begin to self-reinforce, marks the end of the pre-formation phase.[25, 50, 51]

A good example is a start-up exploring different business models during its early days. The founders experiment with various strategies – subscription-based services, one-time sales, or freemium models – without a clear preference for any. After some trial and error, they discover that their freemium model, where basic services are offered for free with premium features available at a cost, is gaining significant traction. Initially, this decision might seem like a stroke of luck, but it sets off a self-reinforcing process within the company. The success of the freemium model begins to shape other aspects of the business, from product development to marketing strategies. This marks the end of the pre-formation phase, where the company's future path begins to take shape around this initial, somewhat random success.

Next, as dominant action patterns begin to emerge during the **formation phase**, it becomes more and more challenging to step away from the initial choices or initial sets of action, thus narrowing the range of options – in effect, there is a push for doing more of the same. While such forces become undeniable, they do not yet converge to a fixed point: some leeway continues to exist. In other words, a path is gradually emerging, with the organisation, its actors, and its practices becoming increasingly dependent on it.[50, 51]

Continuing with the start-up example, the success of the freemium model leads the company to focus its resources on refining and expanding this approach. The founders, who were once open to various business models, now find that their company's growth is increasingly tied to the freemium strategy. New product features are developed with this model in mind, and marketing efforts are geared towards attracting more users to the free service in the hope of converting them to paid subscribers. Although the company still has the option to explore other models, these alternatives become less attractive and less likely as the freemium model continues to succeed. The organisation is now in the formation phase, where its path is solidifying but not yet fully locked in.

Eventually, during the **lock-in phase**, the dominant pattern gets fixed and takes on a deterministic character: alternative solutions are disregarded to keep up with the status quo, with only minor variations on the dominant pattern still being considered. In this phase, the organisation is greatly at risk of becoming inefficient, for it has almost entirely lost out on the possibility of adapting itself to its developing environment and to potentially better alternatives.[24, 35, 50, 51]

In the case of the start-up, the company has now fully committed to the freemium model. Its production systems, marketing strategies, and customer support are all tailored to this approach. Even as market conditions change – perhaps new competitors emerge with innovative business models, or customer preferences shift – the company finds it difficult to pivot away from the freemium strategy. The resources and infrastructure that have been built around this model create a form of inertia, making it nearly impossible to switch to a different approach. The company has entered the lock-in phase, where it is at significant risk of becoming outdated, having lost its flexibility to adapt to new realities.

While path dependency emphasises the importance of seemingly random events or choices solidifying much of a company's further developments, it does not pay much attention to the context in which such choices take place.[26, 50, 51] **Imprinting**, on the other hand, stresses the importance of environmental conditions rather than random historical events or choices: it emphasises how characteristics of an entity shaped during a sensitive moment of its existence can persist for decades, in spite of subsequent environmental changes.[26, 39, 47] During a brief sensitive period, the entity is highly susceptible to environmental influence, making it reflect elements of the environment as it was at that time. These characteristics prove to be highly persistent, with little change to be expected at all. In other words, the imprinted entity finds itself 'stamped' by its initial environmental conditions, leaving it inclined to act, think, or decide according to these initial conditions.[7, 9, 54, 55]

Think about companies that were founded during the height of the dot-com bubble in the late 1990s. During this period, the environment was characterised by aggressive risk-taking, a focus on rapid user growth, and an influx of venture capital. These environmental conditions imprinted themselves on these firms, shaping their culture and strategic priorities. Even after the bubble burst and the broader economic environment shifted towards more conservative business practices, many of them continued to prioritise rapid expansion and aggressive risk-taking, despite the changing market dynamics. In a word, they had been imprinted, and changing their approach proved difficult to execute.

Higher education institutions offer another illustration. Many universities were established during periods when access to education was restricted to the elite, and their curricula and social structures were designed to serve this narrow demographic. Despite the democratisation of education over the centuries and the increasing diversity of the student body, many of these institutions still carry imprints from their origins. This is evident in the persistence of certain traditions, curricula, and organisational structures that were designed to serve a very different societal context. For example, the continued emphasis on classical education in some universities, despite the increasing relevance of technology and vocational training in modern economies, can be attributed to imprinting.

> **Box 8.5 The Point?**
>
> Path dependency and imprinting show the persistence of organisational characteristics and choices, even as the external environment evolves. The concepts help to explain why certain behaviours, practices, and structures remain deeply ingrained within organisations, despite significant changes in their external environment.

## 8.3.2 Escalating Commitment

Building on earlier insights from path dependency and imprinting, the concept of **escalating commitment** highlights a related but more psychologically charged dynamic: the tendency of decision-makers to double down on a chosen course of action, even when evidence suggests that it's failing.[3, 33, 44, 45, 58] In other words, they keep 'throwing good money after bad'[15] – not unlike gamblers relentlessly increasing their bets in the hope of recovering losses.

A striking example of escalating commitment in an organisational context is the case of large-scale IT project failures. Consider a company that invests millions into developing a new enterprise software system, only to encounter repeated technical issues, missed deadlines, and budget overruns. Despite clear warning signs and expert recommendations to halt or pivot the project, leadership remains steadfast in their original decision, pouring in additional resources to 'fix' the problems rather than cutting their losses. Fear of reputational damage, reluctance to admit past mistakes, and the belief that success is just one more investment away keep the organisation locked into an increasingly costly endeavour. In the end, the project may be scrapped after years of wasted effort, illustrating how escalating commitment can lead even rational decision-makers to act against their own best interests.

While escalating commitment may be very damaging to companies, there are three major determinants that explain why it happens:[45]

- Motivation to justify previous decisions – when organisational managers can be held responsible for negative consequences, they will be more likely to justify – and continue – previous choices made. Such motivation is further increased when the internal or external organisational environment demands proof of competence, as is often the case in publicly owned companies.[3, 33, 44, 45, 58] For example, a CEO who championed an expensive market expansion may resist pulling out, even when sales remain stagnant, fearing that admitting failure will damage their credibility. Consequently, the CEO might persist in the taken course, irrespective of the presence of early warning signals that clearly flag its dangers.
- Norms for consistency – next, individuals may model their behaviour according to what is socially and culturally advanced as 'successful' within organisations and society as a

whole. In Western societies, there tends to be a low tolerance for failure, while persistence is often celebrated, with a common belief that overcoming challenges only makes one stronger.[3, 33, 44, 45, 58] Because of such cultural norms, a start-up founder may continue funding an underperforming product not because the data supports it but because pivoting could be seen as weakness, contradicting the entrepreneurial ideal of relentless determination. While it may be the most rational option to pivot, the founder may thus decide to carry on.

- Probability and value of future outcomes – finally, the probability and the deemed value of future outcomes represent decision-makers' rational factors, constituting what can still be expected from the initial action. While the perceived value of future outcomes is often relatively straightforward to assess, the perceived probability of future outcomes has been noted to depend on the efficacy of resources and the persistence of the cause of the setback.[3, 33, 44, 45, 58] For instance, a biotech company developing a groundbreaking drug may continue clinical trials despite repeated setbacks, convinced that one more phase of testing could lead to a major breakthrough. While the potential reward is clear – a lucrative patent and industry recognition – the real challenge lies in estimating the true probability of success. If leaders overestimate the impact of additional resources or underestimate the systemic issues causing delays, they may push forward at great cost, hoping that the next milestone will justify their persistence.

**Box 8.6 The Point?**

While a purely 'objective' type of decision-making would depend only on the probability and value of future outcomes, escalating commitment theory signals such determinants to be often complemented (or even overruled) by variables that are far less objective. The theory explains why students may invest more time and effort in finishing a degree with minimal job prospects over switching to an entirely new field of study. It explains why investors may purchase additional stock even when the share price has plummeted, or why cities may continue to invest enormous sums of money in projects that already proved shaky after the first month.[27, 38, 44, 45] In this sense, commitment decisions may be influenced as much by the need to correct past results as by the goal of achieving future ones.[45]

## 8.3.3 Authenticity and Dealing with Resistance to Change

If the frameworks we've explored so far tell us anything, it's this: resistance is rarely just about the change at hand; it's about what came before it, and how difficult it can be to let go. Path dependency reminds us how current behaviour is shaped by long-established routines. Imprinting shows how formative environments leave lasting marks. And escalating commitment reveals the emotional investments and internalised norms that often keep us tied to old decisions – even when new evidence demands a shift.

In all of these cases, resistance is less a conscious objection and more a reflection of embedded patterns, feelings, and meaning. So, what do we do with that? How do we respond to resistance when it is about not just logic or data but emotions, identity, and the comfort of past choices?

One of the most useful ideas I've come across that helps address this is the notion of **authenticity**. I first encountered it in Peter Block's work, where – writing in the context of consulting engagements – he foregrounded the importance of acting with authenticity when navigating uncertainty and resistance in client relationships.[5] Over time, I have come to believe that the value of his insights extends well beyond consulting; for that reason, I'll include a distilled version of them here, offered as a compass for any leader facing change.

At the heart of Block's approach lies a somewhat uncomfortable truth: you cannot argue someone out of their feelings. And the more you try – the more you explain, rationalise, or push – the more firmly they may dig in. Too often, when encountering resistance, we assume that the problem lies in understanding: if we could just explain things better, or rationalise the plan more clearly, people would come around. But in reality resistance is rarely about a failure to grasp the facts. It's not that employees don't 'get' the change; it's that the change hits something deeper within them, a sense of personal risk. In this sense, resistance isn't a problem to be solved; it's a signal to be listened to.[5]

So how does Block suggest dealing with resistance? Using three steps:

1. Notice resistance when it occurs – the real skill of dealing with resistance lies not in convincing but in noticing. When resistance surfaces, in silence, sarcasm, deflection, or disengagement, your initial job is to identify it to yourself. 'She keeps pushing the deadline back.' 'He's stopped contributing to the discussions.' 'They've gone quiet.' These observations aren't accusations, they're information. Your task is to tune in, not to react.[5]
2. Express what you're noticing – gently reflect back what you're noticing, using neutral language. 'It seems like there's some hesitation around this timeline.' 'I'm getting the sense that this doesn't quite sit right with you.' This is what it means to name the resistance openly. You're not labelling it as good or bad; you're simply offering a mirror and giving people the space to see themselves in it.[5]
3. Let others react – perhaps the hardest part, you stop. You stay quiet. You hold the space. Let the discomfort settle. Resist the urge to explain or fix. Let those who resisted speak, if they want to. Or not, if they don't. The point is not to force a resolution. The point is to remain present, open, and respectful in the face of uncertainty.[5]

When resistance is given space to surface and be voiced, it tends to loosen its grip. It does not disappear altogether, but it ceases to dominate the situation; it remains part of the dynamic, yet no longer determines its course. The key across these three steps is naming your lived experiences in plain, unembellished language and inviting other people to do the same. This doesn't mean that you need to have the perfect words; on the contrary, it means that you need to speak from a place that's real. You might say, 'I'm sensing some hesitation in the room, and I'm not entirely sure what it's about – but I'd like to understand'. Or, 'I realise I'm feeling a bit uncertain about how this will land, and I imagine others of you might be, too'. These kinds of comments don't show weakness; they show authenticity. And, in high-stakes moments, authenticity garners trust.[5]

When you model authenticity, you give others permission to be real too. You lower the temperature in the room. You signal that disagreement is okay, that not knowing is okay, that there's room for vulnerability in the conversation. And, paradoxically, it's this very openness that often accelerates progress. People are far more likely to move forward with change when they feel seen, heard, and understood – not managed.[5]

That is what real change work often looks like: not polished slide decks, not checklists, but these awkward, delicate moments of human engagement. These are the forks in the road – where trust can either deepen or dissolve. Authenticity isn't a tool for manipulating buy-in; it's a posture of respect. And, over time, that posture can often build trust in a way that no clever tactic ever could.[5]

**Box 8.7 The Point?**

Change is hard – not just because it's complex but because people and organisations carry histories, habits, and emotional investments that shape how they respond to it. Authenticity invites us to meet resistance not with persuasion but with presence and honesty.

## 8.3.4 The Law of Diffusion

Alright, so being authentic can go a long way in defusing the explosiveness of resistance. But will it be enough to bring everyone on board? In all honesty, probably not. Then again, it's worth asking whether that's necessary in the first place.

Let's turn to a final tool: the **law of diffusion**. At its core, this framework – advanced by people like Everett Rogers and Geoffrey Moore[29, 32] – reminds us that new ideas, tools, and behaviours don't get adopted by everyone at the same time. Instead, they move through a population in stages, first attracting a small minority of enthusiastic adopters before gradually picking up steam, and eventually reaching even the most sceptical.

This sounds simple enough. But in relation to working with change it can be surprisingly liberating, because if you buy into this logic then the fact that not everyone is immediately on board stops being a cause for alarm. It becomes something to expect. Based on the normal distribution ('the bell curve'), the law suggests that when you introduce something new – whether a product, a behaviour, or a strategic process – roughly

- 2.5 per cent of people will be **innovators** – naturally curious and eager to try new things;
- 13.5 per cent will be **early adopters** – open to new directions, especially if they align with personal values or strategic aims;
- 34 per cent will be the **early majority** and another 34 per cent the **late majority** – more pragmatic, needing evidence, reassurance, or social proof before moving; and
- about 16 per cent will be **laggards** – those who resist change for as long as possible, often for good reason.[29, 32]

What's crucial here is that real momentum doesn't begin until you've convinced somewhere between 15 per cent and 18 per cent of people – roughly the innovators and the early adopters combined. That's the tipping point – it's a psychological and social phenomenon. And it's smaller than most of us think.[29, 32]

This is good news. It means that you don't have to win over the entire organisation to move forward. You don't even need a majority. What you need is a strategic minority – a small but visible group who are willing to adopt the change, test it, speak for it, and make it real in practice. Once they do, others begin to take notice. They see that the change isn't just a theoretical proposal from above; it's something that actual people are trying, adapting, and – crucially – surviving.[29, 32]

The tipping point works not because of volume but because of visibility and credibility. It turns the conversation from 'Why should we do this?' to 'Why wouldn't we?'. And once that shift starts happening, you no longer have to push the change on others – it starts to pull them in.

Importantly, this doesn't mean that the remaining 80 per cent will come along easily or uniformly. Some will need more time. Others will still push back. And a few might never truly buy in. But the diffusion perspective allows you to stop chasing consensus and instead focus your efforts where they matter most: identifying the willing, enabling their success, and letting that success do the talking.[29, 32]

**Box 8.8 The Point?**

Why does this matter for your change efforts? Because too often we try to convince everyone at once – and get discouraged when the middle or the sceptics don't immediately respond. We interpret their hesitation as failure. Or, worse, we try to force alignment, which only hardens resistance. The law of diffusion invites a different approach: focus your energy on the few who are already leaning in. These early adopters aren't just easier to mobilise; they're also your best bet for reaching the rest.

## 8.4 Impact on the Ground

Although a persistence perspective often emphasises the dark side of change, it can have an important impact on how people understand change in an organisational context. Several implications follow from this view; here, I highlight the most important ones.

### 8.4.1 A Persistence Perspective Counterweights (the Need for) Change

First, a major benefit of adding a persistence perspective to your toolkit is its ability to rebalance the scales of the change discussion: specifically, it helps us recognise that what we can and cannot change within organisations is not always within our control. While some aspects of organisational life might be easily adjusted without major repercussions, other elements may lie beyond our direct influence.

Instead of being frustrated by this reality or attempting to disprove it, a persistence perspective encourages us to accept when an organisation is likely to change and when it might (need to) remain stationary. The approach helps prevent managers from becoming caught up in the oversimplified advice that is commonly found in organisational change management.[48] Today, there are far more organisations that aggressively and constantly pursue change than those who avoid it. These companies change rapidly and frequently, often beyond what is sustainable. Executives in such organisations need to closely monitor their operations to ensure that the pace of change does not overwhelm employees or negatively impact customers.[1] As such, understanding the persistence perspective may help managers realise that the most sensible approach is not always to push for constant flexibility but to know when stability is the wisest course of action.

### 8.4.2 A Persistence Perspective Elevates the Level of Change

Next, thinking about change from a persistence perspective redirects our understanding of change to a broader level, beyond the single organisational entity. By shifting the focus from individual firms to organisational populations, the perspective broadens the horizons for those interested in change.

While this reconceptualisation may strike some as a minor redirection of thought, its importance cannot be overstated. Initially, the focus in organisational studies was on individual organisations and their surroundings. This focus was so prevalent that it seemed to be taken for granted that organisations were the appropriate units of analysis.[17] By breaking conceptualisations of change loose from organisational boundaries, a persistence perspective advances a way of thinking that, before its introduction, was not considered in earnest – with industries, sectors, and populations now coming to represent key groups of interest, and organisational survival and death representing fundamental mechanisms through which change is able to take place at all.

### 8.4.3 A Persistence Perspective Legitimises Resistance

Finally, a persistence perspective revalidates resistance to change, transforming it from an unfortunate obstacle into an inherent organisational force. Unlike traditional views that often see resistance as a failure of change management, the persistence perspective considers it a legitimate and expected response within the social context of organisations. Most conventional theories of change have acknowledged resistance as a factor, but rarely have they viewed it as legitimate or acceptable. A persistence perspective, however, sees resistance as a rightful expression of those undergoing change, as they seek to protect their earnt rights and resources.[42] In this sense, the persistence perspective elevates resistance to change as a valid and integral part of organisational life, recognising that it stems from the reality of dealing with organisations as they are, rather than as we hope them to be.

## 8.5 Drawbacks and Pitfalls

As with all perspectives, a persistence perspective is not without its pitfalls. The following challenges should be on your radar when approaching change from a persistence angle.

### 8.5.1 A Persistence Perspective May Seem Incorrect

One common challenge faced by the persistence perspective is the observation of change happening in organisations, despite the perspective suggesting that inertia would prevent it.[20, 37, 39, 51] Examples of change in the world of business are ubiquitous, and many readers of this book will have no trouble thinking of an example they may have experienced themselves. In this way, as organisations do change every so often, what should we make of a perspective that seemingly denies such change in the first place?

Crucial to remark in this respect is that a persistence perspective does not claim that organisations never change at all. What the perspective does emphasise is that (i) change in an organisation is often difficult because of a variety of reasons that are inherent to the organisational context, and that (ii) when change is advanced it should, as far as possible, be limited to those areas that are peripheral to the organisation's activities. While changes to core activities may be forced, they are believed to generally harm the organisation's overall chances of survival. In this way, the persistence perspective should be interpreted not as a rejection of all changes taking place in organisations but rather as a prominent disclaimer on whether such changes might at all be realisable or valuable to the organisation as it is.[2, 19, 31, 57]

> **Box 8.9 Practical Advice?**
>
> For managers and change agents, understanding the limits of what can be changed is just as important as recognising opportunities for change. Focus on identifying areas where change is more likely to succeed without jeopardising the organisation's core strengths. If a change to core activities is necessary, approach it with caution and conduct a thorough risk assessment. Engage in scenario planning to anticipate potential disruptions and ensure that the organisation can adapt without losing its essential identity.

### 8.5.2 A Persistence Perspective Lacks a Sense of Agency

Next, when thinking about change from a persistence angle, it is easy to get sucked into very vague notions of inertia – change cannot happen because 'the system' is preventing it. But who is this system and what is our role in it? Several theories developed from a persistence perspective have been criticised for leaving out direct indications of agency.[13, 26, 28, 49, 51] While several immaterial 'forces', 'factors', or 'determinants' within organisations are pointed towards to explain the firm's immobilisation, seldom do theories deal with more direct indications of who could – if at all – make a difference. Who deepens the ruts in which the organisation finds itself over time, and who could do something to pull it out? In this sense, while theories in the persistence perspective can offer significant structural insight, they can also make you lose out on a sense of agency.

It should be noted that many of the structural factors that persistence theories have raised do contain – albeit implicit – indications of agency. For example, while Hannan and Freeman's indication of political coalitions as an internal determinant of inertia can be understood as a structural factor, it also links to the people trying to keep the organisation stay the same.[17, 18] Similarly, while the theory on path dependency predominantly considers the impersonal, self-reinforcing processes that are at play throughout the organisation's development, it stands to reason that many of these processes emanate from the actions or decisions of particular individuals.[51] In this sense, although the persistence perspective may not have focused directly on agency, it does contain some good stepping stones by way of which to visualise the importance of agentic factors nonetheless.

### Box 8.10 Practical Advice?

Identify the key actors – whether they are individuals or coalitions – who are influencing the organisation's trajectory. Understanding who holds power and how they are using it can reveal opportunities to effect meaningful change, even within a seemingly rigid structure. Empower these actors to make decisions that align with the organisation's long-term goals and ensure that they have the resources and support they need to challenge entrenched practices where necessary.

## SUMMARY

Chapter 8 explored the **persistence perspective on change**, which challenges the assumption that change is always desirable or even possible. Unlike perspectives that treat transformation as necessary or inevitable, this view highlights the significant barriers to change, questioning whether it is truly achievable or if it often serves as mere illusion (see Table 8.1 for an overview).

- ◊ The **development of this perspective** was shaped by two key realisations. First, the difficulty of achieving meaningful change became undeniable, as many organisations struggle to implement or sustain transformations despite extensive efforts. Second, the downside of change became equally evident, with poorly executed initiatives leading to instability and unintended consequences. Together, these insights led to a more sceptical approach – one that sees change not as a given but as something that is often constrained, resisted, or manipulated.
- ◊ At its **core**, this perspective defines change as either unattainable or undesirable. Rather than developing through deliberate intervention, organisations are largely dictated by historical patterns. If change happens at all, the persistence perspective notes it as taking place at the level of the organisational population. Instead of assuming that change is driven by innovation or strategic necessity, this perspective suggests that it is often a form

**Table 8.1 A persistence perspective on change: overview**

| | |
|---|---|
| **Guiding metaphor** | Change as an illusion |
| **The genesis of thought** | |
| Development 1 | The struggle to make change stick |
| Development 2 | Confronting the unintended consequences of change |
| **Unpacking the heart** | |
| Capacity of change | Change as undesirable or unattainable |
| Development of change | History and its projection |
| Drivers of change | The role of the organisational population |
| Aim of change | Window-dressing and personal gain |
| **Extending your toolkit** | |
| Tool #1 | Path dependency and imprinting |
| Tool #2 | Escalating commitment |
| Tool #3 | Authenticity and dealing with resistance to change |
| Tool #4 | The law of diffusion |
| **Impact on the ground** | |
| ( + ) | A persistence perspective counterweights (the need for) change. |
| ( + ) | A persistence perspective elevates the level of change. |
| ( + ) | A persistence perspective legitimises resistance. |
| **Drawbacks and pitfalls** | |
| ( − ) | A persistence perspective may seem incorrect. |
| ( − ) | A persistence perspective lacks a sense of agency. |
| **Related concepts** | |
| ► | Critical theories of change |

of window-dressing, used to create the appearance of progress while serving personal or political agendas.

◊ To better understand the forces that sustain stability, we examined several **key tools**. Path dependency and imprinting explain how historical choices and conditions shape and constrain future actions. Escalating commitment theory illustrates why managers often keep 'throwing good money after bad'. The concept of authenticity reveals how organisations may navigate resistance to change – not with persuasion but with presence and honesty. Finally, the law of diffusion shows why it's reasonable to focus your energy on those who are already leaning in.

- ◊ The persistence perspective makes several important **contributions** to the change conversation. It offers a necessary counterbalance, tempering overly optimistic views of transformation by emphasising the forces that sustain stability. It also elevates the discussion around change, encouraging a more critical examination of when, how, and why change efforts succeed or fail. Additionally, it legitimises resistance, reframing it not as an obstacle but as an inherent and sometimes rational response to change initiatives.
- ◊ Despite its insights, this perspective is not without its **weaknesses**. At times, it may seem blatantly incorrect, particularly when faced with clear examples of successful change. Furthermore, by downplaying agency, it risks portraying organisations and individuals as passive entities bound by history, rather than as actors capable of shaping their own futures.

The persistence perspective connects to broader critical theories of change, offering a thought-provoking challenge to conventional change narratives. While it questions the feasibility and motivations behind transformation, it also raises deeper concerns about whether change is always necessary – or whether, in many cases, stability, continuity, and resistance serve a more vital role in organisational life than is often acknowledged.

## CASE: TO BE OR NOT TO BE . . . A BANK

### The Persistence Perspective in Practice

To be or not to be? It's a great Shakespearian question that has captivated people for centuries. On the surface, it concerns a question of life versus death; yet, delving slightly deeper, it also reflects doubts about how such life should be lived at all, and who the individual who is living it ultimately turns out to be.

For organisations, the question of 'to be or not to be?' matters as much as it does for people. Do we want to exist at all in our present form, or not? Which ways of organising as a group do we consider acceptable, and which ways do we not? Who are we becoming as time goes by, and can we agree to that at all? These are questions that most organisations invariably face as they mature. How they respond to them ultimately defines the fate of all those involved.

One company that has come to exemplify this quintessential struggle quite beautifully is Desjardins, based in Québec, Canada. While the company offers a range of financial services that are not too different from those provided by an average bank, it has repeatedly fought against being considered one; instead, ever since its founding in 1900, Desjardins has toiled to be (and remain) a financial 'cooperative' – a business that is owned and controlled by the people who use its services. At Desjardins, members have a say in how the organisation is run – and how it is not. At the time of writing, Desjardins is the largest financial cooperative in Canada and the fifth largest financial cooperative in the world. It holds over CAN$350 billion in assets, counts more than 7 million members, and employs approximately 50,000 employees. For many Canadians, Desjardins is an organisation to be proud of – as much developed for them as by them.

In this case, we will look into the evolutions of Desjardins, as well as its struggles surrounding how *not* to evolve. Because, after all, to be or not to be – that is the question.

### Origins and Founding by Alphonse Desjardins

At the end of the nineteenth century, French-Canadian citizens of Québec were often treated as second-class by their English counterparts – and one of the most deplorable consequences of that discrimination was that they had very poor access to financial services. In 1900, to fight usury and democratise access to credit, French-Canadian Alphonse Desjardins began creating small savings and loans cooperatives (known as 'caisses populaires'), which were owned and operated by members themselves. These organisations were founded with a strong social mission and cooperative identity, aimed at promoting the economic emancipation of working-class French Canadians.

From the outset, the founder rejected using the terms 'bank' or 'business' to describe the institution, explaining that the word 'bank' was unsuitable because its meaning was entirely at odds with the nature of these institutions. He emphasised that a 'caisse populaire' was not a business or a mere financial transaction service but rather a social and community-focused initiative. Founding principles included notions such as democracy, decentralisation, autonomy, altruism, and prudence. In the decades that followed, these initial directions became highly influential in the strategic and organisational choices made at Desjardins.

### Acceptance of 'Consumer Credit'

By the 1960s, Canadian society had evolved a lot since the days of Alphonse Desjardins. As technology had developed, so had the needs and expectations of the people whom these technologies were meant to serve. Instead of using horse-pulled carriages, people increasingly resorted to cars. Instead of warming their homes with a woodstove, they switched to electric heaters. Instead of spending their time washing clothes manually in a tub, they used a laundry washer.

To finance such 'consumption goods', people increasingly resorted to credit companies and financial institutions. However, at Desjardins, the decision to start offering this kind of credit was long rejected in horror, contrary as that decision seemed to be to the cooperative principles and the group's history of anti-usury. Cyrille Vaillancourt, president of Desjardins in 1963, warned that easy credit for consumption was a trap that ensnared thousands every year. He pointed out that those who engaged in such practices were only interested in collecting higher interest from borrowers. Vaillancourt expressed concern that if the 'caisses populaires' adopted such practices, they would turn into capitalist organisations focused solely on returns, losing their core values.

Two years later, societal evolutions and new technologies proved to be increasingly irreversible. To keep up with the changed demands of their members, Desjardins voted – somewhat reluctantly – in favour of opening up towards 'consumer credit'. It did, however, cause quite the commotion. Emile Girardin, president of the Montréal region at the time, noted that some people criticised the organisation for being too rigid and closely tied to the founder's original doctrine, while others were concerned that its rapid evolution might undermine its cooperative nature. He questioned how to reconcile these differing viewpoints and unite them as a cohesive approach.

In the years that followed, a variety of coping mechanisms developed as ways of answering that question. For some, this included reframing the extension of consumption credit as a means to 'democratise' or 'decentralise' money. For others, it included engaging in extensive rationalisation, stating how Desjardins would rapidly become irrelevant if it did not open to the practice.

### Introduction of Credit Cards

In the 1970s, a similar debacle arose, this time concerning the potential introduction of credit cards. For many traditional banks, credit cards had gradually turned out to be convenient ways of extending small credits to their customers, which they could use as they saw fit. Yet, for Desjardins, the question proved much more delicate, with many members considering credit cards to be at odds with the organisation's founding principle of prudence. In 1974, the group voted strongly against the introduction of credit cards. An editorial in an internal Desjardins magazine at the time summarised the decision by stating that the cooperative nature of the group could not support certain practices of consumer society that led people into debt with high costs.

For seven years, Desjardins refrained from offering credit cards, even though other Canadian financial institutions had already begun providing them to clients in the late 1960s. By 1981, the organisation's stance on the issue had become increasingly untenable. An internal memo highlighted that the 1980s had revealed the precarious state of human evolution, emphasising that cooperatives would need to operate in a world largely shaped by others. As a result, a new vote was held on the introduction of credit cards – and this time the Desjardins members voted in favour.

In the internal corporate magazine that later elaborated on the outcome of the voting, much was being done to make this strategic shift acceptable to even the most cooperative-minded of members. In several elaborate articles, the group's leaders explained how the introduction of credit cards did not mean that Desjardins would become any less concerned about the sage use of credit, nor did it mean that the cooperative practices were replaced with more capitalist ones. Leaders even went so far as to argue that credit cards were not truly cards of credit but rather payment cards – stipulating in as many as seven points why such terminology would in fact be more appropriate. To organisational outsiders, such rhetorical juggling may have seemed somewhat pointless, but to Desjardins insiders, it touched upon the very foundations on which their organisation was vested – including protecting the weak against exorbitant money-lending practices.

### Revising Organisational Structure

By the end of the 1990s, it seemed that competitive forces were again knocking on Desjardins' door. While the company had always displayed great pride in its cooperative governance model and structure – where small, autonomous units clustered together to represent the organisation as a whole – its leaders eventually campaigned to revise this structure to a more centralised one. While this would allow Desjardins to save quite a lot of money and increase the speed of its decision-making process, it would also represent a severe departure from the cooperative model that the organisation had been following for almost a century. As a result, a tough decision had to be made, with external commentators questioning whether Alphonse Desjardins would have been deeply upset by the changes.

For many, however, restructuring Desjardins was seen as the only practical path forward. Several directors noted that the competition was fierce, and that Desjardins needed to cut costs and improve productivity to remain competitive. In such argumentations, it was often emphasised that members needed to understand that certain compromises were essential for the future of the Desjardins Group.

At the beginning of the twenty-first century, Desjardins members voted in favour of restructuring the group. Following this decision, leaders were quick to stress that the restructuring did not conflict with the cooperative principles of democracy and equality. President Béland pointed out that, in his view, the regions had never been as well balanced as they were after the changes. He explained that previously there had been a mix of large and small federations, but the restructuring had created sixteen groups of equal strength, ensuring a more balanced distribution of power and a stronger influence of the 'caisses' within the new structure. Béland later emphasised that the new organisation would firmly rely on the principles established by Alphonse Desjardins, the group's founder.

For some, these statements seemed empty. In 2011, René Croteau, a former executive at Desjardins, released a sharp critique of the group's restructuring decisions in his book *A Cooperative Heritage Disfigured*. The book sparked significant controversy and debate, ultimately highlighting the critical question that Desjardins had been grappling with for over a century: should it continue to be a cooperative or simply evolve into a bank?

### Reflect

1. Why was Desjardins facing such difficulties with the changes described?
2. How were changes coped with at Desjardins? What did the various parties at Desjardins do in order to manage these changes?
3. Do you think that Desjardins changed too much or too little? Why?
4. How may the organisation tackle similar issues in the future?

### Case Study Sources

Croteau, R. (2004). *Un patrimoine coopératif défiguré et dénaturé*. Sainte-Foy: Éditions MultiMondes.

De Keyser, B., & Langley, A. (2025). Sustaining authenticity while enabling adaptation: Discursively navigating strategy-identity tensions over time. *Long Range Planning*, *58*(1), 102533.

Giroux, N. (1993). *Changement stratégique dans une institution: Le cas Desjardins*. Boucherville: G. Morin.

Grondin, P. (1938). *Catechisme des Caisses populaires Desjardins*. Levis: Federation de Quebec des Unions regionales des Caisses populaires Desjardins.

Lamarche, J. (1997). *Le président Béland: Biographie du 8e président du Mouvement Desjardins*. Montréal: Guérin.

Lévesque, B. (1997). *Desjardins: Une Entreprise et un Mouvement?* Québec: Presses de l'Université du Québec.

Poulin, P. (1990). *Histoire du Mouvement Desjardins: Tome I Desjardins et la naissance des caisses populaires 1900–1920*. Montréal: Québec-Amérique.

Poulin, P. (1994). *Histoire du Mouvement Desjardins: Tome II La percée des caisses populaires 1920–1944*. Montréal: Québec-Amérique.

Poulin, P. (1998). *Histoire du Mouvement Desjardins: Tome III De la caisse locale au complexe financier*. Montréal: Québec-Amérique.

Poulin, P. (2000). *Desjardins: 100 ans d'histoire*. Sainte-Foy MultiMondes.

Poulin, P., & Tremblay, B. (2005). *Desjardins en mouvement*. Montréal: Presses HEC Montréal.

## REFERENCES

[1] Abrahamson, E. (2004). Avoiding repetitive change syndrome. *MIT Sloan Management Review*, *45* (2), 93–95.

[2] Barnett, W. P., & Pontikes, E. G. (2008). The Red Queen, success bias, and organizational inertia. *Management Science*, *54*(7), 1237–1251.

[3] Bazerman, M. H., Giuliano, T., & Appelman, A. (1984). Escalation of commitment in individual and group decision making. *Organizational Behavior and Human Performance*, *33*(2), 141–152.

[4] Betton, J., & Dess, G. G. (1985). The application of population ecology models to the study of organizations. *Academy of Management Review*, *10*(4), 750–757.

[5] Block, P. (1986). *Flawless consulting: A guide to getting your expertise used.* Hoboken, NJ: John Wiley and Sons.

[6] Burgelman, R. A. (2002). Strategy as vector and the inertia of coevolutionary lock-in. *Administrative Science Quarterly*, *47*(2), 325–357.

[7] Carroll, G. R., & Hannan, M. T. (2004). *The demography of corporations and industries*. Princeton, NJ: Princeton University Press.

[8] Cool, K. O., Dierickx, I., & Szulanski, G. (1997). Diffusion of innovations within organizations: Electronic switching in the Bell system, 1971–1982. *Organization Science*, *8*(5), 543–559.

[9] DiMaggio, P., & Powell, W. W. (1983). The iron cage revisited: Collective rationality and institutional isomorphism in organizational fields. *American Sociological Review*, *48*(2), 147–160.

[10] Dobrev, S. D., Kim, T.-Y., & Carroll, G. R. (2003). Shifting gears, shifting niches: Organizational inertia and change in the evolution of the US automobile industry, 1885–1981. *Organization Science*, *14*(3), 264–282.

[11] Dooley, K. J. (1997). A complex adaptive systems model of organization change. *Nonlinear Dynamics, Psychology, and Life Sciences*, *1*(1), 69–97.

[12] Fredrickson, J. W., & Iaquinto, A. L. (1989). Inertia and creeping rationality in strategic decision processes. *Academy of Management Journal, 32*(3), 516–542.
[13] Garud, R., & Karnøe, P. (2001). Path creation as a process of mindful deviation. In R. Garud & P. Karnøe (eds.), *Path dependence and creation* (pp. 1–38). London: Lawrence Erlbaum Associates.
[14] Gilbert, C. G. (2005). Unbundling the structure of inertia: Resource versus routine rigidity. *Academy of Management Journal, 48*(5), 741–763.
[15] Guler, I. (2007). Throwing good money after bad? Political and institutional influences on sequential decision making in the venture capital industry. *Administrative Science Quarterly, 52*(2), 248–285.
[16] Hammer, M., & Champy, J. (1993). *Reengineering the corporation: A manifesto for business revolution*. New York: Harper Business.
[17] Hannan, M. T., & Freeman, J. (1977). The population ecology of organizations. *American Journal of Sociology, 82*(5), 929–964.
[18] Hannan, M. T., & Freeman, J. (1984). Structural inertia and organizational change. *American Sociological Review, 49*(2), 149–164.
[19] Judge, W. Q., Hu, H. W., Gabrielsson, J., Talaulicar, T., Witt, M. A., Zattoni, A., … Quttainah, M. (2015). Configurations of capacity for change in entrepreneurial threshold firms: Imprinting and strategic choice perspectives. *Journal of Management Studies, 52*(4), 506–530.
[20] Kelly, D., & Amburgey, T. L. (1991). Organizational inertia and momentum: A dynamic model of strategic change. *Academy of Management Journal, 34*(3), 591–612.
[21] Kimberly, J. R. (1979). Issues in the creation of organizations: Initiation, innovation, and institutionalization. *Academy of Management Journal, 22*(3), 437–457.
[22] Koch, J. (2011). Inscribed strategies: Exploring the organizational nature of strategic lock-in. *Organization Studies, 32*(3), 337–363.
[23] Leonard-Barton, D. (1992). Core capabilities and core rigidities: A paradox in managing new product development. *Strategic Management Journal, 13*(S1), 111–125.
[24] Leonard, D. (1995). *Wellsprings of knowledge*: Boston, MA: Harvard Business School Press.
[25] Mahoney, J. (2000). Path dependence in historical sociology. *Theory and Society, 29*(4), 507–548.
[26] Marquis, C., & Tilcsik, A. (2013). Imprinting: Toward a multilevel theory. *Academy of Management Annals, 7*(1), 195–245.
[27] McNamara, G., Moon, H., & Bromiley, P. (2002). Banking on commitment: Intended and unintended consequences of an organization's attempt to attenuate escalation of commitment. *Academy of Management Journal, 45*(2), 443–452.
[28] Miller, D., & Chen, M.-J. (1994). Sources and consequences of competitive inertia: A study of the US airline industry. *Administrative Science Quarterly, 39*(1), 1–23.
[29] Moore, G. A. (1991). *Crossing the chasm: Marketing and selling high-tech products to mainstream customers*. New York: Harper Business.
[30] Pierson, P. (2000). Increasing returns, path dependence, and the study of politics. *American Political Science Review, 94*(2), 251–267.
[31] Ritala, P., Heiman, B., & Hurmelinna-Laukkanen, P. (2016). The need for speed: Unfamiliar problems, capability rigidity, and ad hoc processes in organizations. *Industrial and Corporate Change, 25*(5), 757–777.
[32] Rogers, E. M. (2003). *Diffusion of innovations* (5th ed.). New York: Free Press.
[33] Ross, J., & Staw, B. M. (1993). Organizational escalation and exit: Lessons from the Shoreham nuclear power plant. *Academy of Management Journal, 36*(4), 701–732.
[34] Ruef, M. (1997). Assessing organizational fitness on a dynamic landscape: An empirical test of the relative inertia thesis. *Strategic Management Journal, 18*(11), 837–853.

[35] Schreyögg, G., & Kliesch-Eberl, M. (2007). How dynamic can organizational capabilities be? Towards a dual-process model of capability dynamization. *Strategic Management Journal*, *28*(9), 913–933.

[36] Schreyögg, G., & Sydow, J. (2009). *The hidden dynamics of path dependence: Institutions and organizations*. New York: Springer.

[37] Schwarz, G. M. (2012). The logic of deliberate structural inertia. *Journal of Management*, *38*(2), 547–572.

[38] Simonson, I., & Staw, B. M. (1992). Deescalation strategies: A comparison of techniques for reducing commitment to losing courses of action. *Journal of Applied Psychology*, *77*(4), 419–426.

[39] Simsek, Z., Fox, B. C., & Heavey, C. (2015). 'What's past is prologue': A framework, review, and future directions for organizational research on imprinting. *Journal of Management*, *41*(1), 288–317.

[40] Sorge, A., & Van Witteloostuijn, A. (2004). The (non)sense of organizational change: An essai about universal management hypes, sick consultancy metaphors, and healthy organization theories. *Organization Studies*, *25*(7), 1205–1231.

[41] Sorge, A., & Van Witteloostuijn, A. (2007). The (non)sense of organizational change continued: A rejoinder to Armbrüster and Glückler. *Organization Studies*, *28*(12), 1887–1892.

[42] Spicer, A., & Levay, C. (2012). Critical theories of organizational change. In D. M. Boje, B. Burnes, & J. Hassard (eds.), *The Routledge companion to organizational change* (pp. 276–290). Abingdon: Routledge.

[43] Staber, U., & Sydow, J. (2002). Organizational adaptive capacity: A structuration perspective. *Journal of Management Inquiry*, *11*(4), 408–424.

[44] Staw, B. M. (1976). Knee-deep in the big muddy: A study of escalating commitment to a chosen course of action. *Organizational Behavior and Human Performance*, *16*(1), 27–44.

[45] Staw, B. M. (1981). The escalation of commitment to a course of action. *Academy of Management Review*, *6*(4), 577–587.

[46] Stieglitz, N., & Heine, K. (2007). Innovations and the role of complementarities in a strategic theory of the firm. *Strategic Management Journal*, *28*(1), 1–15.

[47] Stinchcombe, A. L. (1965). Social structure and organizations. In J. G. March (ed.), *Handbook of organizations* (pp. 142–193). Chicago, IL: Rand McNally.

[48] Sturdy, A., & Grey, C. (2003). Beneath and beyond organizational change management: Exploring alternatives. *Organization*, *10*(4), 651–662.

[49] Suddaby, R., & Foster, W. M. (2017). History and organizational change. *Journal of Management*, *43*(1), 19–38.

[50] Sydow, J., Schreyögg, G., & Koch, J. (2009). Organizational path dependence: Opening the black box. *Academy of Management Review*, *34*(4), 689–709.

[51] Sydow, J., Schreyögg, G., & Koch, J. (2020). On the theory of organizational path dependence: Clarifications, replies to objections, and extensions. *Academy of Management Review*, *45*(4), 717–734.

[52] Tasler, N. (2017). Stop using the excuse 'organizational change is hard'. *Harvard Business Review Digital Articles*, *2*(5), 2–5.

[53] Teece, D. J., Pisano, G., & Shuen, A. (1997). Dynamic capabilities and strategic management. *Strategic Management Journal*, *18*(7), 509–533.

[54] Tilcsik, A. (2013). Remembrance of things past: Individual imprinting in organizations. Doctoral dissertation, Harvard University.

[55] Tucker, D. J., Singh, J. V., & Meinhard, A. G. (1990). Founding characteristics, imprinting, and organizational change. In J. V. Singh (ed.), *Organizational evolution: New directions* (pp. 182–200). Newbury Park, CA: Sage.

[56] Välikangas, L. (2007). Rigidity, exploratory patience, and the ecological resilience of organizations. *Scandinavian Journal of Management*, *23*(2), 206–213.
[57] Vergne, J.-P., & Durand, R. (2011). The path of most persistence: An evolutionary perspective on path dependence and dynamic capabilities. *Organization Studies*, *32*(3), 365–382.
[58] Whyte, G. (1986). Escalating commitment to a course of action: A reinterpretation. *Academy of Management Review*, *11*(2), 311–321.
[59] Young, R. C. (1988). Is population ecology a useful paradigm for the study of organizations? *American Journal of Sociology*, *94*(1), 1–24.

# Part III

# Change in Practice

**IN THIS PART, YOU WILL LEARN TO . . .**

- ▶ organise different perspectives on change in relation to each other;
- ▶ evaluate the relevance of perspectives according to the situation;
- ▶ create informed, adaptive strategies for navigating and leading change in complex environments.

If understanding change requires multiple perspectives, then practising change demands even more – an ability to weave perspectives together, apply them in real-world contexts, and navigate the complexities that arise. In this part of the book, we move from seeing change through different lenses to actively working with those lenses, integrating insights, and overcoming the common traps that can limit our ability to drive meaningful transformation.

Chapter 9 works at bringing perspectives together, exploring how different ways of thinking about change can complement each other. While each perspective offers valuable insights, real-world challenges rarely fit neatly within a single framework. We examine practical strategies for combining perspectives, drawing on their strengths, and managing tensions between them. This is not about forcing alignment but about finding productive ways to engage with different ways of seeing and shaping change.

Chapter 10 puts these ideas to the test by leveraging perspectives for action, illustrating how you can benefit from drawing on multiple perspectives in practice. By stepping into the complexity of a real-world scenario, we uncover what it takes to make the most of perspectives and avoid getting stuck in rigid or one-dimensional thinking.

Together, these chapters provide a practical toolkit for those who want to engage deeply with change. They offer not just a way to understand the dynamics at play but a roadmap for leading change with insight, and a capacity to navigate the unexpected. As we move forward, the challenge is not just to adopt multiple perspectives but to use them in a way that creates impact, fosters learning, and ultimately makes change work.

# 9 Bringing Together Perspectives on Change

## Introduction

Over the course of this book, we have explored seven distinct perspectives on organisational change: (i) the managerial perspective, (ii) the organic perspective, (iii) the tension perspective, (iv) the reactive perspective, (v) the capability perspective, (vi) the paradox perspective, and (vii) the persistence perspective. Each of these perspectives provides a unique lens through which to view the dynamic and often complex nature of change within organisations (see Figure 9.1). As we conclude this journey, the task now is to synthesise these perspectives, drawing together the insights we've accumulated in previous chapters to create a more holistic understanding of organisational transformation.

In this chapter, we will tackle several integrative questions that will help you navigate this synthesis: how can we make sense of the various perspectives we've explored? Are some perspectives more applicable than others in different situations or is there value in embracing multiple viewpoints? How can we effectively use these perspectives to guide our approach to change and what practical benefits do they offer in real-world scenarios? And, perhaps most importantly, what are the potential pitfalls of focusing too narrowly on one perspective or failing to appreciate the broader picture?

This chapter will focus on weaving these individual viewpoints into a cohesive framework that can be applied in practice. We will examine how perspectives can complement each other, showing how different lenses can illuminate different aspects of organisational change. We'll also consider how to balance perspectives, recognising that there is no one-size-fits-all approach to managing change. Each situation may require a different emphasis or combination of perspectives.

By the end of this chapter, you will have not only a deeper understanding of how diverse perspectives fit together but also a practical framework for using them to enhance your approach to change management. The goal is to help you see the big picture – how various perspectives, when carefully considered and applied, can inform and shape your understanding of organisational transformation, making you more adaptable and effective in navigating the complexities of change.

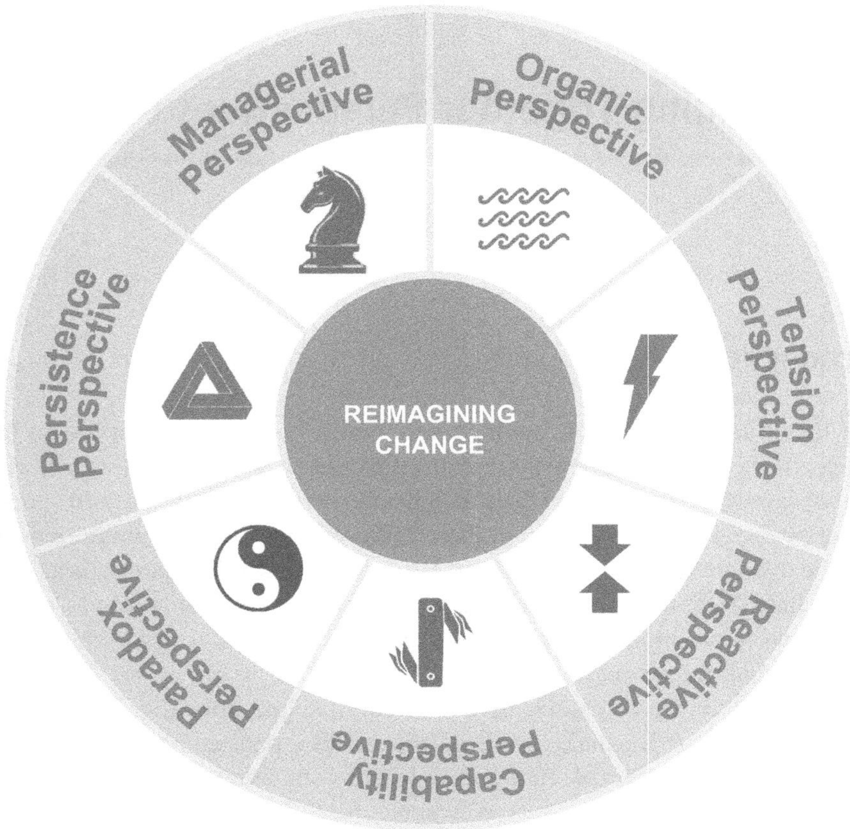


**Figure 9.1** Infographic – perspectives on change: the lens through which we view the world shapes the reality we perceive.

## 9.1 How to Make Sense of Perspectives on Change?

If you've carefully engaged with this book, you will by now appreciate that each perspective provides a distinct and inherently different lens through which to understand organisational change. While all perspectives address the same phenomenon, they diverge significantly in how they conceptualise, appreciate, and interpret change within an organisational context.

For example, a managerial perspective envisions change as a rational, structured process, where leaders plan and implement transitions in a deliberate, top-down manner. In contrast, an organic perspective suggests that change emerges from within, escalating in an ongoing and fluid fashion, often driven by informal adaptations and bottom-up innovation. A tension perspective focuses on power dynamics, emphasising how change is a mechanism for restructuring authority and influence within an organisation. Meanwhile, a reactive perspective ties change to survival, portraying it as a response to crises, external pressures, or existential threats, where immediate action takes precedence over long-term planning.

These differing perspectives underscore the multifaceted nature of organisational change – each serving as a unique set of interpretative goggles that shape how we perceive, analyse, and respond to change. They provide not only different ways of understanding the topic but also distinct vocabularies, frameworks, and potential solutions. Perspectives shape our perception of reality and influence how we define problems, devise strategies, and implement change within organisations.

To illustrate this point, consider a company facing a significant shift in market demands due to rapid digital innovation. A managerial perspective would see executives meticulously planning a response – restructuring departments, implementing new technologies, and reallocating resources to maintain competitiveness. In contrast, an organic perspective would highlight how employees at all levels adapt informally, share knowledge, and innovate in response to new technological trends, often steering the company in unexpected directions. A tension perspective, in turn, would frame the change as a struggle for influence, where different factions within the company – such as IT, marketing, and product development – compete to define the company's digital strategy. Meanwhile, a reactive perspective would depict the company as scrambling to survive, making short-term, urgent decisions without necessarily abiding by a coherent long-term vision. These varied interpretations illustrate how the same organisational reality can be understood and navigated in fundamentally different ways, depending on the perspective adopted.

Ultimately, it's important to understand that the differences among perspectives are more profound than a mere variation in semantics: at their core, perspectives uphold radically different beliefs regarding the nature of reality ('ontology'), as well as how we can hope to distil knowledge from such reality ('epistemology'; see Table 9.1).

For instance, from a managerial perspective, reality is intelligible and orderly, with knowledge of that reality being developed through informed analysis and scholarly logic. Rationality thus stands central, with reality being objectively knowable for all who prove clever enough to grasp it.

From an organic perspective, on the other hand, reality is not fixed but transient, relative to sociality and place. To distil knowledge from such reality, we must work to experience and engage ourselves in social interaction. In this logic, reality is not objectively knowable as much as it proves to be subjectively construable.

According to the tension perspective, reality is rife with contradiction and conflict between opposing views. Knowledge is to be distilled from embracing such contradictions wholeheartedly.

For the reactive perspective, reality is highly uncertain and replete with risk, with knowledge coming from encountering and learning from hardship. Only by stumbling and picking ourselves up can we hope to work out how things truly are.

When turning towards the capability perspective, reality is about what is potential rather than what is. Knowledge emanates from the aspiration to develop – we aspire, and thus we are.

From a paradox perspective, reality is dual – both moving and stable – with true knowledge coming from the pursuit of balance and harmony. Rather than being either black or white, reality is believed to be both at the same time.

**Table 9.1 Ontologies and epistemologies**

| PERSPECTIVE | ONTOLOGY | EPISTEMOLOGY |
|---|---|---|
| MANAGERIAL PERSPECTIVE | Reality is intelligible and orderly. | Knowledge comes from judicious analysis and the use of reason and logic. |
| ORGANIC PERSPECTIVE | Reality is transient, relative to sociality and place. | Knowledge comes from experience and is derived from social interplay. |
| TENSION PERSPECTIVE | Reality is grounded in contradiction. | Knowledge comes from embracing tension and strain. |
| REACTIVE PERSPECTIVE | Reality is uncertain and replete with risk. | Knowledge comes from encountering and learning from hardship. |
| CAPABILITY PERSPECTIVE | Reality is potential. | Knowledge comes from the aspiration to pre-emptively develop. |
| PARADOX PERSPECTIVE | Reality is dual. | Knowledge comes from reaching for balance and harmony. |
| PERSISTENCE PERSPECTIVE | Reality is fixed and self-reinforcing. | Knowledge comes from accepting the limits of one's own possibilities. |

Finally, according to a persistence perspective, reality is fixed and self-reinforcing, with knowledge coming from the acceptance of one's limitations. What we can do is defined by what we can't, and this insight is believed to steer us towards genuine expertise.

Learning about different perspectives reveals that what we learn from organisational change is dictated not solely by the situations we encounter but also by how we choose to observe and interpret them. The choice of perspective influences not only how we define problems but also how we formulate strategies, allocate resources, and measure success. By acknowledging the diversity of perspectives, we can develop a more nuanced and adaptable approach to managing change – one that respects multiple realities and embraces complexity rather than reducing it to a single, one-size-fits-all solution.

## 9.2 Which Perspective Is to Be Preferred?

Given this overview of perspectives on organisational change, a natural question arises: which perspective is to be preferred? As you might expect, the answer is far from simple. Each perspective emphasises different facets of organisational life, making it impossible to declare one to be superior in all situations. Every perspective has its strengths, just as each has its limitations. An organic perspective might be valuable for understanding changes initiated by front-line employees, but it may fall short when addressing the need to balance change within a finely tuned business environment. In such cases, a paradox perspective could offer better insights. Similarly, while a persistence perspective could help explain why an organisation maintains outdated practices, a reactive perspective might be more useful for understanding how it responds to sudden crises. Likewise, a capability perspective may highlight how an organisation can prepare for change, but it might not explain why some changes remain unattainable.

This doesn't imply that any perspective is inherently flawed or leads to incorrect conclusions. Rather, each perspective has its conceptual focus and strengths, with some being more suited to a situation than others. Instead of seeking a single, all-encompassing framework, the key is to apply different perspectives based on the context. If you're a consultant tasked with restructuring an organisation over the next six months, a managerial perspective will likely be your go-to framework. If you're a union representative seeking to understand and leverage internal organisational frictions, a tension perspective may offer more insight. On the other hand, a crisis manager might find the reactive perspective most useful in exploring how adversity can trigger organisational change. These examples demonstrate that no single perspective will consistently outperform the others; each offers a unique lens through which to view organisational realities, suited to specific circumstances.

Furthermore, as each perspective invariably elaborates on aspects of organisational reality while downplaying others, it would be wise to generally complement one 'leading' perspective with several 'supporting' perspectives. What can I add to my general understanding of a case when looking at it from different angles? While most situations tend to incite recollections of the vocabulary used in a 'leading' perspective, this doesn't mean that their interpretation can't benefit from perusing them from other, less obvious points of view. In this way, rather than aiming to prioritise the use of one perspective and do away with the rest, I suggest that change aficionados tap into multiple angles, building a rich understanding of organisational reality by drawing on complementary outsets.

To be clear, such a multi-perspective approach to organisational change is not merely an intellectual exercise; it has practical value in navigating the complexities of real-world change. Organisations are dynamic, multifaceted entities where different stakeholders – leaders, employees, customers, regulators – view change through distinct lenses. A single perspective may align well with one group's interests while overlooking the concerns of another. By integrating multiple perspectives, one can develop a more nuanced strategy that balances competing priorities, mitigates resistance, and fosters more sustainable transformations.

Ultimately, embracing a pluralistic approach does not mean abandoning coherence in favour of conceptual fragmentation; rather, it requires developing the ability to shift between perspectives strategically, much like a skilled navigator adjusting their course based on changing conditions. The challenge, then, is not simply to understand multiple perspectives in isolation but to cultivate the agility to synthesise them effectively. In so doing, change leaders can move beyond rigid, one-size-fits-all models of transformation and instead adopt a more adaptive, context-sensitive approach – one that fully embraces the complexity of organisational life.

## 9.3 How Can Perspectives Aid Us with Change?

Having toiled to master seven different perspectives on organisational change, a valid question is how one can benefit from such knowledge. In this respect, three major points can be noted.

### 9.3.1 Becoming Aware of *Your* Point of View and How This Influences Your Behaviour

First, although their influence is largely concealed from us in day-to-day interaction, perspectives and their baseline logics tend to have significant implications for how we position ourselves in the world and act on that world as it is. For instance, when naturally tilting towards the managerial perspective, you will find yourself inclined to tackle change issues in the most analytic of ways – aiming to rationalise a shift in course as intended and work from there. Similarly, when your predispositions lean more closely towards the persistence perspective, you might be inclined to not bother too much with organisational change at all, considering such efforts to be either harmful or impractical.

How we act is often predicated on the perspective or general logic by which we make sense of the world. In most cases, people don't simply hold opinions; they think and feel through them. Our perspectives remain unnoticed and unexamined until they are brought to light, often operating below our conscious awareness. As a result, individuals perceive reality as certain and unquestionable – not recognising that their understanding of what is 'true' or 'real' is shaped by a specific point of view.[1]

In this sense, an important step towards actively steering one's behaviour is to become aware of the logics and points of view underlying that behaviour: how do I tend to look at organisational reality, and on which baseline assumptions do I generally construct my actions? This is not to say that any 'errors' or 'flaws' are to be detected by reflecting in such a way. Whether you naturally adhere to the organic or to the reactive perspective doesn't make you better or worse as a person. What such an act of soul-searching aims to accomplish is to expose which set of goggles finds itself most firmly installed before your eyes, thus revealing why you act as you do. Hence, by establishing knowledge of the perspectives on organisational change, you have not simply enriched your general views; you have actively gathered the means to find out which set of logics is most indicative of your own interactions with the organisational context in which you live.

### Box 9.1 Practical Advice?

Sounds good? The next few pointers might help you out on how to surface your preferred point of view in practice:

- Conduct a 'perspective audit' of your actions – after each major decision or interaction, reflect on the perspective that seemed most dominant in your thinking. Write down how your perspective influenced the outcomes and whether it was the best approach for that situation.
- Engage in self-reflection and journalling – set aside 10–15 minutes each day to journal about the decisions you made that day. Reflect on the perspectives you leaned on, whether managerial, reactive, or otherwise. Over time, this practice will make your habitual ways of thinking more visible and open to change.
- Seek feedback from others on your approach – ask a peer or a mentor to observe your approach to change. Afterwards, have a candid conversation about how your perspective shaped your decisions, and whether a different viewpoint might have led to a better outcome.
- Identify triggers that activate specific perspectives – keep track of situations where you feel your perspective shift strongly (e.g., during high-pressure meetings or in conflict with others). Note the specific triggers and how they influence your behaviour. This awareness can help you recognise when you are acting based on a default perspective rather than a more nuanced or appropriate one.

## 9.3.2 Becoming Aware of *Others'* Point of View and How This Influences Their Behaviour

Next, it is helpful to realise that others may be looking at organisational reality from quite a different angle from yours. It is widely recognised that change agents and participants in a change process can have differing interpretations and perspectives due to their individual differences, experiences, and roles within the process.[2] In this sense, while you can cuss and fuss about organisational colleagues who 'don't get it', it might not be a question of colleagues being too dim or ignorant to come to terms with your ideas. Instead, it might very well be that your colleagues simply interpret change and organisational reality in a different way.

For example, after reading this book, let us imagine that you have become an arduous believer of the organic perspective on change. In your work environment, you start to notice change initiatives bubbling up all over the place, and you become increasingly worried about how your organisation is drawing on them. While your firm is churning through several major change programmes, little explicit attention is being given to suggestions for change put forward by operational staff. As a result, you see a lot of potential to improve your organisation by tuning in to bottom-up suggestions and decide to present your ideas to the rest of the managerial committee. However, after you have delivered your presentation, many of your colleagues start raising questions, asking if you really expect the organisation to leave its strategic course to the whims of operational staff.

So, what gives? Are your colleagues too dim-witted to get what you are trying to say? Depending on who your colleagues are, the answer is probably no: their cognitive capabilities are perfectly sufficient. Yet, most likely, while your colleagues may be competent enough to understand what you are trying to say, the angles from which they interpret organisational reality are profoundly different. While you may have turned into a zealous believer of the organic perspective, your colleagues might, for example, be tilting quite heavily towards the managerial perspective on change. When viewed through the managerial lens, the ideas you just presented may not look as sensible or grandiose as you consider them to be. From a managerial view, several of your ideas might even sound outright foolish – for isn't it the manager's duty to lead the organisation in its change trajectory, steering with expertise where operational employees lack the knowledge to do so? As such, rather than rejecting your ideas because they are stupid, it is most likely that your fellow managers rejected them because these ideas are silly to them: that is, when evaluated from the point of view that these managers predominantly occupy.

### Box 9.2 Practical Advice?

To become aware of others' point of view, these practices might help you get going:

- Engage in active listening to understand different perspectives – in meetings, pause before responding. Reflect on what others have said without interrupting or preparing a counter-argument in your head. This will help you better grasp their underlying assumptions and perspectives before reacting from your own point of view.
- Reflect on how your own perspective might be distorting your interpretation of others' – after an interaction where you felt a strong emotional reaction (e.g., frustration, confusion, or anger), take a moment to reflect on whether your own perspective might have distorted your interpretation of the other person's actions or ideas. Consider: 'Did I let my own assumptions cloud my judgement of what people were actually saying?'
- Identify the underlying interests and needs driving different perspectives – before presenting your ideas in a meeting, take time to consider what underlying needs might drive the perspectives of your colleagues. Are they concerned with control, efficiency, innovation, or stability? Understanding their motivations can help you tailor your message to resonate with their priorities.

By being aware of individuals' diverse perspectives when discussing organisational change, you can engage in more productive conversations, reducing the risk of conflicts arising from differing views. It will give you better prospects for realising change without gouging someone's eye out in animated discussion.

### 9.3.3 Trying Out Different Angles

Finally, once you have mastered the different outsets on organisational change, you can start switching consciously between different perspectives to see how such shifts impact your understanding of organisational reality as it presents itself. Does this situation make better sense when evaluated from a different angle? By having a broad set of perspectives at the ready, you can apply the logic – or set of logics – that fits a particular situation. In this way, rather than drawing on the framework as a mere body of knowledge, you can actively use it to reconsider the way organisational reality is made sense of – thus changing lenses when the situation requires you to.

#### Box 9.3 Be Aware!

The ability to switch perspectives is not only a cognitive exercise; it opens up new ways of responding to challenges and seizing opportunities that would otherwise remain hidden. That being said, switching perspectives also requires a degree of humility and self-awareness. It demands that you step outside of your own biases and assumptions, acknowledging that no single perspective has a monopoly on truth. It encourages you to question your own tendencies and invites a more nuanced, multidimensional view of the organisation and the challenges it faces. Essentially, it's about moving beyond the safety of familiar thinking to engage with the complexity and richness of organisational life – where multiple truths can coexist, often leading to more innovative and effective solutions.

## 9.4 What to Avoid When Dealing with Perspectives?

When considering how to effectively utilise perspectives, it is important to avoid two common pitfalls. Let's look at them now.

### 9.4.1 Developing a Crush

First, having read through the chapters of this book, it is possible that you have by now developed a preference for a particular perspective. Maybe you feel somewhat captivated by the emphasis on the potentiality of the capability perspective; or perhaps you fancy putting the catharsis logic of the tension perspective to the test. While such preferences are perfectly normal, I would nevertheless warn you not to let yourself get dragged into them too much.

Before you know it, you will become so attached to the perspective in question that the use of other perspectives will start to look absurd and pointless – even when the situation in question would benefit from such a shift in angle.

Most of us will have some experience with this phenomenon: your friend or supervisor returns from a dedicated training event or course, only to have fallen in love with the new logic preached there. While they start treating everything as a nail for their newly acquired hammer, they are simultaneously driving everyone else nuts with their overly zealous application of knowledge to situations for which the insight in question is ill-suited. As a result, they quickly kill all support for the (potentially interesting) insight they accumulated, with intense frustration and harsh words often preceding a complete fallout in the organisation as it is.

I advise you not to take this course in respect of the perspectives on organisational change here set out. Invariably, we will all encounter situations in which one perspective is preferred over others, but rarely will such a perspective suit us uniformly. Traps occur when an established way of thinking stops being effective, causing frustration, inadequate responses, and unhelpful actions. When a previously useful mindset becomes counterproductive, continuing to rely on it can leave individuals stuck, making it more difficult to break free. In essence, a person can become ensnared by their own logic.[1]

### Box 9.4 Practical Advice?

Here are a few tips to avoid the pitfall of developing-a-crush:

- Regularly question the fit of your preferred perspective – in every decision-making process, intentionally assess whether you are leaning too heavily on a familiar perspective. If so, consider deliberately adopting a different one to test if it leads to new insights.
- Seek diverse opinions and challenge your own view – engage in a 'perspective-swapping' exercise with a colleague or mentor. Take turns presenting your reasoning from one perspective, then ask the other person to challenge that reasoning with a different perspective.
- Experiment with 'perspective switching' in real-time – next time you are analysing a change initiative or organisational challenge, try to approach it from a perspective you typically avoid. If you're drawn to a rational, managerial approach, try viewing the issue from an organic perspective instead, and note how it shifts your understanding and action plan.
- Recognise when 'crushing' becomes counterproductive – if you experience frustration in a discussion, pause and ask yourself: 'Am I being too rigid in my thinking?' Acknowledge this and actively try to open your mind to other approaches.

By integrating these practices into your approach to organisational change, you will avoid the pitfall of developing an overzealous attachment to a single perspective. This flexibility not only helps you remain effective and adaptable in different situations but also enhances your ability to navigate the complexity of organisational dynamics with a balanced, comprehensive approach.

### 9.4.2 Losing Sight of the Woods for the Trees

Second, while you should be wary not to fall in love with a single perspective, you should be equally careful not to get lost in the plethora of perspectives available. In many situations, not all perspectives are evenly useful, and prioritising which perspectives to draw on is often necessary to actively advance your understanding.

Imagine that you find yourself in a crowded meeting room, discussing a particularly thorny issue. Given the complexity of what is at stake, no answers are obviously right or wrong. As a result, all attendees take turns expressing their views on the matter, with severe discussions often emerging when views clash. As the afternoon develops, you start to feel increasingly overwhelmed – ideas tumble around in your head, with arguments pro and contra ricocheting against one another. As the meeting comes to a scheduled closing point, all attendees step out of the room, puzzled about whether or not a decision has been reached: after all your arguments and discussions, what is the organisation going to do with the issue?

The example illustrates what I would like to refer to as a pitfall of indecisiveness – or the act of losing sight of the woods for the trees. While all perspectives on organisational change discussed in this book can offer meaningful outsets from which to make sense of reality, be careful not to become overwhelmed by the variety of interpretations available: for when doing so, no valid interpretation will in the end remain.

#### Box 9.5 Practical Advice?

To help you avoid losing sight of the woods for the trees, here are some tips:

- Clarify your objective before diving in – at the beginning of any change-related discussion, jot down your key objective or goal. Periodically check back to this note throughout the discussion to ensure that you are not getting sidetracked by less relevant perspectives.
- Identify key priorities and focus on them – when faced with any example of organisational change, ask yourself: 'Which of the perspectives I know will most likely help me to make sense of at least half of the problem?' Narrow your focus to the perspectives that will help resolve or advance the most critical components of the issue.
- Simplify and synthesise – after exploring various perspectives, take a few minutes to write down a summary of the main points from each viewpoint. Then, look for commonalities or contradictions. Try to consolidate these insights into a simpler framework that guides your next steps, rather than getting bogged down in every nuance.

By implementing these strategies, you can avoid the trap of becoming lost in the complexity of multiple perspectives. Instead of being overwhelmed, you will be able to synthesise the most relevant viewpoints and stay focused on the larger goal, ensuring that the discussion leads to actionable insights and decisions, rather than confusion and indecision.

### Box 9.6 The Point?

I recommend that you approach the perspectives discussed in this book with moderation. Avoid using only one perspective for every situation but also avoid becoming overwhelmed by using all perspectives at once. When drawing on perspectives, moderation is key.

## SUMMARY

Chapter 9 explored the multifaceted nature of perspectives on change, offering insights into how understanding and engaging with different viewpoints can play a crucial role in managing and facilitating change effectively.

- It began by discussing how various **ontologies and epistemologies** shape the way individuals perceive and engage with change. These foundational frameworks influence not only how we understand reality but also how we approach the methods and strategies for implementing change. The chapter emphasised that perspectives are deeply tied to our worldview, and that recognising the influence of these perspectives is the first step in navigating change successfully.
- Next, the chapter addressed the question of **which perspective is most suitable** in the context of change. It argued that no single viewpoint should be deemed universally superior; instead, perspectives should be viewed as complementary. The appropriateness of a perspective is context-dependent, and the ability to adapt and shift viewpoints based on the situation is key to effective change management.
- We then explored **how perspectives can be used to our advantage** during the change process. The importance of self-awareness and understanding how our own viewpoint influences our behaviour was highlighted, as was the need to be aware of how others' perspectives shape their actions. By acknowledging these dynamics, individuals can foster better collaboration, communication, and decision-making. The chapter also suggested that experimenting with different perspectives can uncover novel solutions to challenges during times of change.
- Finally, the chapter concluded with a **cautionary note on dealing with perspectives**. It warned against developing a 'crush' on one particular viewpoint, which can lead to tunnel vision and hinder the ability to see the broader picture. Similarly, it cautioned against losing sight of the overall goal by becoming too focused on minute details, stressing the importance of balancing detail-oriented thinking with a holistic view of the situation.

In sum, this chapter provided a comprehensive understanding of how multiple perspectives can enhance the process of change, urging you to remain adaptable, open-minded, and self-aware in your approach to navigating complex organisational transformations.

## REFERENCES

[1] Ford, J. D., & Ford, L. W. (1994). Logics of identity, contradiction, and attraction in change. *Academy of Management Review*, *19*(4), 756–785.

[2] Van de Ven, A. H., & Sun, K. (2011). Breakdowns in implementing models of organization change. *Academy of Management Perspectives*, *25*(3), 58–74.

# 10 Leveraging Perspectives for Action

## Introduction

While the accumulation of theory may be intellectually stimulating for some, I suspect that for most of us the real excitement lies in seeing how theory can be applied to solve real-world problems. In this final chapter, we will bridge the gap between theory and practice by exploring how the perspectives on change we've developed throughout this textbook can be actively used to benefit organisations in motion. We'll focus on applying these perspectives to a concrete business case to demonstrate how theoretical frameworks can be leveraged in practical, organisational contexts.

This chapter will guide you through two related practical processes: (i) interpreting or making sense of a change case; and (ii) advancing or developing our own instances of change. While both processes are grounded in the same multi-perspective approach that has underpinned this entire text, they differ in purpose and execution. The first process equips you to understand and navigate change that is already unfolding or has taken place, whereas the second supports you in shaping and operationalising change moving forward. Together, these processes form two complementary work streams – one centred on interpretation, the other on activation.

Through the lens of a fictionalised case, this chapter will illustrate how you can move from theoretical understanding to practical application, showing you how to use the perspectives discussed in previous chapters to either make sense of or advance real-world organisational change. By the end of this chapter, you will understand not only the techniques for actively interpreting and working with change but also how to shift between perspectives depending on your role. So, let's dive in and explore how to turn theory into practical tools, ultimately helping you navigate organisational change with more clarity and confidence.

## 10.1 The Case

Sagecom was founded by a small collection of IT enthusiasts, led by the charismatic trio Bob Ross, Steven Sacherson, and Andy Jacobs.* At its inception, the organisation had set out to

* This case is inspired by the author's observations at Sagecom and informal conversations with its employees. While it draws on real experiences, certain details have been adapted, combined, or fictionalised for narrative clarity and confidentiality. To protect privacy, pseudonyms have been used for both the company and the individuals involved.

address a gap in the market that Ross, Sacherson, and Jacobs had noted: the offering of customised help to businesses implementing enterprise resource planning (ERP) systems. While such integrative IT systems had become increasingly in vogue in the 1990s, Ross, Sacherson, and Jacobs had observed many firms struggling to configure the software to their business setting. To help alleviate such issues, Sagecom was founded, employing a handful of IT consultants who would focus on customising ERP solutions to the client's every desire.

While Sagecom's initial start had been somewhat difficult – with Ross, Sacherson, and Jacobs toiling tirelessly to make a name for their new-found company – the firm soon started to expand internationally. As Ross enjoyed good connections with some ERP devotees in France and China, Sagecom speedily opened offices in these two countries. Although the number of people employed was still modest, it gradually became clear to the industry that Sagecom was here to stay: customers enjoyed working with the young firm, and it was increasingly recommended among digital executives. Ross was proud that the France and China offices were kicking off successfully – after all, he had been the one to introduce the option to the firm and had thus felt largely responsible for its eventual success or failure.

After a couple of years, it became clear that Ross's introduction of the France and China opportunity had proven emblematic of what had gradually turned into the 'Sagecom way': if opportunities arose, employees were encouraged to act on them, eventually funnelling such ideas into successful ventures. For their part, Ross, Sacherson, and Jacobs had frequently broadened Sagecom's horizon in ways that no one could have foreseen in earlier years. Rather than basing themselves on 'strategy', 'scenarios', or 'blueprints', they had successfully promoted many ideas over the years that were based on their ad hoc conception of where the industry needed them to go. In this regard, Sagecom came to supplement its initial focus on ERP implementations with a wide variety of digital 'solutions' and 'templates', based on the experiences and opportunities employees had found themselves presented with. In small talk, employees even began to refer to themselves as 'digital cowboys', who lived under a 'can-do attitude' and rode wherever the rising and setting of the sun would take them.

As time went by, this rising and setting of the sun could be interpreted quite literally. As Sagecom gradually expanded its geographical reach to countries all over the globe, it became increasingly difficult for headquarters to keep up with each office's working day, rhythm, and pace. As each region was somewhat different in wants and needs, it was decided that a localised model would serve Sagecom best. This way, regional employees could adapt themselves most satisfactorily to the requirements of their concrete business setting and work to benefit their actual clients. It was an exciting time, and Ross, Sacherson, and Jacobs relished every moment of the Sagecom journey.

Yet, as the years went by, it became clear that the Sagecom journey was also becoming increasingly difficult to maintain. As the numbers of employees and senior partners grew larger and larger – with the group eventually pushing through the threshold of 2,000 employees – several of the early enthusiasts started to complain that the 'cowboy feel' was gradually slipping away. Although employees were still officially encouraged to seize emerging opportunities, Ross, Sacherson, and Jacobs had started to progressively crack down on major suggestions made by anyone but their closest confidants: as the firm had expanded to a size where it became impossible to know everyone by name, Ross, Sacherson, and Jacobs had become increasingly uneasy about allowing Sagecom to be directed by the overall collective. As a result, they had become increasingly reliant on their status as founders to draw decision-making power back to headquarters, effectively blocking any course they considered out of line with Sagecom's original direction. Some of the partners even remarked that Sagecom was turning into something like the United Nations, with 'a lot of talk being exchanged, but nothing substantial ever changing'.

While Sagecom continued to perform quite well in terms of financial results, this sensation of deadlock became worse as the years went by. Although many customers still relied on the firm for the customisation of their ERP systems, many employees started to feel that they could no longer rely on the firm in the way they used to. The overall vibe and tendency to develop 'wherever the sun would take us' was noted to have largely disappeared, with many complaining that the firm now rarely 'put its money where its mouth is'. While changes were often publicly announced, many noted how the firm repeatedly dropped the ball in terms of implementation. As the actual follow-up of initiatives was largely absent, many employees continued to stick to how they had done things in the past. As a result, things tended to stay more or less the same at Sagecom, with employees becoming increasingly proficient in the set of activities that guaranteed high revenues in the short run and the firm gradually turning into what some of the initially hired managers silently referred to as 'a creature of habit'.

Some ten years after Sagecom's founding, this culminated in the firm encountering a major crisis. While Sagecom had become highly competent in offering on-premises implementations of ERP systems – with over 80 per cent of its revenues stemming from such work – software packages increasingly came to turn towards cloud solutions. For Sagecom, this sudden change in software approach came with a devastating impact: as the firm had long disregarded anything but its initial source of success (i.e., on-premises work), it had not anticipated this shift to the cloud in its official directions. As a result, Sagecom lost out on many major contracts to the extent that the firm was – at one point – on the brink of bankruptcy. Luckily, however, some of Sagecom's more entrepreneurial types had been sensing that the cloud would one day start overruling on-premises solutions, and covertly developing expertise in their spare time. Soon, these gumptious men and women were charged to push Sagecom to the next level, with resources being reinvested in cloud capabilities and digital whiz kids being drawn in. After a year of precarious crisis management, Sagecom started getting back on track: cloud contracts were reeled in and financial prospects were on the mend. Everyone heaved a sigh of relief: Sagecom was going steady once again, but the firm's future had been hanging by a thread.

To prevent such major crises from happening ever again, Ross, Sacherson, and Jacobs experienced significant pressure from other partners to systematise and open up strategic decision-making. It was decided that extensive 'strategy exercises' would, from now on, be conducted every five years. In such exercises, partners from all global offices would get together and try to figure out the firm's potential problems and solutions to such problems, redirecting the firm wherever necessary. Large consultancy firms would be hired to lead such strategy exercises, as these organisations were believed to have access to market data and developmental expertise that Sagecom did not. Concretely, this meant that Sagecom executives would fly over every five years for a week of retreats in the Swiss Alps, after which follow-up conversations would be carried out by means of voice over internet protocol (VoIP) software. Having pondered the potential problem for about a month or six, consultants would deliver to Sagecom a roadmap of what to do, after which the firm would work on improving its organisational performance in the coming five years.

During the first of these strategy exercises, a significant concern involved the firm's governance, structure, and use of resources. For many partners not related to Sagecom's headquarter offices, it had long been challenging to get the needed resources. While headquarters often emphasised that they were not the dominant party within the group, they were criticised for often propagating themselves as exactly that – with one international partner even quoting from the George Orwell classic *Animal Farm*: 'At Sagecom, it often seems as if "all animals are equal – but some animals are more equal than others".' In this sense, partners started to increasingly search for an organisational set-up that enabled it to be more flexible in daily operations, allowing it to pick up on trends as they developed in particular regions, and quickly readjust the means and processes of the affected Sagecom office in accordance.

After long and arduous discussions, the Sagecom partner group decided to erect the 'Sagecom Innovation Center'. This entity – which would function separately from Sagecom's operational activities – would serve as a firm-specific incubator for promising ideas, being bestowed with an independent budget to stimulate the development of hopeful ventures. In this way, it was believed that the Sagecom group would reel in the best of two worlds: being able to continuously optimise the operational business by retaining focus on day-to-day activities, while also becoming more flexible by allowing promising ideas to flourish.

However, this decision did not go far enough for many international partners to address standing concerns on headquarters dominance. According to these partners, while the occasional idea as incubated would be able to thrive more easily, more conventional decision-making power would still be concentrated primarily within the headquarter group. Yet, as international partners were out-debated in discussions on the issue – especially when founders Ross, Sacherson, and Jacobs started to weigh in on the argument – the affair was dropped from the official agenda.

Backdoor conversations on the topic became increasingly animated: as international partners had noted that others were struggling with the same issues they had long thought themselves facing alone, some created dedicated online groups in which international managers could voice their concerns about the Sagecom centralised direction. In this way, international partners soon started to feel increasingly organised, with several motions being covertly prepared for shifting decision-making power more equally across Sagecom offices.

Eventually, pressures looming below the Sagecom surface were picked up by Margaret Steele, a prominent member of the firm's independent advisory board who had come to serve as a business guru in countless successful firms over the years. For Steele, the noted supremacy of headquarters in decision-making was irreconcilable with professional business-doing. After having talked personally with many of the international partners, Steele wrote a letter to all managing executives at Sagecom, voicing her concerns regarding the organisation's decision-making processes. In her final statements, she presented the organisation with an ultimatum: either the firm would alter its approach to strategic decision-making or she would leave Sagecom's advisory board. Given Steele's reputation, this was not a minor threat to consider.

One day, having lunch, Ross, Sacherson, and Jacobs stayed silent for a while and looked each other in the eye: change was, once again, coming to Sagecom. As it had always done, one way or the other – and as it would probably always continue to do. They smiled and prepared themselves.

## 10.2 How to Interpret Change in Practice

Having visited the Sagecom case, I expect many readers will find it tempting to read it as a clear example of one particular perspective – with the perspective in question being considered 'the' way to appreciate how Sagecom has over the years come to develop. For others, on the other hand, there will be a tendency to interpret the Sagecom case as a stage on which all different perspectives chaotically intersect and compete, with the most significant challenge being to focus on what is going on. In both instances, we tend to get stifled by the views we entertain – either because we don't allow views other than the one we are most fond of or because we don't allow any priorities guiding our way. In the next few sections, I will highlight how you can systematically interpret or make sense of cases of change.

### 10.2.1 Going Broad: Developing a Story Canvas

In the first stage, I would advise you to keep your horizon broad: which perspectives might help in coming to terms with the case as observed? Developing what I call a **story canvas** can help: Table 10.1 provides an example of what such a canvas could look like.

As seen in the story canvas, the Sagecom case can be interpreted in various ways. What we emphasise and omit will be related to how we choose to look at the case.

When we, for example, look at the case from the angle of the managerial perspective, we tend to see an organisation that is trying to figure out how to improve its performance rationally. We will be particularly drawn in by the observation of the organisation systematically evaluating its strategy every five years and by the observation that internal and external expertise is often hinged on to guide the organisation's actual change efforts. Here, failures to get things moving will be attributed to Sagecom's rational analyses proving incomplete – for example, lacking the notion of who will conduct follow-up on change or overlooking particular market trends that will prove important for future business-doing – or to employees not acting in full accordance with the change plans advanced.

However, a very different image will materialise when we look at the Sagecom case from an organic angle. Now, we will see an organisation that has long developed according to chance and opportunities, with executives and employees acting on their gut feel and intuitive sensation of the right thing to do. 'Cowboys' were encouraged to seize the day, and developments in France and China proved the result of random social connections rather than rational analyses. While Sagecom gradually 'professionalised' its way of doing things – with partner meetings and strategic evaluation seemingly overwriting its initial 'can-do attitude' – this standardisation of activities largely seemed to function as a layer of varnish, with actual changes still being made on account of random occurrences taking place within the organisation's social sphere.

**Table 10.1 Sagecom story canvas**

| | | |
|---|---|---|
|  | Managerial perspective | Sagecom has been trying to rationally come to terms with issues as popping up, using internal and external expertise to improve its organisational performance over time. Changes are introduced in a structured way, according to the outcome of judicious analysis, as exemplified in its five-yearly exercises. |
| 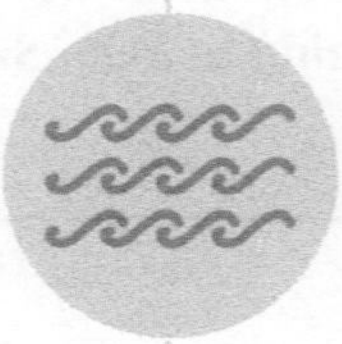 | Organic perspective | Sagecom has been developing continuously, according to the opportunities and experiences its membership base has come to encounter over time. Decisions to grow the firm in a certain direction are often the outcome of random occurrences taking place in the broader social sphere, with Sagecom incrementally attuning itself to the context in which it operates. |
|  | Tension perspective | At Sagecom, tensions have long been building within the socio-political scene: while headquarters long represented the dominant voice within the organisation, international offices have gradually become more intent on a revision of decision-making power. Nowadays, these tensions seem to have nearly reached a point of culmination, with Steele catalysing frustrations. |
|  | Reactive perspective | Faced with a severe crisis, Sagecom changed in ways it simply did not seem capable of when all was going well. Reacting to a shift of the environment towards cloud solutions, Sagecom safeguarded its very survival by letting its resources – briefly – manage themselves. |
|  | Capability perspective | Sagecom is on a quest to become a more flexible firm throughout. It is involved in serious discussions about how to manage resources more proactively and let go of stifling habits. |
|  | Paradox perspective | Sagecom is struggling to harmonise the activities it currently executes with the developments it should be working towards. Changes are often overruled by routine, resulting in a disbalanced firm. In later years, Sagecom has tried to restore this balance by erecting a separate innovation centre. |
|  | Persistence perspective | While change is often announced at Sagecom, actual developments of the firm are rare. Sagecom is consistently keeping close to the fundamentals laid down by its founding figures Ross, Sacherson, and Jacobs. Change programmes have little effect other than to allow executives to have a chat with expensive consulting companies during trips to the Swiss Alps. |

When looked at from the paradox perspective, another very different Sagecom stands out. Now, we see an organisation that repeatedly struggles to harmonise change with ongoing operations. Although change programmes were repeatedly announced, the organisation seemed keener on perfecting what it had been doing for many years – investing in the exploitation of current activities while increasingly neglecting exploration into new domains. As a result of such disbalance, the organisation eventually found itself in stormy waters, from which it emerged only by capitalising on the new grounds of cloud implementations. In later years, ongoing harmonisation between current efficiency and future developments was looked after explicitly by founding a separate Sagecom innovation centre, aiming to keep Sagecom operations focused while simultaneously allowing innovations to thrive.

### Box 10.1 Be Aware!

As the story canvas displayed in Table 10.1 illustrates, many other interpretations of the same case can be made: in the Sagecom case, we can discern elements of all perspectives on organisational change as theoretically discussed. Note that this might not always be the case: in other practical examples, while we might discern clear elements of some perspectives, we might also be unable to observe any clear connections to others. It is the exploration of different perspectives that is the essence of this first stage of drafting a story canvas – which perspectives can offer relevant insights and which might prove less useful? What is essential in this first stage is thus not to conclude on any one perspective early on or to go overly detailed yet, but to set out alternative ways by which the case can be made sense of.

## 10.2.2 Going Deep: Developing a Storyline

In the second stage, we delve deeper into the interpretation that might be most relevant to our particular interest. This choice should not be based on preferring one perspective over others; rather, it should be made based on the specific conditions we, as observers, find ourselves in. What do we hope to learn from the case and how do we relate to its settings?

Say we fulfil the position of a Sagecom employee, newly promoted to lead one of the international offices. From this context, the tension perspective might be the most pertinent to dig into, given that our story canvas indicates that this position is most closely related to issues of socio-political difference. Building on the elements highlighted in our story canvas, we can now look into developing a more detailed **storyline**, as displayed in Figure 10.1.

Initially, Ross, Sacherson, and Jacobs founded the organisation and came to lead it as a rather charismatic trio. By making some successful calls – such as growing the company internationally into France and China – their 'can-do' leadership style quickly became consolidated, with employees increasingly respecting Ross, Sacherson, and Jacobs for their insight and apparent gut feel. As time passed, this manner of taking care of things even implicitly developed into a 'Sagecom way', giving further credit to the approach initialised by Ross, Sacherson, and Jacobs.

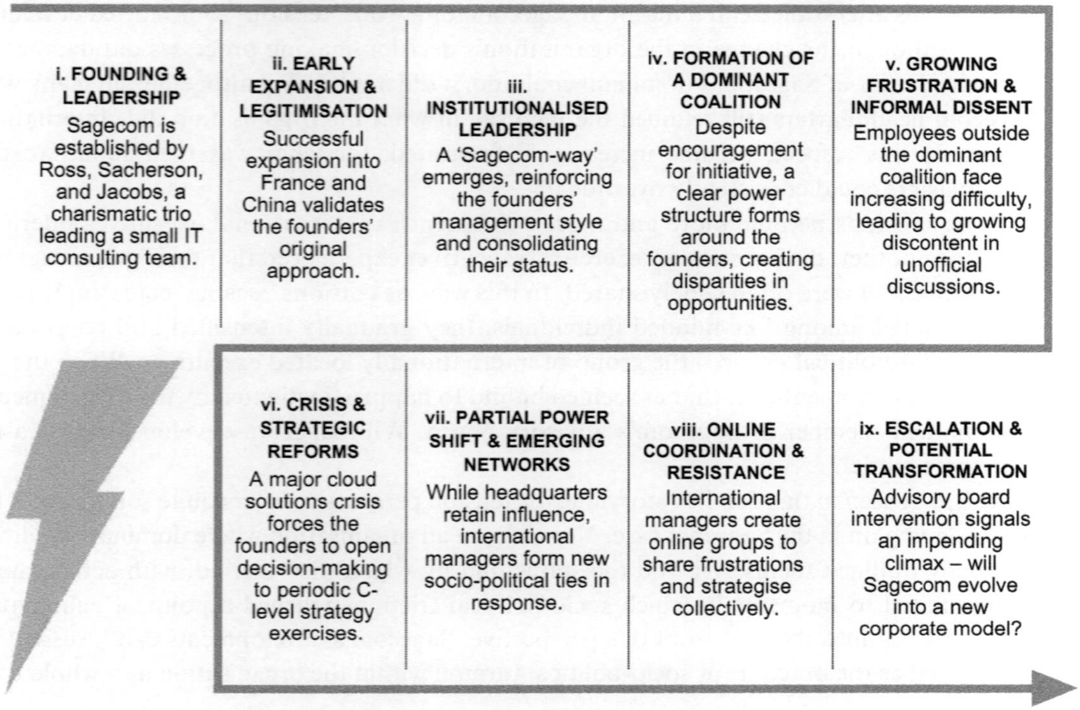


**Figure 10.1** Sagecom storyline: tension perspective.

Gradually, the founding trio thus established itself quite firmly as the organisation's ultimate decision-makers, to the extent that their (dis)approval effectively made (or broke) propositions. Although executives and operational employees were still publicly encouraged to pursue opportunities autonomously, it became increasingly clear that the absence of support by Ross, Sacherson, and Jacobs inevitably spelt defeat. In this sense, a clear distinction arose between those who enjoyed the favour of Sagecom's founding figures and those who did not – between those who were 'in' the dominant coalition and those who were 'out'.

This rupture between Sagecom's dominant coalition and the rest of its employees led to the build-up of feelings of frustration and resentment among those who considered themselves bereft of actual decision-making power. Yet, although hallway conversations turned increasingly sour, little real change was to be noted: while tensions continuously increased, they didn't yet reach a level at which they could overcome the power of Sagecom's standing coalition.

These tensions came to fruition when Sagecom experienced a major external shock, which functioned as a trigger to dissatisfaction long since building: the notion of having been close to bankruptcy propelled Sagecom executives to push for a change in decision-making processes. This catharsis of tensions long present within the organisation's socio-political fibre toppled the predominance of Sagecom's initial decision-makers and systematised strategy according to exercises in which all executives could participate.

While this alteration cleared the air at Sagecom for a while, tensions soon started developing again. Although the change in the organisation's decision-making processes did dampen the exclusive power of Sagecom's dominant coalition, it did not break it altogether: in many ways, Sagecom headquarters still retained the final say in what the organisation did. International offices, in this respect, became increasingly frustrated, for what was their input worth if headquarters could consistently override it?

These tensions became more and more prominent as international executives interacted with one another: during strategy exercises, executives experienced that their grievances were not unique and were often widely shared. In this way, as tensions became increasingly shared and validated among like-minded individuals, they gradually intensified and consolidated a new socio-political group – the group of internationally located executives. When the case ended, a new moment of catharsis seemed bound to happen, instigated by the involvement of a prominent member of Sagecom's advisory board. Will Sagecom develop towards a new corporate model?

As can be seen in this detailed storyline, the tension perspective offers quite some insight into what is going on in the Sagecom case. Now, we see an organisation where dominant coalitions gradually outlined themselves and the status quo by which they thrived, with actual change being limited to moments in which socio-political frictions reached a point of culmination. When delving into the case from this perspective, Sagecom's developments can be essentially interpreted as the outcome of socio-political turmoil within the organisation as a whole.

### 10.2.3 Going Rich: Developing an Actual Story

Finally, after having developed both the broader story canvas as well as the detailed storyline that is most suited to our situation, we can now look into the merging of both: how can we fill in the blanks of our detailed storyline by making use of the elements we highlighted in our story canvas? By doing this, we should be able to combine both the advantages of **going broad** – that is, retaining the most holistic understanding of our case – with the advantages of **going deep** – that is, making sense of the case details coherently.

To illustrate this final stage, let us continue developing our example. In our initial stage of drafting the story canvas, we discovered that many perspectives offer a meaningful take on the Sagecom case. In our second stage of drawing a more detailed storyline, we then focused exclusively on further developing the tension perspective, given that this perspective accorded most closely with our hypothetical situation of you representing a newly appointed employee at one of Sagecom's international offices. In this third and final stage, we will now complement our tension perspective with elements of other perspectives that might fill in the blanks we still experience when looking into our case: we complement our initial primary perspective with several secondary perspectives.

While the choice of these secondary perspectives will once again depend on your particular situation and desired answers, it will most often be propelled by the questions still arising after drafting your detailed storyline. What issues can I not (or only partially) make sense of when interpreting the case from the current perspective? In our example, this could include questions such as: how come Sagecom typically drifted back to a 'dominant' setting, even after tensions

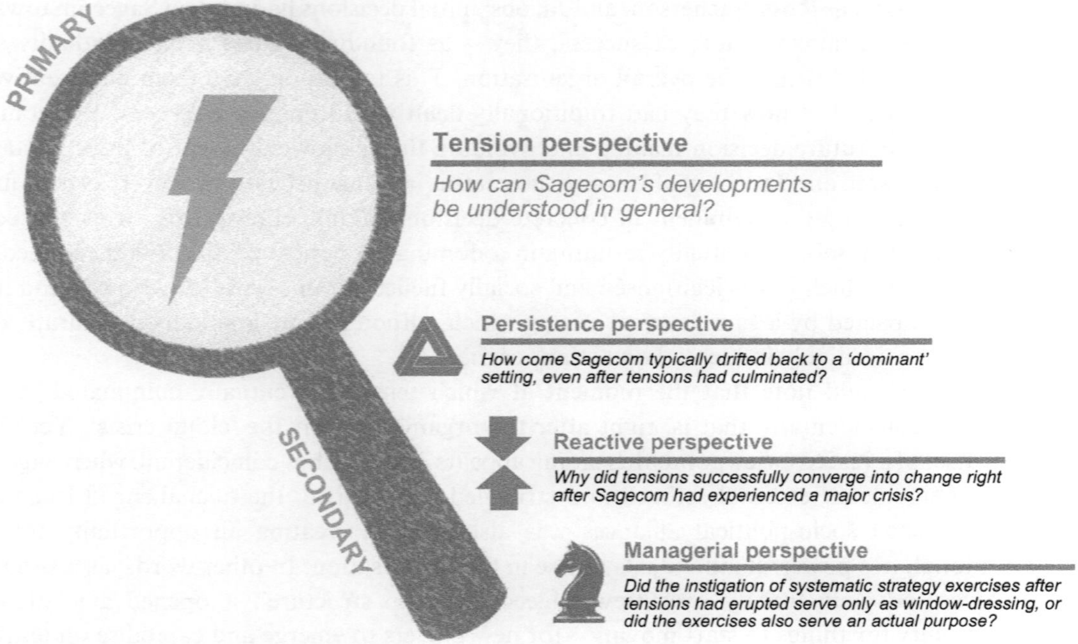


**Figure 10.2** Sagecom story: bringing perspectives together.

had culminated? Why did tensions successfully converge into change right after Sagecom had experienced a major crisis? And did the instigation of systematic strategy exercises after tensions erupted serve only as window-dressing, or did the exercises also serve an actual purpose? Recalling the hypothetical situation we find ourselves in, these questions seem to be some of the more pertinent that will need answering if we are to successfully wrap our heads around the situation laid out to us. To answer them, however, we must turn to perspectives other than the tension perspective. In Figure 10.2, I have visually highlighted the complementary use of relevant secondary perspectives.

First, we could note that Sagecom had repeatedly drawn back to states of status quo, irrespective of all disseminated discourse on seizing opportunities. The persistence perspective might show us the way here. By adding to our case interpretation from this logic, we might understand that initial environmental conditions and the founding figures had left quite the mark on Sagecom as it was. For instance, when Sagecom was founded, we could note that environmental conditions strongly favoured the strategic directions that Ross, Sacherson, and Jacobs almost intuitively opted for. While the early success of such a move had proven instrumental in putting the firm on the map, our persistence goggles also highlight it as the eventual cause of the firm dropping out on market trends in later years: as routines and capabilities were attuned towards the delivery of on-premise solutions, it became increasingly difficult for Sagecom to make sense of a reality in which cloud alternatives would take over.

Furthermore, as Ross, Sacherson, and Jacobs' initial decisions had pushed Sagecom towards a seemingly sustainable state of success, they – as founding figures – had gradually seen themselves reified within the overall organisation. This reification gave them an incentive to remain consistent in how they had traditionally dealt with things at Sagecom. By retaining consistency in future decision-making and avoiding the acknowledgement of prior mistakes, Ross, Sacherson, and Jacobs could ensure their status in future ordeals. However, as their input became increasingly pre-eminent in concrete decision-making, shrewd executives started to lean in more closely – eventually resulting in a dominant political coalition that retained the status quo by which it was legitimised and socially fuelled. In this sense, Sagecom found itself strongly impacted by a foundational setting which, although now gradually inaccurate, continued to prove highly influential on actions carried out.

Next, we could note that the moment at which tensions eventually culminated seemed strangely coincidental – that is, right after the organisation hit the 'cloud crisis'. Yet, from the outset of a reactive viewpoint, this timing appears anything but coincidental: when Sagecom faced a significant external setback and struggled for survival, the unchallenged leadership of established socio-political alliances was also shaken, creating an opportunity for less traditional, less powerful individuals to rise in the organisation. In other words, as a situation of severe adversity briefly overthrew Sagecom's 'deep structure', it opened a window of opportunity for things to start moving – for new players to emerge and capitalise on tensions long since slumbering. In this sense, the reactive perspective can help us understand the timing of tensions as having converged into change at Sagecom – not so much as a random occurrence but as being sparked by the powerful motor of adversity and hardship.

Finally, when looking into the changes emerging after Sagecom's cloud crisis, it is easy to do away with the instigation of strategy exercises as being nothing more than an effort at window-dressing – advanced to appease the non-dominant coalition into the idea of actual development. Yet, when peering at our case through the managerial lens, we could also observe a firm that is genuinely trying to structure its approach to organisational change by relying more profoundly on logic and rational debate, working to consistently improve its performance over time. Although arguably imperfect at first, such developments did offer non-dominant executives fora for meeting each other and nurturing socio-political ties beyond the formerly available ones. In this sense, while the instigation of strategy exercises might strike the critical observer as somewhat meaningless or rigid, it should be noted that its creation nevertheless served the fruitful development of tensions quite significantly, advancing change at Sagecom in ways beyond those initially intended.

### 10.2.4 Reiterate: Redrawing the Story (if You Want To)

In the final stage, you would do well to evaluate the outcome of your interpretation exercise. Have I gathered the insights that I was aiming for – or can I, according to the situation I currently find myself in, make sense of the case in a more coherent and explanatory way? As this book has highlighted time after time, no single perspective on organisational change will consistently deliver 'the' answer. Instead, each perspective shines its light on different aspects of a given change situation, and it is up to us to decide which aspects that should be. In a final effort, we can thus reiterate our case interpretation, emphasising a different outset as the primary perspective (Stage 2) or complementing our initial primary perspective with different secondary perspectives (Stage 3). While many different combinations can often be made, the relevance of each iteration will mostly depend on the context in which we find ourselves and the questions in which we are most interested.

## 10.3 How to Advance Change in Practice

Having explored how change can be interpreted in practice, we now turn to a more active question: how can change be advanced? Before we embark on that journey, however, a brief but important word of caution.

Humans, by nature, are not particularly comfortable with uncertainty. That's not just anecdotal; it's a well-established finding across behavioural research. When faced with ambiguity, people tend to take predictable steps to reduce discomfort: they prefer small, certain gains over larger but uncertain ones; they follow social cues in unfamiliar settings to avoid standing out; and they often cling to flawed information simply because it feels better than having none at all.

In most texts on organisational change, I've often seen these tendencies discussed in the context of how people respond to change – the idea being that because people dislike uncertainty they'll naturally push back against the unfamiliar. Here, however, I want to highlight a slightly different point: uncertainty-aversion doesn't just shape how people respond to change; it also shapes how they initiate it. When trying to advance change, people will often favour a structured approach – even if it's flawed – over working with a more complex (and uncertain) range of options. And that instinct matters deeply for how we can realistically make change efforts unfold in practice.

For example, when working with people on the change perspectives set out in this book, I always – at some point – received the question of how to use them: meaning, how to leverage their knowledge to advance or operationalise our own instances of (organisational) change. I often responded to these questions by emphasising how each perspective offers a different angle to the change problem, and how a best-practice approach is almost per definition excluded because of the multifaceted nature of change. I explained that perspectives each offer different ways of making sense of change, and that with such differences in interpretation come different practices. When I was in the mood, I even extended into the beauty of such kaleidoscopic reality, where shifting lenses can lead to dramatically different versions of organisational life.

It rarely worked. When people were polite, I'd get something of a half-baked nod and an upside-down frown, visibly flagging their lingering dissatisfaction with my response. When people were more forthright, they would keep pushing for more: yes, we hear you, multifaceted, sounds great. But what to do? How to make it work in practice?

Over time, I've come to realise that these calls for more structured guidance shouldn't simply be shrugged off, even if delivering on them wouldn't be fully consistent with the real-life complexities of organisational change. For at their core they relate to something deeply human: our preference for clarity over uncertainty, even when we know that such clarity may never fully capture the richness and ambiguity of real-world situations.

So, in response, I'll offer here what I consider to be a 'pretty good' approach to advancing change in practice (see Figure 10.3). I cannot emphasise enough that it's not a best practice: as the real-life complexities of organisational change go well beyond what any single model can offer, it is only one viable way of approaching change for practice. Many others may be possible, and, depending on the situation, may even make more sense. Still, I believe that this roadmap offers a helpful way of drawing together the different perspectives explored in this book into a coherent and manageable form for action. Imperfect, yes, very much so, but hopefully useful in a lot of situations. And, for now, that will have to do.

## 10.3.1 Setting Course

In the first stage of advancing change, you may want to start by getting to grips with the basics – what's the course you aim to set out, and could you realistically leverage the behaviour and insights of existing organisational members to help you with that? Here, both the managerial and the organic perspectives have much to offer.

### 10.3.1.1 Vantage Point #1: Managerial Perspective

When faced with the challenge of advancing change, most of us instinctively seek to make the process more manageable. That's perfectly reasonable – developing a plan is often a very useful first step. As outlined in Chapter 2, frameworks such as Lewin's three-stage model, Kotter's eight steps, or McKinsey's influence model can offer early clarity and structure.

What's not reasonable, however, is stopping there. In practice, I'd wager that at least three out of four change initiatives never move beyond this first step. A plan is drawn up, a blueprint is announced, and off we go, without much further thought. While this approach offers the comfort of order, it rarely survives the messiness of reality. Not because the plan is necessarily bad at its core. Not because people are automatically resistant. But because relying solely on a managerial perspective ignores too much of the complexity and multifaceted nature that define real-world change. Without integrating other perspectives, even the most polished plan is likely to falter.

Remember that approaching change from a managerial angle is only one way of making sense of it: it is certainly a useful step – but it's only a step. If it is the only perspective being utilised, it will make everything that falls beyond its scope seem nonsensical – such as those who do not acknowledge the almighty guidance of an expert group, or those who prioritise existing operations over proposed new initiatives. In most cases, that does not mean that these people's reactions necessarily are nonsense; it simply means that they are nonsense to you, given the limited vantage point that you occupy.

Guiding questions to consider:

- How can I anticipate or plan the change at hand?
- Which existing change models might be relevant to this situation?

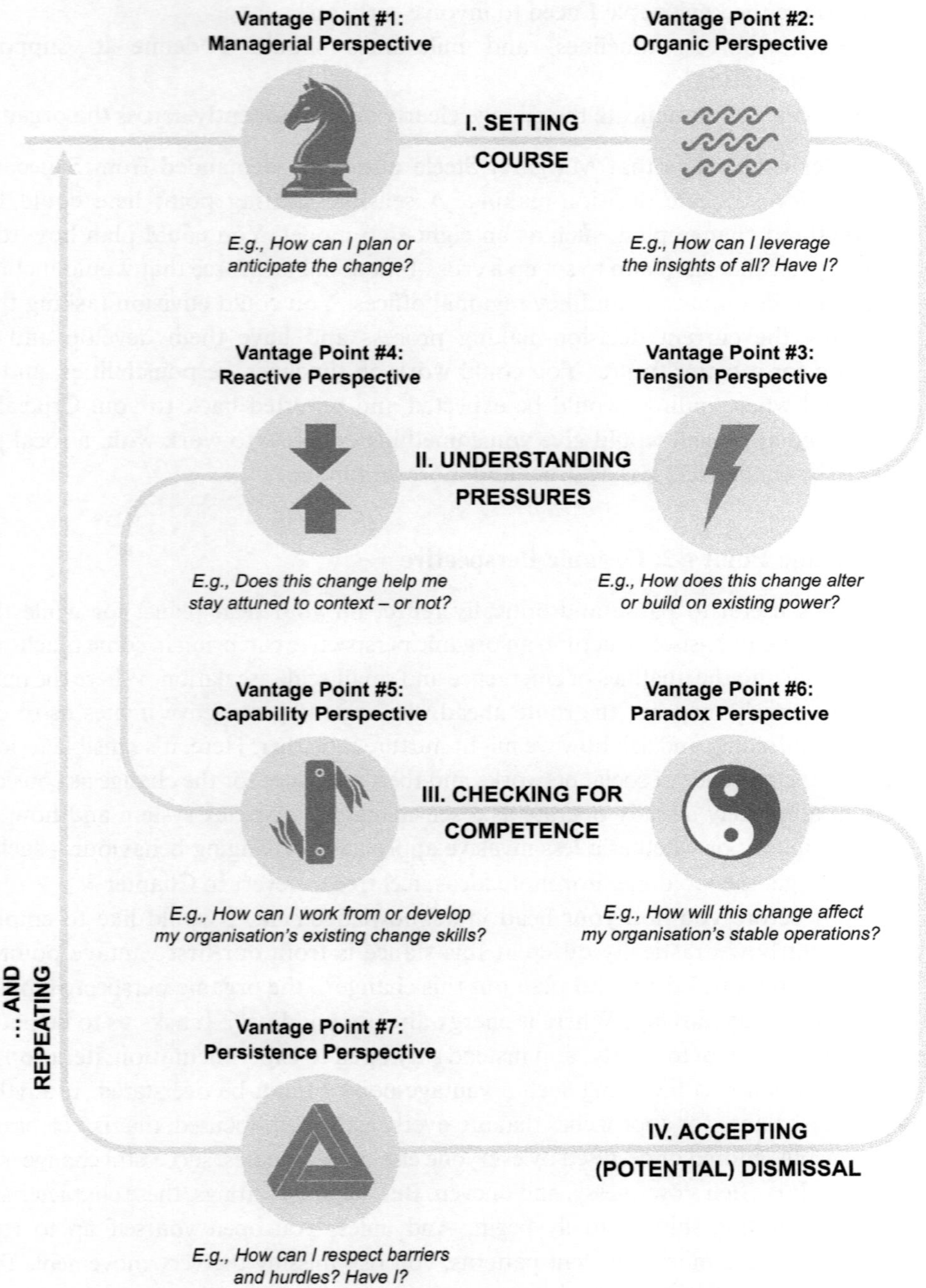


**Figure 10.3** The change perspective roadmap.

- Who are the key people I need to involve early on?
- What resources, timelines, and milestones should I define to support structured implementation?
- How can I communicate the change clearly and consistently across the organisation?

Consider the change that Margaret Steele ultimately demanded from Sagecom – a revised process for strategic decision-making. A sensible starting point here could be to develop a structured change plan, such as an eight-step model. You could plan how to explicate the urgency to others and aim to set up a cross-functional taskforce that would include representatives from headquarters and key regional offices. You could envision tasking this group with mapping the current decision-making process and have them develop and communicate a vision for a better future. You could work on timelines, responsibilities, and definitions of how and when findings would be expected and reported back to you. Crucially, this initial structured approach would give you something concrete to work with: a focal point that will make the change feel less abstract and more within reach.

#### 10.3.1.2 Vantage Point #2: Organic Perspective

Next, it's useful to pause and critically reflect on your neat plans: for while the managerial perspective emphasises structure, an organic perspective can bring in some much-needed balance by looking into the qualities of emergence and small-scale escalation. Where the managerial mind seeks to clearly map out the route ahead, the organic perspective invites us to observe what's already unfolding and ask how we might nurture it further. Here, it's sensible to look into things such as the presence of social networks and their relevance for the change as considered; how the organisation may already operate as a self-managing complex system and how this will affect your proposal; or whether a less invasive approach to changing behaviour – such as nudging – may also get the job done. For more ideas, feel free to revert to Chapter 3.

Now, before you nod your head in acknowledgement, I would like to emphasise just for a moment how drastically different this stance is from our first vantage point. Rather than asking, 'How can I drive and plan out this change?', the organic perspective pushes us to ask, 'What's already moving? Where is energy already building?'. It asks us to be patient – to resist the urge to control too early, and instead stay open to experimentation, iteration, and learning.

The relevance of including such a vantage point cannot be overstated. If anything, it acts as a counterbalance for approaches that are overly leadership-focused, that is, celebrated by those at the top, but ignored or despised by everyone else. In most cases, successful change is not uniformly smooth. It is often slow, messy, and uneven. But, in many settings, these characteristics are vital to how real, lasting shifts actually begin. And unless you open yourself up to recognising and supporting these more emergent patterns, you risk missing the very movements that make a lot of change possible in the first place.

Guiding questions to consider:

- How can I leverage the insights of all? Have I?
- Where are actions relevant to a change already happening, even if informally or below the radar?

- Which informal practices, routines, or conversations seem to carry the seeds of the change that I'm looking for?
- How can we create space for experimentation without needing to control outcomes too soon?
- How can I stay attuned to shifts in energy, language, or behaviour that signal organic momentum?

In our case example, with your structured plan for shifting strategic decision-making in hand, you may want to look into ways to better tailor it to the specificities of the organisation: what could you do to better tap into Sagecom's undercurrent? You could, for example, map out the social network of the organisation, which makes you realise that Steele – although a business guru – has a very loose connection within Sagecom as a group. This would make it unlikely for people to change their behaviour based solely on her observations. Or, you could consider whether Sagecom already functions as a complex adaptive system (CAS) – in which case, any radical interventionist programme may do more harm than good, and small tweaks to context may be preferable. Initiatives like these may also help you to realise that, although you may think that you understand things better than everyone else, you most likely don't. Despite having a clear plan, you may not fully grasp the lived realities of those on the ground. Stay open. Consider how the organisation's own people may already be experimenting with small, practical shifts for navigating the existing strategic decision-making – and how these efforts could inform, adapt, or even do away with the grand plan you have in mind.

## 10.3.2 Understanding Pressures

Once you have a basic understanding of your envisioned change process and the way in which it could benefit from the insights of all organisational members, you may want to start thinking about the pressures that your change will either build on or feed into. Here, the vantage points of both the tension and the reactive perspectives can offer excellent footing.

### 10.3.2.1 Vantage Point #3: Tension Perspective

As soon as you have a sense of how your change might be enacted – from both a managerial and an organic angle – it's important to examine the power dynamics your change is likely to either lean on or disrupt. Some elements of the existing power structure will lie outside your immediate influence. In those cases, your best move is simply to recognise that power is there, understand where it resides, and remain aware of how it might shape the path ahead. But not all dynamics are fixed. Some can be moderated or redirected. In both cases, the insights from Chapter 4 may prove particularly helpful.

At times, a proposed change may easily gain traction because it resonates with tensions that have been simmering beneath the surface – frustrations, rivalries, or inefficiencies that many have quietly endured. In such cases, the change can serve as a release valve, offering people a legitimate reason to get behind something new. There's nothing that shifts as easily as a system people are already rooting against. Use that energy wisely. But tread carefully: don't opportunistically attach your change initiative to any source of tension simply because it's there. Misreading the underlying issue – or falsely instrumentalising it for your own agenda – can backfire dramatically, eroding trust and inviting severe resistance once people realise the (perhaps unintentional) ruse.

More often than not, however, your change is going to threaten someone's turf. Whether explicitly or subtly, organisational changes almost always translate into shifts in influence. Someone, somewhere, is likely to feel disempowered or sidelined by what you're proposing. That's why it's crucial to surface potential power clashes early on. Identify where power shifts might be happening, not just in theory but in terms of individuals or groups who may feel that their voice, autonomy, or control is at stake. If you leave these tensions unaddressed, they can quietly (or loudly) undermine your efforts later. But if you recognise them head-on, you can create the possibility of moving forward without igniting unnecessary conflict. In most cases, acknowledgement, respect, and empathy go a long way.

Guiding questions to consider:

- What unresolved tensions currently exist within the organisation? Does the proposed change align with or push against these tensions?
- Who stands to lose power, influence, or status as a result of this change? Who stands to gain it?
- How are these individuals or groups likely to respond – openly or beneath the surface?
- How can I engage with them constructively to reduce defensiveness and foster buy-in?
- How can I make space for productive tension without fuelling unmanageable conflict?

In our case example, as you've come to terms with a first notion for changing strategic decision-making at Sagecom, a constructive next step may involve figuring out where power resides in the organisation – not just formally but informally as well – and how this might affect your envisioned change. For instance, as the proposed change aims to create a more inclusive and decentralised structure, it quickly becomes clear that certain senior figures at headquarters – especially those who have long held informal influence over strategic direction – will likely perceive the move as a potential dilution of their authority. From there, you could then consider how to engage with those whose roles might be most affected – not with platitudes but with genuine dialogue (see Chapter 4's dialogue theory framework and stakeholder mapping for inspiration). By acknowledging discomfort directly and making space for mutual adjustment, you may transform a potential stand-off into an opportunity for shared ownership. Ignoring this tension, by contrast, will likely result in quiet obstruction or visible pushback, both of which will stall or sink your change before it even truly begins.

#### 10.3.2.2 Vantage Point #4: Reactive Perspective

Beyond gradually building tensions, it's equally important to consider the more immediate challenges coming from the environment. Ask yourself, 'Will the change I'm trying to advance help the organisation remain attuned to its context – or not?' And even if it seems well aligned, are current conditions favourable for launching this change right now? Chapter 5 offers several tools and ideas to help guide these reflections in greater depth.

One critical factor to consider here is timing. A change initiative might make perfect sense on paper, but still fall flat because the current environment simply doesn't allow it to take root. For example, you may propose offshoring as a way to reduce costs, only to find that new trade restrictions or tariffs render the move financially unsound. Or you may want to launch a new service line, only to realise that a sudden spike in demand for core operations leaves your team too stretched to execute it well. These kinds of mismatch don't mean that your original proposal was inherently flawed, but they do reveal how vital it is to consider external conditions and opportunity windows. Change that ignores context – and how it already pressures your organisation to respond without you directing it – is rarely successful, no matter how well designed.

Just as importantly, you'll want to reflect on how the change you're advancing could affect your organisation's capacity to respond to future shocks. Some initiatives that seem strategic in the moment – such as outsourcing key capabilities or eliminating redundant resources – may leave your organisation more fragile in the long run. In this sense, a reactive perspective invites you not just to adapt to current shocks but to think carefully about the long-term resilience of the system you're reshaping. Ask not only, 'Is this smart now?', but also, 'What will this make us more or less able to do later on?'.

Guiding questions to consider:

- What predicaments (e.g., market, regulatory, technological) are currently influencing the organisation?
- Is now the right time to pursue this change – or would it be wiser to wait for a better opportunity window?
- How will this change affect the organisation's capacity to respond to unforeseen events in the future?
- Could this initiative unintentionally reduce organisational flexibility or resilience?

With the Sagecom decision-making model, you may want to conduct a close reading of the environment before moving forward: are you currently in a time of 'equilibrium' or 'punctuation' – or what kinds of adverse challenge is your firm already required to respond to right now? A reactive perspective prompts you to pause and reassess whether this really is the right time to push through such an overhaul. For example, if several key regions are currently in the middle of dealing with heightened regulatory scrutiny due to radically new data protection laws, it might suggest that your timing is problematic. Implementing a new governance model under these circumstances risks distracting local leaders from urgent compliance and business continuity issues. Moreover, you may want to consider whether the proposed structure – which would rely heavily on decentralisation – might reduce the firm's flexibility to react swiftly to grand challenges in the future, or whether it would enhance it. When negative, these insights don't necessarily invalidate the initiative, but they may suggest the need to stagger implementation, build in local adaptation windows, or prioritise resilience alongside reform.

### 10.3.3 Checking for Competence

Next, after understanding pressures, you may want to check how your change would draw on, improve, or undermine your organisational competences, both dynamic and stable. The capability and paradox perspectives will be the most useful ones to help you out here.

#### 10.3.3.1 Vantage Point #5: Capability Perspective

Once you've identified a realistic path for change that takes both gradual power dynamics and more sudden setbacks into account, the next critical question becomes: 'Is your organisation equipped to deliver on this change?' Does it have the necessary experience, skills, systems, and adaptive capacity to make the change work, not just in principle but in practice? Tools like the dynamic capabilities framework and the strategic agility model, discussed in Chapter 6, can help you assess this more systematically.

As straightforward as this may sound, organisations often skip this step. Time and again, I've seen major change programmes launched without any serious consideration of whether the organisation is capable of carrying them out. It's madness – and it's avoidable. Think of it like assigning a random person a marathon next week without ever checking whether they're trained. Sure, they might make it. But they might also collapse halfway through (and, more likely than not, they will). The same applies to organisations. Implementing sweeping change without understanding your group's capability for change is a recipe for backlash and breakdown. Don't cut corners here.

However, more than just assessing your organisation's existing competence in relation to change, you may also want to look into how your initiative will realistically affect such competence for future use: will your change initiative help the organisation become more adaptable in and of itself, or will it potentially undermine such skill? Not all change builds change capabilities. Sometimes, a change that looks reasonable in the short term may clip an organisation's wings for adaptation in the longer term – because it renders leadership more divided, because it freezes up resources, because it cuts down on people who know what's happening in the marketplace ... Tread carefully and design with long-term learning in mind.

Guiding questions to consider:

- Does the organisation have experience with changes of this scale or nature?
- What skills, resources, or systems are already in place – and what might be missing?
- Are we asking people to do things they've never done without preparing them first?
- Could this initiative deplete resources, stretch people too far, or undercut organisational confidence?
- Will this change enhance our capacity to adapt in the future, or diminish it?
- How can we build change capability through the change process – not just for this initiative but for what comes after?

For example, as you get a clearer understanding of how to move forward with Sagecom's change in strategic decision-making, it's best to ask whether the organisation has the capacity to implement and sustain such a shift. On paper, the idea of changing briskly to a decentralised strategic model sounds compelling. In practice, however, it may be that Sagecom has little experience with shifts that alter its core decision-making model. Its resources may be too locked up to make it happen in practice, or its leadership team may not truly agree on it (despite committing at face value). A capability perspective thus prompts you to step back and ask, 'Are we able to realise this change and, if not, how can we build the skills and systems that will help us get there?'. One option might be to pilot the new model in a few regions with relatively stronger leadership benches, providing targeted coaching and support along the way. This would allow the firm to strengthen its experience with the change before scaling up – and to learn where cracks might appear. Just as importantly, an approach like this could open space to reflect on whether the change would build longer-term adaptive capability across the group, for example by building more leadership unity, or whether it would create resentment and isolation instead.

#### 10.3.3.2 Vantage Point #6: Paradox Perspective

At this point, it's worth considering – and acknowledging – your organisation's stable competences: can your organisation keep doing what it currently does well while changing? This is where the paradox perspective becomes especially valuable – helping you manage the harmony between stability and transformation, continuity and disruption. For deeper insight into this contradictory balancing act, see Chapter 7.

When you're focused on driving change, it's easy to lose sight of the value of the familiar. Established routines and reliable operations start to feel invisible, as if they run themselves. They don't. Their smooth functioning depends on the competence of people, systems, and technologies that have been carefully fine-tuned over time. These processes only appear to be self-sustaining because, behind the scenes, your organisation is constantly working to keep them up.

Change initiatives, even when they don't directly target certain operations, inevitably affect them. Whether through diverted time, depleted energy, budget reallocation, or shifts in attention, change always introduces strain for existing ways of doing things. That doesn't mean that you shouldn't proceed. But it does mean that you need to ask: 'Is this change worth the disruption it may cause?' And, perhaps more importantly: 'How can I design and pace this initiative in a way that safeguards – or even strengthens – the operational foundations we rely on every day?' In the end, the real challenge is not choosing between continuity and change but learning how to carry both, at once, without letting either drop.

Guiding questions to consider:

- How might this change initiative impact our competences for stable operations, even indirectly?
- Are we assuming that existing systems will 'just keep running' during the transition?
- What trade-offs will this change require in terms of time, attention, or resources?
- Could the pursuit of change unintentionally undermine what currently works well?
- How can we maintain business continuity while advancing this initiative?
- How might we design this change to reinforce rather than erode our current strengths for doing things?

For instance, at Sagecom, you may want to pause on your excitement for the reform and ask yourself: 'Will the company be able to keep running as usual while undergoing this change?' It may be that Sagecom's regional teams are already juggling heavy delivery schedules and navigating growing client demands. While the proposed governance model would aim to decentralise decision-making and foster agility, the transition itself could stretch teams thin, especially if it introduces confusion around roles or adds layers of coordination before people are ready. A paradox perspective would thus prompt you to step back and ask: 'How do we introduce the new without breaking the old?' You might decide to run the new process as a 'shadow structure' alongside the old one for a limited time, testing ideas and gathering feedback before making a full shift. Or you might phase the rollout, starting with one business unit to refine the model before scaling. This kind of thinking doesn't just protect current operations; it gives your change effort the breathing room it needs to mature without destabilising the business it's meant to strengthen.

### 10.3.4 Accepting (Potential) Dismissal . . . and Repeating

Finally, you're up for what may be the hardest thing of all: accepting when a change initiative, despite all good intentions, may not be in the organisation's best interests. Here, the persistence perspective offers excellent understanding.

#### 10.3.4.1 Vantage Point #7: Persistence Perspective

After having established a fairly multifaceted understanding of the change initiative you're aiming to advance, take one final moment for explicit and grounded reflection: What barriers and hurdles can you realistically expect along the way – and have you taken them seriously? More broadly, how has your organisation become shaped and imprinted by its past? What paths has it become dependent on? And which forces of inertia – structural, cultural, cognitive – might be holding it steady where it stands? Chapter 8 will help you navigate these kinds of question in greater depth.

It is absolutely critical that you engage with these questions with brutal honesty and that you don't automatically treat their outcomes as roadblocks waiting to be cleared. Some you can clear: in such cases, having anticipated the rigidity early on will allow you to meaningfully engage with it. Let people express what they're feeling and why they'd be resisting your change; acknowledge and name such resistance in a neutral way; and allow people to respond. During this process, it's crucial to always be authentic: put into words what you're experiencing and allow people to do the same. It's not about manipulating people around your change proposal; it's about establishing the trust for people to live the change themselves.

Yet some constraints may not be so malleable. There are moments when the sources of persistence are so deeply woven into the organisation's fabric – into its identity, values, systems, or relationships – that trying to uproot them wholesale could do more harm than good. At such times, the wiser course may be to adapt your initiative to fit the contours of what exists – or to park it entirely. If your proposed change threatens to unravel what the organisation holds as core, you may find that the cost of moving forward outweighs the benefits. In these moments, recognising limits is not a failure; it is a mark of change maturity. What matters most is that your change initiative grows out of – not away from – the organisational soil it depends on to survive.

Guiding questions to consider:

- What routines, values, or norms have become deeply embedded in the organisation over time?

- Which structural, cultural, or emotional forms of inertia could slow or block the change, even unintentionally?
- Am I treating resistance as something to be managed or as a signal worth listening to?
- What aspects of the current system are genuinely non-negotiable and am I willing to respect them?
- Could this initiative be adapted to better align with the organisation's underlying path dependencies?
- Am I being honest about what might not be changeable and what that means for the initiative?

For example, as your proposed overhaul of Sagecom's decision-making process nears its final design, it becomes crucial to pause and reflect not just on what is desirable or possible but on what may ultimately be endurable. A deeper dive into Sagecom's historical DNA reveals a legacy of centralised leadership that has, over the years, become tightly woven into the fabric of how the company operates. While decentralisation might make perfect sense in general, it's worth noting that past attempts to delegate authority to regional hubs were quietly walked back after inconsistent results and political fallout. Those past failures have left scars, not just in processes but in people's collective memory. This insight doesn't necessarily mean that the change should be abandoned, but it may need to be rethought. For instance, rather than rolling out a sweeping new model across the entire organisation, these insights may confirm your earlier idea of piloting the change in a smaller, lower-stakes unit to build credibility and learn from within. Recognising that resistance seldom stems from stubbornness but rather from deeply held beliefs about what has protected the firm in the past may help you engage with these barriers respectfully and adaptively.

#### 10.3.4.2 . . . And Repeating

Ideally, you would work your way through each of these vantage points – and the distinct perspectives they offer – before moving ahead with any substantial change. And once you've decided whether or not to proceed, you would loop your insights back to the beginning, refining your course and starting over again. As your change initiative takes shape and unfolds in practice, repeatedly revisiting the perspective roadmap will help prevent getting locked into a dominant logic or narrow way of thinking. Change doesn't unfold in a straight line – and neither should your thinking.

It's tempting to see this process as overly laborious – something to shortcut in the name of clarity or efficiency. And, to be fair, it is hard work. Genuinely shifting perspectives on the same issue is not just an intellectual exercise; it's mentally and emotionally taxing. You don't simply tick a few boxes and call it done. Instead, you're asked to truly reframe how you think about the problem, and to enter unfamiliar or even uncomfortable ways of seeing. More often than not, this means bumping into things that disrupt what you had hoped for or believed in. It can feel like your carefully crafted plan – neatly laid out in polished slides – is coming undone. The allure of reverting to a simpler, more linear approach can be strong.

I urge you to resist that temptation. Because, while this process complicates, it also deepens. It keeps your thinking honest, your design grounded, and your change initiative much more likely to stick. In a world defined by complexity, thoughtful multi-angled iteration is not a detour; it is the path forward.

## SUMMARY

Working through the Sagecom example, Chapter 10 illustrated how perspectives can be actively tapped into to either better interpret or advance change in practice. As discussed, two main approaches are to be considered:

◊ When **interpreting change in practice**, you want to avoid falling into the ruts of your dominant perspective early on. To do this, three stages of interpretation can help. In the first stage of going broad, the case observer develops a broad interpretation of the case according to multiple perspectives, drafting a story canvas. In the second stage of going deep, the case observer pushes further into the most relevant perspective according to their situation or context, drafting a more detailed storyline. In the final stage of going rich, the case observer merges the outputs of their former efforts, filling in the blanks still featured in the storyline by drawing on relevant secondary perspectives marked within the story canvas. The story that eventually emerges can then be evaluated: either it meets the needs of the observing party or it is reiterated from a different outset.

◊ When **advancing change in practice**, the change perspective roadmap offers a grounded way to proceed while respecting the complexity of change as a phenomenon. Rather than relying on a single framework or viewpoint, it invites you to look at your change initiative through a variety of lenses, with each vantage point bringing its own questions and insights, helping you stress-test your assumptions, uncover blind spots, and refine your thinking. Crucially, it encourages not a one-off diagnostic but an iterative mindset: work through each perspective before you act, and return to them as your initiative evolves. The roadmap offers no guaranteed answers, but it does provide a structure for navigating complexity with greater clarity, humility, and depth.

By showcasing the use of theoretical perspectives in a practical context, I hope to have provided you with some indication of how to put this book to actual use – eventually allowing you to turn good theory into veritable practical tools.

# Index